BRAZIL'S LULA

"I love this guy. He's the most popular politician on Earth."

Barack Obama, London, April 2, 2009

BRAZIL'S LULA:
THE MOST POPULAR POLITICIAN ON EARTH

Ted G. Goertzel

BrownWalker Press
Boca Raton

Brazil's Lula: The Most Popular Politician on Earth

BrownWalker Press
Boca Raton, Florida • USA
2011

ISBN-10: 1-61233-505-5 *(paper)*
ISBN-13: 978-1-61233-505-6 *(paper)*

ISBN-10: 1-61233-506-3 *(ebook)*
ISBN-13: 978-1-61233-506-3 *(ebook)*

www.brownwalker.com

Front cover photograph courtesy of Agencia Brasil/Marcello Casal, Jr.

Cover design by Shereen Siddiqui

Publisher's Cataloging-in-Publication Data

Goertzel, Ted G.
Brazil's Lula : the most popular politician on earth / Ted G.
Goertzel.
p. cm.
ISBN: 978-1-61233-505-6
1. Lula, 1945- 2. Brazil. President (2003- : Lula). 3. Brazil—Politics
and government—2003-   I. Title.
F2538.5.L85 G64 2011
981.06`5092—dc22

2011928346

TABLE OF CONTENTS

Introduction.. 1

CHAPTER ONE
An Abusive Father and a Courageous Mother... 5

CHAPTER TWO
Coming of Age in São Paulo... 11

CHAPTER THREE
The Struggle for Workers' Dignity... 15

CHAPTER FOUR
The Long Struggle for the Presidency.. 23

CHAPTER FIVE
Keeping the Economic Ship Afloat... 39

CHAPTER SIX
Vote-Buying and Corruption Scandals... 53

CHAPTER SEVEN
Ending Hunger with Family Allowances... 69

CHAPTER EIGHT
Rural Development, Land Reform and the Environment....................... 81

CHAPTER NINE
From Participatory Budgeting to Advisory Councils.............................. 95

CHAPTER TEN
Building National Self-Esteem with Foreign Policy............................... 99

CHAPTER ELEVEN
Winning Reelection in 2006... 117

CHAPTER TWELVE
Making Brazilian Capitalism Boom.. 133

CHAPTER THIRTEEN
Socialism, Economic Solidarity and Micro-Capitalism......................... 151

CHAPTER FOURTEEN
Electing a Successor... 165

CHAPTER FIFTEEN
The Son of Brazil in Power.. 191

Index... 213

ACKNOWLEDGEMENTS

Special thanks are due to Laura Randall, Anthony Spanakos, Eduardo Piragibe Graeff, Fernando Henrique Cardoso, and anonymous reviewers who read and commented on versions of the entire manuscript. João Paulo Peixoto, Claudio Weber Abramo, and the late and much missed Antonio Carlos Pojo do Rego, are much appreciated for their comments on chapters. Eduardo Graeff, Denise Paraná, Izabela Freire, Gabriel and Clelia Bolaffi, and José Julio Freire went out of their way to help in arranging interviews and making practical arrangements.

Thanks are due to Adhemar Alteiri, Carlos Alberto, Carlos Roberto Takao Yoshioka, Cassio Pennachin, Celecicino de Carvalho Filho, Claudio Couto, Dagmar Freire, Danielle Ardaillon, David Fleischer, Eiiti Sato, Fernando Gabeira, Fernando Pimental, Francisco de Oliveira, Frederico Jayme, Frei Chico, Glaucio Soares, Jorge Hage Sobrinho, John Goertzel, Jose Genoino, Marcelo Ottoni Durante, Rogerio Arantes, Ronald Rocha, Sônia Miriam Draibe, Tulio Kahn, Virginia Cestari, and Yves Zamboni-Filho.

A special acknowledgement to Sue Ellen White for copy editing the manuscript and for helpful suggestions on the content and presentation.

INTRODUCTION

Tens of millions of Brazilians were jubilant when Luiz Inácio Lula de Silva was inaugurated president of Brazil on January 1, 2003. He promised that "hope has finally conquered fear and it is time for Brazil to blaze a new path." Workers' Party supporters had waited a long time to see him in Brasilia's Palace of the High Plains. A lathe mechanic and union leader by trade, he was the first president from the working class and the first without a college education. One of his friends, Frei Betto, a Dominican friar and liberation theologist, captured the mood:

> He appeared. Then the speech. "Change." A liturgy of confirmation. From this day forward the vines will bear fruit, burying all angry feelings; the flowers will give nectar in abundance; milk and honey will run freely through the slums at the edge of town, fattening rickety babies, restoring the teeth of the old, educating the youth, and distributing justice as if it were hot bread until all are satisfied.[1]

History is full of charismatic leaders who disappointed their followers. But eight years later, Lula ended his presidency more popular than he started. The economy was booming, inequality and poverty were down and Brazil was looking forward to hosting the Olympic Games. More than 80 percent of Brazilians rated Lula's government as "good" or "excellent" in national polls in 2010. Barack Obama called Lula the most popular politician on earth.[2]

Lula's presidency was a triumph, but not the kind of triumph many of his supporters had expected or wanted. Corruption scandals plagued his government. The Workers' Party, which had been an innovative vehicle for democracy and popular participation, became another vehicle for careerist politicians. Lula's market-friendly economic policies were much like those of the so-called "neoliberal" government that came before. Some of his most loyal and enthusiastic supporters felt betrayed and left the Workers' Party.

---

[1] Frei Betto, *A Mosca Azul.* Rio de Janeiro: Rocco, 2006, p. 26.
[2] *Huffington Post*, "Obama: Lula is 'Most Popular Politician on Earth', April 2, 2009. *New York Times*, March 18, 2011.

But the activists who abandoned Lula found themselves on the margins of Brazilian society. Author Denise Paraná called Lula the "Son of Brazil" because his roots are in deep in Brazilian mass culture, and his sense of what the Brazilian people want and will accept has been outstanding.[3] Other Latin American leaders, such as Venezuela's Hugo Chávez and Bolivia's Evo Morales, also have roots in their countries' mass cultures. But they tend to antagonize their middle classes and exacerbate social divisions. Lula has a very Brazilian preference for social harmony. He has been remarkably successful in appealing to Brazilians of very diverse class backgrounds. His Brazilian approach to leadership has much to offer a world too often torn by class and ideological antagonisms.

I bought Denise Paraná's book, *Lula: O Filho do Brasil [The Son of Brazil]*, in the São Paulo airport in 2002 and wrote an enthusiastic review.[4] On a trip to Brazil in 2006 I got in touch with her to find out if she was planning a sequel. I was eager to get her views on how Lula's presidency was working out. Denise said she was not able to do a sequel to her book. She had been a strong supporter of Lula and the Workers' Party for many years and was troubled by the corruption scandals during his first term as president. She was busy with other commitments, but I sensed that she was not ready to grapple with the contradictions of Lula's presidency. She suggested that I might do a sequel myself. This book is the result, one that expresses my views, not hers.

Previously, I had written a biography of Lula's predecessor, published as *Fernando Henrique Cardoso: Reinventing Democracy in Brazil.*[5] As *New York Times* reporter Larry Rohter observed, "since the collapse of a right-wing military dictatorship in 1985, two figures have dominated politics in Brazil above all others: Fernando Henrique Cardoso and Luiz Inácio Lula da Silva."[6] Fernando Henrique and Lula were allies in the democratization movement that ended the military dictatorship. They were then competitors in the democratic politics that followed. Cardoso defeated Lula in two presidential elections in 1994

[3] Denise Paraná, *Lula: O Filho do Brasil*. São Paulo: Editora Fundeão Perseu Abramo, 2002. Quotes from *Lula* in the Introduction and Chapter One are translated from this book.

[4] Ted Goertzel, "The Making of Lula of Brazil," Brazzil Magazine, May 2003. http://www.brazzil.com/p135mayo3.htm.

[5] Ted Goertzel, *Fernando Henrique Cardoso: Reinventing Democracy in Brazil*. Boulder: Lynne Rienner, 1999.

[6] Larry Rohter, *Brazil on the Rise*, New York: Palgrave, 2010, p. 252.

and 1998. Then Lula defeated candidates from Cardoso's Social Democratic Party in two elections in 2002 and 2006. Lula's Workers' Party candidate, Dilma Rousseff, defeated the Social Democratic candidate in 2010.

Together Fernando Henrique and Lula governed Brazil for 16 years in which the country made remarkable progress. There is intense rivalry between Lula's Workers' Party and Cardoso's Social Democratic Party, but it is rivalry within a shared democratic commitment. This book examines that rivalry as it plays out in several different policy areas.

This is the first full biography of Lula de Silva, including his childhood, his years in the labor movement, his four campaigns for the presidency, his two presidential terms and the election of his successor, Dilma Rousseff. It explains Brazil's remarkable success in weathering the economic crisis of 2008. Its focus is on Lula as a personality and on his leadership style, and how they have impacted Brazilian society. The story has personal drama and controversy, enhanced by many quotations from Lula and other Brazilian observers.

Lula's model of leadership contrasts sharply with that of populist Latin American leaders who aggravate social class and international conflicts. His distinctively feminist personal style, rooted in his early childhood experiences, is a model for twenty-first century political leaders everywhere.

CHAPTER ONE
AN ABUSIVE FATHER AND A
COURAGEOUS MOTHER

In his first interview with Denise Paraná, Lula was quite frank about the privations of his childhood, saying, "the first thing I remember, when someone asks me about my childhood is exactly the fact that I did not have a childhood." He told of living in a tiny house without electricity or running water, of squatting around a wood stove to eat mush, beans and manioc flour. Meat was an occasional treat when one of his brothers killed a guinea pig or a pigeon, or his mother killed a chicken. Rice was a luxury reserved for when someone was sick.

This kind of poverty was widespread in the Brazilian northeast at the time, and it gave Lula a bond with the Brazilian masses not shared by any previous president. Lula's personality and life history may have been even more affected by the fact that his father abandoned the family shortly before he was born. Lula adamantly refused to model himself on his father who he viewed as a failure. Having a father who is a failure can have advantages in life; research shows that father failure is common in the childhoods of eminent people.[7] Two American presidents, Barack Obama and Bill Clinton, were also resentful of their fathers (or stepfathers) and had very close relationships with their mothers.

Successful mother's boys learn to share their feelings and empathize with others, and develop practical skills in human relations and problem solving. Not having to compete with a father for their mother's attention in childhood may help them build self-confidence. Not having to submit to the father's authority, or rebelling against it, may help them to move quickly through adolescence into career paths that suit their own talents and inclinations. In Lula's case, his father returned to his life when he was nine and he had to deliberately rebel against him, with his mother's support.

Lula is quite explicit about adopting a maternal model of leadership. In a 2010 campaign speech he said:

---

[7] Victor, Mildred and Ted Goertzel and Ariel Hansen, *Cradles of Eminence*, 2nd ed. Scottsdale, Arizona: Great Potential Press, 2003.

The best example I can give of the art of governing is the art of being a mother. Governing is nothing more than acting like a mother taking care of her family, assuring everyone the right to have opportunities. Incidentally, the word "govern" is really wrong. I don't know which philosopher invented the word "govern," it should be "to care for."[8]

According to the dictionaries, the word "govern" implies exercising authority and enforcing rules. This is a stereotypically masculine approach to life, implicit in the traditional upbringings and legal and military training of most of Brazil's past presidents. In contrast to many other leaders, Lula is a feminist, not just in ideology but in his personal style. He freely shares tender feelings and is uninhibited about breaking into tears on public occasions. This is very much the opposite of the stereotype of the Latin American ruler. Lula did not get this style from his regional or social class background or from Brazilian culture; he got it from his mother. He is not so much the son of Brazil as the son of a remarkable Brazilian single mother.

In the interviews with Denise Paraná, Lula sometimes offers excuses for his father, saying, for example, that his father may not have heard Lula's younger sister ask for a piece of bread when he gave it to his dog instead. He expressed admiration for his father's strength and potency and gives him credit for treating both his families equally, which is not how his older siblings remember it. But he also expresses intense resentment of occasions such as when his father denied him an ice cream bar on the grounds that he didn't know how to eat it. It was true that he had never eaten ice cream, but Lula thought he should have been allowed to make a mess of it if the other children were having it. He also recalls that his father saved his leftover breakfast pastry in a special tin for himself rather than sharing it with his wife or children, who were given cheaper bread.

Lula's references to his mother are not the least bit ambivalent. He is filled with admiration for her courage in overcoming overwhelming odds to give the family a chance at a decent life. He readily breaks into tears when recalling her, and regrets only that she didn't live long enough to see his full success in life. His brothers and sisters, interviewed by Denise Paraná, shared his worshipful admiration

[8] Malá Menzes, "Lula fala em Deus e vingança no Piauí," *O Globo*, October 15, 2010. http://www.senado.gov.br/noticias/OpiniaoPublica/inc/senamidia/notSenamidia. asp?ud=20101015&datNoticia=20101015&codNoticia=481646&nomeOrgao=&nomeJornal=O+Globo&codOrgao=47&tipPagina=1.

of their mother and resentment of their father, both of which seem well deserved.

As the youngest in a large family, during his most formative years, Lula may have been forced to mature early. His mother simply did not have time to dote on him and solve all his problems for him. This may be what he meant by saying he did not have a childhood. In another sense, however, the fact that his mother couldn't watch over him every minute left him free to have the kind of unstructured childhood sometimes denied to middle-class children. He bonded closely with his siblings, especially his brother Frei Chico. As soon as he was old enough, he played all sorts of games and sports with neighborhood children, developing leadership skills on the neighborhood soccer field. He had a good mix of maternal support and autonomy for personal growth.

After his mother moved from the northeast to São Paulo when he was nine, he had to assert himself against his father's authority, although his older brothers suffered more from his father's abuse. His mother thought Lula's father had asked her to come to São Paulo because of a manipulative letter sent by one of her sons who was already there. She arrived to discover that her husband was still living with her cousin and several children he had fathered with her. He supported both families, a fact which Lula admired, but his older siblings make it clear that he favored the children of the second family. Lula is clear that they were all much better off when his mother broke with his father and set up a household of her own even though they were living in a miserable shack with almost no furnishings or belongings. The poverty was less of an ordeal than living with an abusive father who beat his older brothers and stalked his mother after the breakup.

As Lula entered adolescence, he made a deliberate decision not to model his life on his father but to fulfill his mother's ambitions that he get an education and pursue a skilled occupation or profession. When he became a father, he resolved not to subject his children to the kind of treatment he had received from his father. As Denise Paraná concluded, "Lula used all of his energies to escape the destiny of his father, to avoid falling into the repellant 'fount of ignorance' that Aristides [his father] represented to him."

If Aristides was a fount of ignorance, Lula set out to be a fount of knowledge, obtained from formal schooling, courses offered by the union movement and informal reading. If Aristides was a tough guy, Lula resolved to be gentle and accommodating. If Aristides was a womanizer, Lula set out to be a devoted husband and father. In the Metalworkers Union, he chose to work with the social services department, helping workers and their families with practical problems. For Lula, getting along with people from all walks of life is a matter of personality and philosophy of life, not political ideology. Lula's worldview is fundamentally Christian, not Marxist. This is obscured by the fact that he keeps his religious life private and respects the separation of church and state. A Roman Catholic, he repeatedly emphasizes his appreciation of all Brazil's religious groups, including the evangelicals and the Jews. He chose an evangelical Protestant as his running mate. His is not a narrow, sectarian Christianity; it is a theology of compassion for other human beings. Frei Betto says:

A devotee of Jesus and of Saint Francis of Assisi, Lula likes to pray, he has the habit of making the sign of the cross before his meals, and he never misses the Mass of the Worker celebrated every first of May at the central church in São Bernardo do Campo. At the same time he protects his faith with the same discretion that he protects his family from the scrutiny of the media.[9]

Lula says he has a strong aversion to making enemies, another way in which he models himself on his mother:

I am a man who learned not to have enemies. Obviously, someone can be my enemy, but I am not his. When someone reaches 60, he is already thinking of the other life; anyone who is Catholic has this preoccupation. I do not want to create any animosity that might cause the "Man" to be in doubt about receiving me there above; I want to guarantee my space. Therefore I do not have time to make enemies. I do not care if a governor is from the PMDB, if he is of the PT, the PSDB, the PFL [political parties], I don't want to know if he is Jewish, if he is evangelical, if he is …. I want to know the following: does he govern? Are there people in that state, in that city? Then they have equal right with everyone else in this country. That's how it is.[10]

[9] Frei Betto, "O Amigo Lula," America Latina en Movimiento, October 28, 2002. http://alainet.org/active/2675&lang=es.
[10] Lula da Silva, "Discurso na cerimônia alusiva à coleta do primeiro óleo da camada do pré-sal na Plataforma P-34," September 2, 2008.
http://www.info.planalto.gov.br/static/inf_briefdiscusos.htm.

This is a personal value, rooted in his admiration for his deeply religious mother, *dona* Lindu, from whom he also inherited his admiration of the dignity that comes from not needing the trappings of wealth or power. He remained loyal to her values by continuing to live simply in an apartment in a working class suburb of São Paulo, without domestic servants, long after he could have afforded more.

While Lula modeled himself in many ways on his mother, his assertiveness in dealing with large groups and standing up to authorities may owe more to his father. His mother was completely overwhelmed by his strength in confronting the power of the authoritarian state as a union leader. His success as a leader was rooted in his mother's gentle courage tempered with his father's tenacity. As Lula put it, "I took a little of the perversity of my father, and a little of the goodness of my mother."

CHAPTER TWO
COMING OF AGE IN SÃO PAULO

When Lula was seven, he was told his father had sent word that he wanted Lula's mother to join him in the state of São Paulo. Actually, the invitation came from Jamie, one of Lula's older brothers who took advantage of their father's illiteracy to insert his own wishes in the letter. Believing the message was from her husband, Lula's mother sold the farm in the northeast and all her belongings and loaded the family onto the back of a truck for the 13-day journey south. For the seven-year-old Lula, it was a great adventure. He saw his first bicycle at the town where they left the northeast. When they took a taxi on arrival in São Paulo, it was his first automobile ride. His father's greeting wasn't warm. Lula remembers him complaining that they hadn't brought his dog. Aristides wanted them all to go to work, not to school. And Lula did work, as a shoe shiner, selling fruit on the street, and delivering dry cleaning. He also had a great time playing games with the other kids in the neighborhood. They played with tops and kites and sling shots and, most of all, they played soccer.

But his mother insisted that they also go to school and Lula completed the third and fourth grades and then passed the entrance examination to go to vocational school to become a lathe mechanic. After his parents separated, he had no further contact with his father, only hearing about him occasionally from his uncles. He didn't miss his father much, saying "He was not one of those fathers who gave his children reason to miss him."

Lula very much enjoyed schooling, especially the vocational school. The curriculum was five months in the classroom, a month's holiday, and then six months in a factory. He was the youngest worker at his first factory job and the other workers treated him well. One of the older workers, a black man he knew as "Old" Barbosa, took him under his wing and taught him the tricks of the trade. There was a soccer field next to the factory, and Lula was an excellent player and team leader. He says that he was an introverted child in general, and that it was only on the soccer field that he became more extroverted. Even there, however, he wasn't a fighter or a smart aleck; he thought that when you are a good leader you don't need to fight with people.

He also had his first sexual experience as a young worker of 16, he later told an interviewer from the Brazilian edition of *Playboy*:

Playboy: Did you have many girlfriends?

Lula: No, I was very shy, awkward. I wasn't dating, I didn't have time, I worked a lot.

Playboy: How old were you when you had your first sexual experience?

Lula: Sixteen.

Playboy: Was it with a woman or a man?

Lula: What is this? With a woman, of course! But at that time pederasty was much more common than it is now. At that time, a boy of 10 or 12 years already had sexual experience with animals …

Playboy: And the woman who initiated you, do you remember her?

Lula: I went to one of these houses in São Paulo. A friend took me.[11]

Later he learned that people were saying that he had had sexual experiences with animals, but he says "I never had any reason to say no I had not done so. It was never my passion to have relations with animals."

When he brought his first paycheck home to his mother he "felt like the owner of the world." The industrial economy in the suburbs of São Paulo was growing, and there was a demand for skilled workers. Lula changed jobs several times, seeking better pay or working conditions. He left one job when the boss insisted he work on Saturday. The family was going on a picnic, so he left after lunch and didn't come back.

One day he was working a night shift with little supervision. A screw broke on the press he was using and it fell and smashed his finger. He waited until the owner arrived at six in the morning to go to the doctor. At the hospital, they amputated the finger. He says he had a complex about the missing finger, but he did get a workman's compensation payment that allowed the family to buy some furniture and a small piece of land.

One day, when Lula was 15, he showed up at the factory where he was working and found the boss standing in the door. The boss sent the workers home because other factories were on strike and he

---

[11] *Playboy*, Brazilian Edition, July 1979.

thought picketers might come from those factories. Lula went with some of the older workers in a company truck to see what was happening at other factories. Two thousand picketers had massed in front of the factory where his sister Maria was working. When the owner refused to shut down, they kept pushing on the factory wall until it collapsed. Then the owner closed the factory and when the workers left the picketers formed a "Polish corridor" and harassed them. At another factory, Lula saw the workers attack an owner who threatened them with a gun. He believes the owner died. On another occasion, when the police used horse cavalry to break up a demonstration, he saw the strikers throw marbles on the street to trip the horses. He found these events exhilarating. He wasn't angry at the bosses, but he thought they should pay more.

Later on, Lula concluded that the violent actions by the unions were actually a sign of weakness. He thought that a well-organized strike didn't need to use violence. If the large majority of workers supported a strike, you didn't need pickets, just one or two people to keep an eye on things. He felt it was more effective to use gentle persuasion than Polish corridors.

Things got more difficult in the economic crisis of 1965, after the military *coup d'état* of 1964. Lula and his brothers were out of work and he got up at six every morning to walk from factory to factory seeking work. The long waits at the factory doors, only to be turned down, were depressing.

Lula's first serious girlfriend, Lurdes, lived two doors away. He had known her and her brothers for 10 years, but had thought of her only as a friend. One day when he was 22 he decided to ask her for a date, and they got along very well. She worked in a textile factory and she discouraged him from joining a labor union because she had heard of people getting in trouble with the police. But his colleagues urged him to join, and he finally decided it would be worth the risk. At the time he had no political consciousness, only a desire to save up money so he and Lurdes could marry and buy a house. He joined the union in April 1969, and married one month later.

With help from the union social services fund, he was soon able to realize his version of the Brazilian dream: to own a house close to a bakery, a bus stop and a pharmacy. Lurdes got pregnant and he was very happy, even though the house was on a muddy street that flooded whenever it rained and had open sewers. Then, in the seventh month of her pregnancy, Lurdes became ill. He took her to the hospital, but the doctors misdiagnosed her and didn't treat her for hepatitis. He told the doctors she was very ill, but they didn't listen to him and sent him home. He returned the next day, bringing baby clothes, only to find that his wife and son were dead.

Lula was depressed for two years after Lurdes' death in 1971. His friends had moved on and he couldn't hang out at Lurdes' mother's house as he used to. He sold the house and moved into a kitchenette apartment, planning to live alone, but his mother left his sister's house and moved in with him. She didn't think he should be alone. He went three years without dating, and then went into a phase of wanting to date a different woman every night. During this period he dated a nurse named Miriam Cordeiro who became pregnant with his daughter Luriam. But by the time he knew that Miriam was pregnant he had fallen in love with a young widow, Marisa Letícia, whose husband had been murdered while working as a taxi driver. Lula adopted her young son, Marcos Cláudio, who was too young to remember his biological father. He was the same age that Lula's son would have been. Marisa wasn't eager to marry at first; she wanted to have her own career. But Lula assured her that they could both work after their marriage in 1974.

Lula's long marriage to Marisa produced three additional sons, Fábio Luís (born in 1975), Sandro Luís (born in 1979), and Luís Cláudio (born in 1985).

CHAPTER THREE

THE STRUGGLE FOR WORKERS' DIGNITY

Lula was recruited into union activism by his older brother, Frei Chico, who was active in union circles. He got his union card in September 1968 and has always remembered the number, 25968. Frei Chico wanted Lula right away to run for a spot on the governing board of the metalworkers union because they needed someone from his factory. He wasn't much interested, but Frei Chico and his friends talked him into it.

Lula found the acrimony of union politics disquieting at first, but with time he was drawn into it. Frei Chico kept dragging him to union meetings and encouraging him to take courses. After Lurdes' death union activities were something to distract him and get him out of the house. The union offered short courses on topics such as labor law, leadership skills and workers' rights. Lula signed up for just about every course that was offered, and read heavily in union newspapers and pamphlets. He also took courses on marriage enrichment through the union's social services department. With all these courses, he was gradually filling in the gap he felt from not having had more schooling.

Lula had a knack for making friends on both sides of factional disputes within the union. There were important strategic issues. The more conservative leaders were focused on getting benefits from the system without antagonizing the authorities. The more radical ones wanted to confront the system and demand change. Lula saw merit on both sides, and was often able to get both sides to endorse him in union elections, or at least not to oppose him vigorously. He was naturally gregarious and always focused on practical matters rather than arguments over principle. He also volunteered to work in the union's social services department where he got to know a lot of workers and their families. Indeed, he met Marisa Letícia there when she came into the social services department for help. He had already heard of her from her father.

In 1969, Lula was elected as an alternate director to the governing board (*diretoria*) of the Metalworkers Union of São Bernardo do Campo, an industrial suburb of the city of São Paulo. He continued to work as a lathe mechanic while holding this position, but in 1972 he was elected to a full-time position as titular director with responsibility for the department that helped members with social services, legal problems and unemployment insurance issues.

The legal department had not been a traditional route to union leadership, and the established leaders didn't realize that Lula was using it to build a political base until it was too late for them to stop him. When workers had a problem, or doubts about joining a strike action, they felt comfortable coming to him.

Unions were highly regulated by the military government, using laws that had first been passed in the 1930s, inspired by Italian fascism. The unions provided some services for workers, including vacation colonies and medical assistance, but were largely constrained from negotiating wages and working conditions directly with employers. These matters were referred to labor courts that were generally sympathetic to the employers. Some of the union leaders had become soft with comfortable careers in the labor bureaucracy and generally tried to restrain the workers. Lula's sympathies were with younger, more militant leaders who wanted to push the limits of what was allowed, mostly by calling strikes. But he managed to maintain good personal relationships with both the cautious older leaders and the more militant younger ones, and was elected president of the union in 1975.

Moving into leadership so quickly was stressful for Lula because he was not accustomed to public speaking and felt inhibited by limited formal education. The first time he was asked to give a speech, at the inauguration of a union school, he spent a week writing out a short talk. Then the leader who had invited him spoke first and anticipated everything he had to say. All he could say was "Listen, folks, after Paulo's speech the union school is inaugurated."

He asked a close friend with more formal education, Dr. Maurício Soares, to help him write his inaugural speech. Lula says he had difficulty even reading it aloud in front of the crowd. The content was carefully calibrated to balance criticism of capitalism with equal criticism of Soviet-style socialism. This reflected Dr. Maurício's Christian socialist views which Lula shared. They didn't yet have the term "Third Way" but that was the substance of their ideology: seeking a third way between the two global extremes. The language was flowery, reflecting Dr Maurício's literary skills.

It was not a speech that Lula could have written, and he was shaking so much he had to sit down to give it. But Brazilians are accustomed to ornate rhetoric on ceremonial occasions, and the speech was suitable for an event that included the governor and the state secretary of labor. Lula wore a suit, vest and tie, a fact that was remarked on in the press because it was so unusual to see a worker dressed that way on a public occasion.[12] By dressing up and giving an ornate speech, he was asserting that organized labor was a respectable, dignified part of Brazilian society. Lula's mother was there as was his pregnant wife. He cannot remember what his mother said at the time, but he believes she was frightened. The criticism of socialism in Lula's 1975 speech was not just for the dignitaries to hear. Lula says that:

> The truth is that we had serious criticisms of the actually existing socialism. Our struggle within the PT [Workers' Party] – and after the fall of the Berlin wall, this changed a lot, and it changed also because there are other currents within the PT – this was because we did not accept the Soviet model as an alternative model of society, we did not accept it. We criticized socialism because we did not accept a socialist society without freedom of expression, without the right to strike, without opposition political parties. I already had all this information. It was not possible to speak of democracy with only one party, with unions that cannot make strikes, without people who can criticize the party in power. At this time we already made all those criticisms.

The mid-1970s were a transitional period in Brazilian politics. The military had seized power in 1964, and had suppressed the radical student and armed guerrilla movements that grew up to oppose them. But by the mid-1970s, pressure was mounting for a return to democracy. The military had set up a two-party system with an official pro-government party, ARENA, or the National Renovation Alliance, and a semi-official opposition party, the MDB or Brazilian Democratic Movement. This worked for them when the government was popular, but when people got tired of military rule, they naturally started to vote for the opposition party. Support for the MDB was growing, especially in São Paulo. Opposition candidates started to approach the unions for votes, and some union leaders were elected to political offices. In 1974, the union reluctantly supported the MDB candidate for governor of São Paulo, Orestes Quércia, because

---

[12] *Folha Online*, "Lula demorou 13 dias para ir de PE a SP e quatro eleições para chegar à Presidência."
http://www1.folha.uol.com.br/folha/especial/2002/governolula/presidente-biografia.shtml.

they couldn't stomach the ARENA candidate. They were surprised when Quércia won with their support.

Lula's base was the region known as the "ABC": the booming industrial suburbs of Santo André, São Bernardo do Campo and São Caetano do Sul on the outskirts of the São Paulo metropolitan area. The economy in the ABC was booming, led by multinational auto companies such as Mercedes Benz, Volkswagen, Ford and General Motors. The skilled workers in the ABC were the highest paid in Brazil and demand for their labor was strong. The labor activism of the 1970s wasn't born of desperation and misery; it was born of hope caused by things getting better. The belief that they could work together to make their lives better.

Workers' Party historian Laís Abramo says that the underlying goal of the strikes was "to restore the dignity of the workers." Just as the student activists had done, the workers sought to "assert their collective subjectivity against the authoritarian state and the despotism of the entrepreneurial class."[13] The specific issues at each workplace differed, but that wasn't important because the drive was to stand up for workers' rights. There was a chain reaction as each strike inspired strikes at several others.

There were radical groups that thought the time had come for social revolution. Some small revolutionary groups had survived the years of repression in underground cells. Others were newly organized. Frei Chico joined the Communist Party in 1971, and he spent his time in meetings of small clandestine cells. Lula thought the time was ripe for a mass movement operating in the public. He urged his brother to join him in open confrontation with the authorities, but Frei Chico remained loyal to the Party line at the time.

Part of Lula's strategy was to keep the workers' movement a workers' movement, led by workers, rather than merging with revolutionary movements of students and intellectuals. The multinationals were accustomed to working with organized labor in other countries, and they urged the government not to provoke the workers. Some of the revolutionary groups sent members to take jobs in factories so they could become union activists and push the movement towards revolution. Although these worker-students tried to fit in with the ordinary workers, they usually gave themselves away. One

[13] Laís Abramo, "O Resgate da dignidade: Greve Metalúrgica em São Bernardo (1978)," Fundação Perseu Abramo, April 19, 2006. http://www.fpabramo.org.br/o-que-fazemos/memoria-e-historia/exposicoes-virtuais/o-resgate-da-dignidade-greve-metalurgica-em-sao.

day, some workers drew Lula's attention to a Japanese-Brazilian worker who used perfect Portuguese. They suspected he might be a police agent, so Lula went over and talked to him, telling him people thought he might be an agent because he didn't talk like someone who carried iron bars in a factory for a living. He advised him to go back to school and become an electrical engineer. Then he could help people by raising production. On another occasion, he saw a young woman working at the Volkswagen factory go into a bar and order a *pinga* (a sugar cane liquor). He thought that wasn't the drink a worker would order coming off shift.

Keeping workers in the leadership was important for the movement's public relations. The press and the public were used to students and intellectuals who became radicalized. An independent mass workers' movement was a new phenomenon, and many people sympathized with their struggle to improve life for their families. The liberal politicians who were campaigning for a return to democracy saw the workers' movement as a useful ally.

Every year, the unions had to negotiate adjustments in wages to compensate for increasingly high inflation rates. As the press covered these issues, Lula's image appeared regularly in the papers and on television. Bearded, often carrying a few extra pounds and bit disheveled, he became a media icon of the São Paulo industrial worker. He was coming up in the world, and in 1975 he was invited to travel to Tokyo for an international congress of Toyota workers. He didn't enjoy the trip much; he was short of spending money and didn't care for Japanese food.

And what was worse, while he was in Japan he got the news that Frei Chico had been arrested by the dreaded DOPS – the Department of Political and Social Order. On a stopover in the United States on his way back from Japan, he got a call from the São Paulo Secretary of Labor warning him that it would be safer for him not to return to Brazil. But Lula had no link to the Communist Party and he decided to come back. He was not arrested on landing in São Paulo, so he took the union's lawyer with him to Second Army headquarters to try to find his brother. They kept them waiting five hours and told them nothing. It took 30 days for the family to find out where Frei Chico was.

It was a dangerous time, and nobody knew how things would turn out. The military leaders were still in control of the federal government, but they were divided among themselves as to how long they should remain in power and how they could make the transition to back to democracy. The workers had strong support in the São Paulo state government, which controlled most of the police forces. But the military loomed over them, and it controlled the federal security forces.

The workers kept pushing and pushing, the strikes got larger and larger, and the authorities kept pushing back. In 1979, federal authorities officially "intervened" in Lula's union and Lula was officially out of office. But the strikes continued. In 1979, more than 100,000 workers participated in what the press of the time called "the largest work stoppage in the history of Brazilian unionism."[14]

In response, the DOPS, the state security police, arrested Lula and seven other union leaders. He was treated reasonably well while in prison, never tortured as his brother had been. The purpose of the arrest was to pressure the workers to return to work, not to extract information about a clandestine organization. Lula's mother was ill at the time and she died of cancer while he was in prison. The prison officials escorted him out of the prison to visit her grave.

Close to 2,000 people gathered around the cemetery during the burial, supporting Lula and demanding his release from prison. He was released after only 30 days, although he was sentenced to 3 ½ years for "inciting to collective disorder." The sentence was annulled a year later, and state public security secretary observed that, "his political future is now guaranteed and he could easily be elected deputy or senator."[15]

But how to make the transition into politics? Up until now, Lula had always thought it better to be an "apolitical" union leader. Becoming a politician would require joining a political party. Choosing a party was a complex decision because the military government had reconsidered its decision to mandate a two-party system. The two-party system had the unintended consequence of uniting the opposition, at least for electoral purposes. So the military government changed the law to allow multiple parties.

Fernando Henrique Cardoso and many of the progressive intellectuals decided to re-register the MDB as the Party of the Brazilian Democratic Movement (PMDB). They hoped to maintain the unity of the opposition. But many other progressive intellectuals and activ-

[14] Folha Online, "Lula demorou 13 dias para ir de PE a SP e quatro eleições para chegar à Presidência,"
http://www1.folha.uol.com.br/folha/especial/2002/governolula/presidente-biografia.shtml.
[15] Ibid

ists thought the time was ripe for a new Workers' Party. After extensive meetings and discussions, Lula decided to join with this group. The core support for the Workers' Party came from the unions of the ABC, but it was not formally linked to the unions. In addition to union members, it attracted land reform activists, environmentalists, feminists, gays and liberation theologists. The party did not label itself "socialist" but there were explicitly socialist tendencies within it. Its internal structure was strongly democratic, with many organized factions, and democratic internal elections.

Frei Chico and Lula disagreed over the party issue. The Communist Party thought it better to work within the PMDB and wait until the Communist Party could be formally registered. Frei Chico (José Ferreira de Melo) got his nickname, which means "friar," because his bald spot made him look like a friar, not because of any religious tendencies. Lula was the religious one. Frei Chico later regretted not joining the Workers' Party because he might have had a career as an elected official if he had. Lula thought so. But it was the Communist Party that kept him from joining, not the Workers' Party.

The Workers' Party was a vibrant membership organization, different from most Brazilian parties which were primarily electoral vehicles for prominent politicians. Members were required to contribute a portion of their income to the party and asked to be active in committees and activities. At the beginning, it was not primarily an electoral vehicle for Lula or any of the other prominent leaders; it was more like a social movement and it inspired admiration from around the world.[16]

The Workers' Party was very active in the mass movement to allow Brazilians to vote directly for president of Brazil, the *Direitas Ja* campaign. The military government had set up an electoral college system that favored small, rural states. The *Direitas Ja* campaign lost and the 1984 presidential election was run under the electoral college system. The Workers' Party abstained from the election on the grounds that the rules were unfair. But the PMDB did put up a candidate and the opposition current was so strong that their candidate, Tancredo Neves, won even under the old rules. The rules were then changed, and Lula ran in the direct election for president of Brazil in 1988.

---

[16] Margaret Keck. The Workers' Party and Democratization in Brazil. New Haven: Yale University Press, 1992. Wendy Hunter, The Transformation of the Workers' Party in Brazil, 1989-2009. New York: Cambridge University Press, 2010.

CHAPTER FOUR

THE LONG STRUGGLE FOR
THE PRESIDENCY

Two hundred thousand people gathered in Brasília on New Year's Day 2003, hoping to witness a turning point in history. For the first time in its 500-year history, Brazil had a left-of-center president from the working class. Lula's life story offered something for everyone. Leftists were inspired by a courageous working-class leader who successfully fought the corporations, the military government and the labor bureaucracy. Conservatives saw his life as a triumph of hard work and individual achievement, as proof that the poor could succeed in Brazil's market economy and as a victory for pragmatism over radicalism. No one was quite sure what he would actually do as president of Brazil. The most important thing was that he would be doing it.

Brazil and Lula had come a long way since 1964 when President Jânio Quadros had unexpectedly resigned and his leftist vice president, João Goulart assumed the presidency. The military seized power and ruled dictatorially for a quarter of a century. But democracy was restored and by 2003 there was no risk of military intervention. The currency had been stabilized, and the country was adapting to the new global economy. Business leaders, in Brazil and elsewhere, were mildly apprehensive about a leftist president, but willing to be reassured. Everyone accepted the election results as valid and outgoing president Fernando Henrique Cardoso made the transition as smooth as possible.

Lula lost his first try at elective office, a run for governor of the state of São Paulo in 1982 on the Workers' Party ticket. He won election to the Brazilian federal congress in 1986 with a very large vote. The 1986 election also made him a delegate to the constituent assembly that wrote Brazil's new constitution in 1988. The constituent assembly was what really interested him. Reflecting back on this period he said, "I never wanted to be a congressman, never. The only thing I wanted in life was to be a member of the constituent assembly, and once the constituent assembly was over I left, perhaps with other pretensions."[17]

---

[17] Lula da Silva, "Discurso na solenidade comemorativa dos 20 anos da Constituição Cidadã," October 22, 2008.

The "other pretentions" were to run for president. He never sought office as a mayor or governor, but aimed right for the top. The 1989 elections were a golden opportunity, for the first time Brazilians would vote directly for president. Lula appeared on the scene as "a scruffy bearded figure calling for radical change under the symbol of his party's red star."[18] He won 17.8 percent of the vote on the first round, ahead of his leftist rival Leonel Brizola, who got 16.5 percent. But both of them were behind Fernando Collor de Mello, a telegenic northeastern governor who ran a slick media campaign paid for by business contributions. Collor got 30.6 percent in the first round. In the runoff, Collor got 53.0 percent and Lula got 46.96 percent.[19] It was a remarkably strong showing and Lula's supporters blamed the defeat on the mass media.

After he was elected, Collor de Mello imposed a radical anti-inflation plan that included freezing all the bank accounts in the country, allowing only small withdrawals. It worked for a short time, and then collapsed. When he was impeached for corruption and replaced by his lackluster vice president, Itamar Franco, it seemed that Lula's time had come.

But an old tension between "tacticians" and "strategists" reemerged within the Workers' Party leadership. The tacticians wanted to focus on winning the election and were willing to moderate the campaign message to that end. The strategists saw little point in winning the election without a mandate for the profound changes the country needed. The tacticians were eager to rely on professional political consultants. The strategists wanted the campaign to be firmly controlled by the party's political leadership.

After his loss in 1989 to a candidate with a slick media-oriented campaign, Lula was eager to hire Brazil's best-known political consultant, José Eduardo Mendonça. "Duda" Mendonça, as he is universally known, was renowned for his skill in working with the emotional side of politics. He had been remarkably successful in making his clients attractive to the public, even when the candidate was not a naturally affable person like Lula. He helped the conservative politician Paulo Maluf get elected governor of São Paulo in 1992 by promoting him as a caring person with a heart despite his stiff demeanor

---

http://www.info.planalto.gov.br/static/inf_briefdiscusos.htm.

[18] Wendy Hunter, *The Transformation of the Workers' Party in Brazil*, 1989-2009. New York: Cambridge University Press, 2010, p. 1.

[19] Wikipédia, Anexo:Lista de eleições presidenciais no Brasil, http://pt.wikipedia.org/wiki/Eleições_presidenciais_no_Brasil#1989.

and conservative ideology. He had also helped Carlos Menem win the presidency of Argentina in 1989. But the Workers' Party vetoed Duda, and Lula allowed his campaign to be coordinated by a team of three Workers' Party leaders. His program was a patchwork of ideas from different factions and interest groups within the party.[20] Even so, Lula might have won in 1994 except for a single issue: the massive inflation that ate away at workers' earnings and made rational economic life difficult. Brazilian currency lost as much as half its value every month, so people had to run to the store to spend their paychecks as soon as they got them. Many anti-inflation plans had been tried and all had failed. The Workers' Party leadership did not focus on the inflation issue because it did not fit into their ideological framework. Monetary stability was usually thought of as a right-wing issue. In a book published in 1995, two English leftists who were strong Lula supporters and opponents of capitalist economics reached a reluctant conclusion:

> Notable in its absence [in the Workers' Party Program] was any specific reference to the vexed question of hyperinflation ... the party still had a working-class mentality, born out of decades of wage bargaining, which found it impossible to imagine that a national agreement between employers and the government for eliminating inflation could serve the interests of workers. So the National Meeting demanded, instead, monthly wage increases, failing to see that this would merely feed inflation in a self-defeating cycle.[21]

The middle and upper classes had indexed bank accounts and other financial mechanisms to cope with inflation. The Workers' Party wanted to give the workers similar coping mechanisms. But automatic wage and bank account adjustments just made inflation worse and there was a danger of the financial system collapsing altogether. President Itamar Franco was at his wit's end after two of his finance minister appointees had failed to control inflation. Finally, in desperation, Franco persuaded sociologist Fernando Henrique Cardoso to take the finance minister job. Cardoso had been a leader in the Senate and was serving the Franco government as foreign minister. He was highly respected by insiders but not a charismatic leader well known to the public.

---

[20] Paulo Markun, O Sapo e o Príncipe. Rio de Janeiro: Objectiva, 2004, p. 253.
[21] Sue Branford and Bernardo Kucinski. Brazil - Carnival of the Oppressed: Lula and the Brazilian Workers' Party. New York: Monthly Review Press, 1995, p. 67.

At the time, the finance ministry was considered a kiss of death for a politician's career because the inflation problem seemed to be unsolvable. Nobody expected Cardoso to solve the problem; they just hoped he could stabilize it and keep the system from collapsing altogether. But, to everyone's surprise, Cardoso put together an anti-inflation plan that worked.[22] He became an instant celebrity as a result, so the Social Democrats and the Liberal Front Party nominated him to run against Lula for the presidency.

They promoted Cardoso as a hero who slew the dragon of inflation, and it worked. Cardoso published his anti-inflation plan, the *Real Plan*, in the *Diário Oficial* in March, just before resigning as finance minister to run for president. In May, the polls showed Lula with more than 40 percent of the vote and Cardoso with 16 percent, with the rest undecided or split among other candidates. Inflation was running over 40 percent a month. The *Real Plan*'s first effects were felt in June, when monthly inflation was down to 6.8 percent. In July, the old money was changed for new *real* notes. Then inflation went down to under 2 percent a month and stayed there. It was a stunning accomplishment, done without freezing bank accounts or imposing price or wage controls as previous failed attempts had done. There were no losers; everyone seemed to be ahead.

The Cardoso campaign crafted a simple campaign strategy that Cardoso described as follows:

> In my experience as a campaigner, everything is symbolic. You have to create a myth and tell the same story over and over, repeating who is good and who is bad. In our case, it is the new currency. And what is bad? Inflation! And what is good? Stability! And this is what I did. At every opportunity, I repeated the principal myth.[23]

The Workers' Party's leaders included some of Brazil's best known economists who assured Lula that Cardoso's plan was another temporary fix, conveniently timed to come out just before the election. Previous plans had stopped inflation temporarily with emergency measures, but had not followed through with the budget cuts and reforms needed to keep inflation down. In the election

---

[22] For Cardoso's life history see Ted Goertzel, *Fernando Henrique Cardoso: Reinventing Democracy in Brazil*, Boulder: Lynne Rienner, 1999, or the updated Portuguese translation published by Saraiva.

[23] Interview with Istoé, reprinted in Suassuna, Luciano e Novaes, Luiz Antônio. Como Fernando Henrique foi Eleito Presidente. São Paulo: Editora Contexto, 1994.

campaign, Lula and the Workers' Party attacked the *Real Plan* as a deceptive plot against the working class. But people did not want to hear that message. Business leaders and the mainstream media loved the plan, as one might expect, but so did the workers who had more real money in their pockets all month. Every week, Cardoso went up in the polls and Lula went down. By election time in October they had reversed positions. Cardoso won the 1994 election on the first round with 54 percent of the vote against Lula's 27 percent; the rest divided among other candidates.

Cardoso's victory was a devastating shock to Lula and the Workers' Party. They felt they deserved the presidency and had been cheated out of it twice. But they also began to worry that their strategy was fundamentally wrong. Two weeks before the 1994 election, when it was apparent they would lose, Lula observed:

> We can't hide from it any more. This thing of the worker and the party of the worker does not work. The Workers' Party is not going to win an election without having a candidate of the middle class.[24]

When Cardoso became president the Workers' Party leaders kept waiting for his plan to fail as Collor de Mello's had. But for the four years of his first term, the Cardoso government managed to keep inflation down without imposing austerity on the workers. Poverty declined because the poor had been the most vulnerable to inflation and gained more from their money holding its value from payday to payday. The country often seemed to be on the brink of financial disaster, especially when the Mexican and then Russian currency failures shook the world system, but Cardoso's team managed to avoid a collapse.

The economists kept pointing to problems, especially an increasing national debt and disappointing economic growth. Finally, in 1998, the Cardoso government was forced to devalue the *real* after wasting billions of dollars on artificially sustaining it. Once again, the country seemed to be on the brink of collapse, this time just before the 1998 election. Once again, Lula and the Workers' Party believed that their time had come. They thought that Cardoso's "neoliberal" policies were exposed as failures. But the internal factional disputes within the party frustrated Lula's efforts to unite around a more effective political marketing plan. He berated his Workers' Party com-

---

[24] *Veja*, October 12, 1994, pp 65-66.

rades, asking them how they would ever arrive at a better society "when we have so much hate among ourselves."[25] The voters were reluctant to change captains in the midst of a storm. They needed reassurance, and Lula's rhetoric was not reassuring. To many voters, it seemed as if he was cheering Brazil's failures. He seemed to be happy every time unemployment went up or the stock market tumbled. The radical policies Lula and the Workers' Party proposed – breaking with the global economy, defaulting on debts and returning to a state directed economy – risked a return to hyperinflation. Cardoso projected the image of a wise, experienced captain keeping a steady hand on the ship of state. He won re-election on the first round with 53 percent of the vote.

Lula and the left were devastated by the 1998 vote. On leaving his apartment after the election, Lula told the press:

Fernando Henrique Cardoso is the executioner of the Brazilian economy, responsible for one of the greatest economic disasters in the history of Brazil. I find it almost incomprehensible that the victims would vote for their own executioner.[26]

But things did not turn out as badly as Lula's economists had led him to expect. The economy stabilized and even grew a bit. Land redistribution was up and poverty, although still severe, was down. Although Cardoso's personal popularity in his second term was low, the Workers' Party's polls showed that people were not ready for radical change. Lula had lost three presidential elections when he used radical rhetoric against candidates that were soothing and reassuring. He decided he needed to use a different approach if he wanted to win.

Fernando Henrique Cardoso claims to have played a role in changing Lula's thinking. Although they are political competitors, they are also comrades from the days of the struggle against the military dictatorship. About two months after the 1998 election, Cardoso got a message that Lula would like to talk with him. The message came through informal channels so Cardoso assumed that Lula wanted a discreet meeting. He called him personally and set up a confidential meeting, along with Cristovam Buarque, the Workers' Party governor of Brasília and a good friend of both of them.

[25] Paulo Markun, O Sapo e o Príncipe. Rio de Janeiro: Objectiva, 2004, p. 277.
[26] Jornal do Brasil, October 5, 1998.

Lula had never been in the presidential palace, so Cardoso gave him a tour and said "maybe someday you'll be living here." Cardoso remarked that Brazil was in a difficult situation and that it would be good if they kept in touch. Lula responded, "Yes, it is very difficult. I think we are heading toward a tremendous crisis." Cardoso responded that his government would act firmly to prevent a crisis. But even if there were one, it would not lead to the working class taking power, as he sensed Lula was expecting. He suspected that Lula was being misled by Workers' Party intellectuals who were still expecting the collapse of capitalism that Karl Marx had predicted as long ago as 1848.

Cardoso knew this way of thinking well from his youthful involvement in Marxist circles and his academic study of Marxist theory. He also understood that Lula's background was different. He told Lula he realized that:

> In your past you were never a socialist, but Cristovão was a socialist, and so was I. We were taught, years ago, to expect there would be a tremendous crisis, the uprising of a new society, a new political system, and the working class taking power. That is what I sense you are expecting. Still.
>
> All that is gone, Lula. The Berlin Wall is gone. So is the Soviet Union. There is no historical alternative now. So if there is a crisis in Brazil, there will only be disaster. The crisis will be pure misery. You still have intellectuals in your party who think otherwise, but they're leading you down a disastrous path." [27]

Cardoso believes that something changed in Lula's mind on that night, that he was never quite as combative. Of course, Cardoso didn't tell Lula anything he had not heard many times before. But hearing it in the presidential palace from the rival who had defeated him twice may have had a special impact.

As Lula pointed out in his interviews with Denise Paraná, he had always been critical of the "actually existing" socialism of the Soviet bloc. Many of Lula's closest associates in the Workers' Party had been members of armed guerrilla organizations in the 1970s. But the revolutionary left was suppressed and democracy came to Brazil through nonviolent political compromises, something most of the

---

[27] Fernando Henrique Cardoso with Brian Winter, *The Accidental President*, New York: Public Affairs: 2006, pp. 241-243.

radicals had believed was impossible.[28] As the world changed, many of the Workers' Party leaders changed their thinking. Lula thought this was normal. He explained:

> When God created human beings, he made the head round so that ideas can circulate. We can change our minds every now and then. I've had to adjust to reality and work on the basis of that reality and not my aspirations.[29]

A dramatic example of this circulation of ideas occurred in the late 1980s when a group of Workers' Party activists were invited to visit East Berlin by the Communist government of the time. While they were there, the masses stormed Communist Party headquarters. The activists' natural sympathies were with the masses in the streets, not with the bureaucrats in power. When this was followed by the collapse of the Soviet Union and the adoption of market economics in China and India, many of them concluded that the future organization of society would be "capitalism in its globalized form, or neoliberalism."[30]

One of Lula's closest associates, José Genoino, was the Workers' Party's candidate for governor of São Paulo in 2002. He lost that election, but was elected national president of the Workers' Party, and later was reelected to Congress. Genoino had fought with Maoist guerillas in the Brazilian interior along the river Araguaia where the states of Goiás, Pará and Maranhão come together. He was captured, imprisoned and tortured. After democracy was established, he was elected a federal deputy for the Workers' Party from São Paulo. Genoino's belief in Chinese socialism was shaken in 1989 when he watched television coverage of:

> The scene on Tiananmen Square when students were massacred singing the International and Beethoven's Ninth Symphony, and the tanks of the socialist state rolled over them. I spent the whole night without sleeping, remembering colleagues who died in Araguaia and who, when they died, took China as their reference point.

---

[28] Jorge Castañeda, *Utopia Unarmed: The Latin American Left After the Cold War*, New York: Vintage, 1994.
[29] Larry Rohter, "Brazil's Leader Steps Gingerly onto the World Stage," *New York Times*, May 31, 2003.
[30] José Maria de Almeida, in Felipe Demier, editor, *As Transformaões do PT e os Rumos da Esquerda no Brasil*, Rio de Janeiro: Bom Texto, 2003, p. 137.

I was born in a generation that preached the end of the exploitation of man by man; I defended a communist society, I believed in the viability of a perfect society [but now] I am not against profit, the market, some services being privatized and Brazil being inserted in the world.[31]

Another of Lula's closest associates, José Dirceu, was president of the Workers' Party until he resigned to join the Lula government in 2002. Dirceu was about to be elected head of the National Student Union in 1968 when the police raided the union's secret convention in Ibiúna in the interior of the state of São Paulo.[32] He was imprisoned, and then released in a prisoner exchange when a group of urban guerillas kidnapped United States ambassador Charles Burke Elbrick in 1969, an event recounted in the movie *Four Days in September*.[33] Dirceu went into exile in Cuba and was eager to return to Brazil as soon as possible, but the Cubans thought returning would be suicidal. His underground contacts in Brazil agreed that he was too well known to survive there. So he went to Chile until he had to flee from the coup d'état of 1973. He escaped to Mexico and then to Europe where he studied economics.

Dirceu had been banished from Brazil by the military government, but never felt comfortable living out of the country. Finally, the Cubans agreed to help him to return in 1975 after he had undergone plastic surgery and been trained to function with a new identity. He reentered Brazil with a false Argentine passport and five thousand dollars in cash. When he learned that several of the contacts the Cubans had given him had been arrested, he settled into a new identity in as "Carlos Henrique Gouveia de Mello" in a small community in the interior of the state of Paraná. He married and, after finding that he was not cut out for work in agriculture, sustained himself with small business ventures, developing a familiarity with ordinary Brazilians.

Dirceu remained underground until an amnesty in 1980 allowed him to surface. By that time his worldview had moderated and he participated in the founding of the Workers' Party. He was the par-

[31] José Genoino, "Entrevista," in Fernando Portela, *Guerra de Guerrilhas no Brasil: A Saga do Araguaia*. São Paulo: Editora Terceiro Nome, 2002, p. 29, 30, 31.

[32] Jos"e Dirceu and Vladimir Palmeira, *Abaixo a Ditadura*. Rio de Janeiro: Garamond, 1998. Paulo Markun, *O Sapo e o Príncipe*. Rio de Janeiro: Objetiva, 2004.

[33] The movie *Four Days in September* is based on a book by Fernando Gabiera, *O Que É Isso, Companheiro?* Rio de Janeiro: Guanabara, 1988.

ty's national president during the 1990s, and was elected a state deputy and then a federal congressman. As a congressman, he was co-
sponsor of the legislation to establish a Parliamentary Commission
of Inquiry into corruption allegations against President Collor de
Mello.

Lula was surrounded by activists and intellectuals such as
Genoino and Dirceu who had adjusted their thinking to the global
shift away from "actually existing" socialism. The party leadership
was also familiar with survey research showing that support for market-oriented reforms, including stabilizing the currency and bringing
in foreign investment, was much broader than they had thought. A
2002 survey, for example, found that 70.5 percent of Brazilians believed that "large foreign companies" were good for Brazil.[34] At the
same time, Brazilians favored a strong government to maintain stability and orderly growth. They did not want radicalism from the
right or the left. They wanted what the slogan on the national flag
promised: order and progress.

An analysis of the Brazilian electorate by political scientist André
Singer, son of Workers' Party economist Paul Singer, found that the
Brazilian electorate fell into three fairly consistent ideological groups:
left, center and right.[35] Lula had shown that he could rally the left
voters. He had no hope of rallying those on the right. The key to
winning were the voters in the "center," voters who could be swayed
by a candidate that seemed reasonable and appealing.

The Workers' Party campaign rhetoric in the 1990, 1994 and
1998 elections rallied the voters on the left, but failed to convince
enough of the voters in the center to join them. It gave more weight
to the opinions of party activists than to professional political consultants. This was understandable for an internally democratic party
that responded to its members. But Lula did not want to go into history as a four-time loser. He wanted to win the presidency in 2002.
He told the party leadership he would not run again unless he could
do it his way. That meant he had to be free to build as broad a political coalition as possible, including alliances with parties that were not
on the left. And it meant he had to formulate a message, a "myth,"
that could be sold to the middle-class voters who had been alienated

---

[34] Pew Research Center. Views of a Changing World, June 2003
http://pewglobal.org. The Brazilian survey was a face-to-face probability sample of
1000 adults 18 years of old and older. The interviews were conducted between July 2
and August 8, 2002.
[35] André Singer, *Esquerda e Direita no Eleitorado Brasileiro*, São Paulo: EDUSP, 1999.

by radical rhetoric in past elections. This time he adamantly insisted on political consultant "Duda" Mendonça at the helm.[36] Duda Mendonça was the ideal person for crafting a new image to appeal to the Brazilian center. His focus was on personality, not ideology or public policy. As he explained to a conference of public relations specialists:

> When I started out in political marketing, it was done primarily by journalists. It was very cold and unattractive. I was the one who introduced emotion to it. The formula worked. Brazilians are profoundly emotional. I showed the political experts that it was possible to make an interesting and attractive program without losing anything in terms of content.[37]

Lula was a natural for this approach because he is a naturally expressive person who communicates his feelings easily. As Mendonça describes it:

> I did not change Lula. My effort was to show that Lula could be himself. The Lula who had appeared in previous campaigns – bad humored, brave faced, rancorous – was a lie. If I had some merit, it was to convince him to go on television as he is. To cry, laugh, wink his eyes, be seductive, tell jokes.[38]

Mendonça started by having Lula record his own extemporaneous answers to questions. Then Mendonça smoothed out the wording and put Lula's speeches on the teleprompter, a device Lula had never been willing to use before. The teleprompter enabled him speak directly to a camera without appearing to read a text. Mendonça had Lula repeat his statements over and over until they became natural. Each statement was recorded, and by the end of the process, Lula agreed that the final version was much better than the first.

[36] Adolpho Queiroz, et al., "De Quintino Bocaiúva a Duda Mendonça: Breve História dos Marqueteiros Políticos no Brasil Republicano. http://reposcom.portcom.intercom.org.br/dspace/bitstream/1904/17464/1/R1210 -1.pdf. Dudo Mendonça, Casos & Coisas. São Paulo: Livros Globo, 2001. Rubens Figueiredo and Ciro Coutinho, "A Eleição de 2002," Opinião Pública, Campinas, 9:93-117, October 2003. http://www.scielo.br/scielo.php?script=sci_arttext&pid=So104-62762003000200005&lng=pt&nrm=iso&tlng=pt.
[37] Duda Mendonça, remarks during the 19th Creative Publicity Week, São Paulo, 2005. Quoted in Queiroz, op cit.
[38] Paulo Markun, O Sapo e o Príncipe. Rio de Janeiro: Objectiva, 2004, p. 332.

After the campaign was over, Fernando Henrique Cardoso praised this effort saying, "Duda's work with Lula was constructive because he perceived Lula as he was and reinforced his natural characteristics. Lula liked it because what was presented was authentic."[39] Duda Mendonça's market research showed that the ideal candidate would be someone like Lula personally, but with a stronger record of achievement. Lula had no dramatic accomplishment to use as his campaign myth, such as Cardoso's slaying the dragon of inflation. He had never been a governor or a senator and had little of the experience Brazilians usually expect in a presidential candidate. His strong points were his inspiring personal history, his effectiveness as a union leader, and his personal charisma. People liked him and believed that he felt their pain because he had lived it. To be elected, he had to convince middle-of-the-road Brazilians that he was past his radical youth and ready to be a mature statesman. He had to reassure the middle class and the business community that he was no threat to their economic interests, while letting the working class and poor know he still had them in his heart.

He also had to look presidential. Lula's stocky frame and short neck and arms made him look awkward in off-the-rack suits. So he got tailored ones that fit perfectly. Personal stylist Nazareth Amaral taught him how to tie a perfect Windsor knot in his silk ties. His hair and beard were carefully trimmed by his usual barber; age had given them a salt-and-pepper look that conveyed wisdom and maturity. In public appearances and television advertisements, he was frequently surrounded by advisors with doctorates in economics and extensive administrative experience to give voters confidence that he would be guided by expert advice.

This shift in image was important for the average voter, but it was not enough for the more sophisticated political actors, especially businessmen and investors with substantial economic interests at stake. They needed a more explicit statement of what Lula's policies would be. In May 2002, Lula met a group of his top advisors in a Portuguese restaurant in Riberão Preto, a small city in the interior of the state of São Paulo, to work on a statement to reassure important opinion leaders. This effort was not led by Duda Mendonça – he looked at a draft of the statement but refused to comment, saying it was a political and not a public relations document. It was prepared

---

[39] Markun, op cit., p. 354.

by a group of Lula's closest political advisors – the men who would play key roles in his administration once he was elected.

One of these advisors, physician Antônio Palocci, the mayor of Riberão Preto, was preparing to take over the political direction of Lula's campaign effort. Palocci was a former Trotskyist who had become convinced of the need for a "modern vision of the economy," getting away from "magical formulas and glittering proposals."[40]

Other leaders at the meeting were José Dirceu, then the national president of the Workers' Party; Aloizio Mercadante, then the party's candidate for senator from São Paulo; José Genoino, then the party's candidate for governor of the state of São Paulo; Zeca do PT (José Orcírio Miranda dos Santos), the governor of the state of Mato Grosso; and the economist Guido Mantega.[41] These leaders were all part of the moderate, pragmatic *Articulação* faction within the Workers' Party, as was Lula.

The Workers' Party had a committee working on an election platform, but its meeting was not until July and it would take time to hammer out a compromise. The leadership group couldn't wait. They needed to issue a statement quickly to reassure business leaders and the middle class that Lula would not disrupt the economy if he were elected. To reassure this sophisticated audience, they needed more than the rhetoric often used in party platforms. They decided they needed to make a firm commitment on four technical economic issues.

First, the Lula government would honor all contractual commitments made by the previous government, including commitments to international lenders. Second, it would control inflation. Third, it would maintain a floating exchange rate. And fourth, it would maintain a "primary budget surplus" (a surplus before making payments on debts) so as to be able to service Brazil's debts. The leaders debated committing themselves to a four percent primary budget surplus, but Lula opposed promising a firm number. Instead they pledged to keep it high enough to honor all commitments without increasing the internal debt.

The problem with these promises is that they sound very much like the "neoliberal" policies of the previous government, policies the Workers' Party had repeatedly denounced. For the general public, the party's campaign argument was that this model had failed and

[40] Antônio Palocci. *Sobre Formigas e Cigarras*. Rio de Janeiro: Objectiva, 2007, p. 57.
[41] Ibid., Chapter Two.

that what Brazil needed was change to a "new model." Rhetorically, the challenge was to promise the public change while promising the business leaders continuity.

The solution was to promise change in vague but dramatic rhetoric while promising continuity in the more precise but boring details. This was done in a document called the "Letter to the Brazilian People" which was signed by Lula personally, not by the Workers' Party. It was crafted in a series of meetings at the *Instituto Cidadania*, the Workers' Party's think tank in the city of São Paulo. Other leaders who were involved included previous campaign leader Luiz Gushiken, journalist André Singer and the general secretary of the Workers' Party, Luiz Dulci. They approved a final draft on June 22, 2002, and Lula released it at a meeting with over a thousand people and dozens of journalists.

In the letter, Lula assured the Brazilian people he would preserve the financial stability Cardoso had brought them and revive the nation's economic growth.[42] He promised to improve the lives of working people without imposing sacrifices on any class or group. He promised "changes" in the economic model to improve living standards, but without specifying what these changes would be. At the same time, he reassured the public that "this transition is naturally premised on respecting the country's contracts and obligations." Sophisticated listeners and readers knew that this meant paying the country's debts. This meant he would have to be at least as fiscally conservative as Fernando Henrique Cardoso had been. As his advisor Luiz Gushiken observed:

> This was a moment of *realpolitik*, in the midst of an electoral campaign that had been sometimes characterized by dreams and fantasies. It was a moment of division between real, precise political discourse and dreams of future intentions. It was our understanding of the crisis the country faced at this point in time, and a clear statement of our commitment to the responses that the situation demanded.[43]

On the campaign trail, Lula replaced the harsh polemics of his 1998 speeches with mellow platitudes. His new slogan, promoted by Duda Mendonça's consulting team, was *Lulinha, Paz e Amor* or *Lula: Peace and Love*. The press immediately labeled it the "Lula-lite" campaign. It worked like a charm.

---

[42] The "Letter to the Brazilian People" is at http://www.pt.org.br/.
[43] Markun, op cit., p. 337.

Political scientist Alberto Carlos Almeida did a study of the 2002 vote. He found that "the personality of the candidate is the strongest determinant of electoral choice."[44] But personality is not everything. Voters also want to feel comfortable with the candidate's political perspective. Almeida found that Brazilians in 2002 were uncomfortable with unconstrained market economics and preferred that the government take a strong role in the economy. In 2002, Lula found the right mix of personality and ideology. He promised unspecified changes under the careful guidance of an empathetic, understanding leader, while reassuring the business community he would respect their need for economic stability.

The leftists in the Workers' Party hoped that, once elected, he would go back to being the Lula of his previous campaigns, railing against neoliberalism. But that was a campaign strategy that had failed, not a reflection of his actual beliefs. *Lula: Peace and Love* actually fitted his personality better.

His leading opponent was José Serra of the Social Democratic Party. José Serra had a courageous record as an opponent of military dictatorship. He had performed brilliantly as minister of health under Cardoso, forcing the American drug companies to back down on the price of drugs for AIDS. He was an experienced, effective administrator, having served as planning minister and health minister in the Cardoso government. But he lacked Lula's good looks and personal charm, and he couldn't shake his association with the Cardoso government. People were tired Cardoso's insistence that they face up to unpleasant realities and difficult problems. Lula made no such demands and Brazilians wanted to believe that he could deliver on his promises.

In a survey conducted just after the first round of the 2002 elections, voters ranked Lula higher on every item except the ability to avoid strikes.[45] Seventy-seven percent thought he ranked highest on running a clean campaign without attacking his adversaries, compared to 11 percent for José Serra, 9 percent for Anthony Garotinho and 3 percent for Ciro Gomez. The voters thought that Lula would be best to create jobs, that he had the best plan for government, was the most honest and trustworthy and that he would do most for the poor. They thought he had the most experience to govern Brazil and

[44] Alberto Carlos Almeida, *Por Que Lula?: O Contexto e as Estratégias Políticas que Explicam a Eleição e a Crise.* São Paulo: Record, 2006, p. 258.
[45] These data are from a 2002 election survey reported by Almeida, Ibid.

was the best prepared and competent, despite the fact that he had never held an executive office. They also believed that he would be best at controlling inflation, although ending inflation had been done by Cardoso over Lula's objections. As political scientist Alberto Carlos Almeida interpreted the data, "the majority, at that time, believed that Lula would even be able to make it rain when water was needed, and to make the sun shine when heat was needed."[46]

Fernando Henrique Cardoso found Lula's popularity frustrating. He thought the Workers' Party had changed its politics without going through the necessary self-criticism. He felt it was deceitful to adopt the Social Democrats' ideas without giving them any credit. He complained that Workers' Party candidates were unwilling to pin themselves down, never specifying exactly what they planned to do. He said:

> They need to say what they are going to do with Brazil. They say they are against what is happening now. But are they going to renationalize industry? Are they going to restructure the debt? How are they going to lower the interest rate? How are they going to reconcile the proposed salary increases with the control of inflation? The agrarian reform is left up in the clouds. Lula says he is going to negotiate everything, but he never explains exactly what. He is going to negotiate to achieve what? What is his position? We are going into an election in which people are voting for images, not for policies. We have no idea which way we are going.[47]

Cardoso's frustration was understandable, coming from a college professor and policy analyst. But as a politician, Cardoso had learned that elections are not won by writing coherent policy documents. They are won by creating a myth and by telling the voters over and over and who is good and who is bad, as Cardoso did in 1994. After eight years of difficult transitions under Cardoso, Brazilians liked Lula's myth of the poor boy from the northeast who would slay the neoliberal dragon. They gave him 61 percent of the vote in the second round of the election against José Serra.

---

[46] Almeida, Ibid, p. 30.
[47] *Revista Época*, Edição 230. http://revistacpoca.globo.com.

CHAPTER FIVE
KEEPING THE ECONOMIC SHIP AFLOAT

Lula' inaugural speech promised dramatic changes for the better, claiming that he would be instituting a new model of politics:

"Change," this is the key word, this was the great message from Brazilian society in the October elections. Hope has finally conquered fear and Brazilian society has decided that it is time to blaze a new path. Faced with the exhaustion of a model that has produced stagnation, unemployment and hunger instead of growth; faced with a culture of individualism, egoism and indifference towards others, and the disintegration of families and communities; faced with threats to national sovereignty, the dire precariousness of public security, the lack of respect for the aged and the despondency of youth; faced with an economic, social and moral impasse; Brazilian society chose change and began, on its own, to promote the necessary changes. [48]

But skeptics observed that the speech offered very few clues about what the "change" would actually be. There was only one concrete promise: a campaign to "end hunger in our country." Lula spoke movingly, saying "if, at the end of my term, each Brazilian is able to eat breakfast, lunch and dinner, I will have fulfilled my life's mission." This vision was made poignant by the fact that Lula had grown up hungry.

Everyone could agree on ending hunger, but people wanted much more than that. Fully 86.4 percent of the respondents in a 2002 survey said they were "dissatisfied with the way things are going in the country today." [49] Nearly half were concerned about the economy, almost a quarter with crime and more than ten percent with political life. Runners up were health and children and education. Housing, international affairs, science, technology or the environment hardly merited a mention. Fully 85 percent of the respondents

---

[48] "Discurso do Senhor Presidente da República, Luiz Inácio Lula da Silva, na cerimônia de posse," Congresso Nacional, 1 January 2003.

[49] Pew Research Center. Views of a Changing World, June 2003, http://pewglobal.org. The Brazilian survey was a face-to-face probability sample of 1000 adults 18 years of old and older living in urban areas. The interviews were conducted between July 2 and August 8, 2002.

rated the country's economy as bad or very bad. They wanted economic growth that would benefit everyone, not only the hungry.

Brazil's economic growth had been disappointing since the 1970s, especially when compared to countries such as China, India, Chile and South Korea. Those countries had adopted the kind of market-friendly policies that the Workers' Party had long denounced as "neoliberal." And the previous Brazilian governments had already adopted many of these same policies.

Many people assumed that "change" meant reversing "neoliberalism," since that is what the Workers' Party had long promised. But what exactly would that mean? One analyst condensed the changes the anti-neoliberal left wanted into three key demands: redistribute income, nationalize important firms and stop paying the foreign debt.[50] Of these three, making payments on the debt was the most urgent because payments come due every month and markets react instantly to any hint of default.

Lula's Rubicon? Lula's whole presidency was constrained by one key strategic decision – the decision to stick with market-friendly economic policies. This meant using tax revenue to pay the nation's debts instead of to fund massive increases in social spending. It meant he couldn't do a large-scale land reform because he needed the revenue from commercial agricultural exports. It meant he had to allow economic development in the Amazon and other environmentally sensitive regions instead of converting them to nature preserves. It meant he had to welcome foreign investment and co-opt business elites into working with his government. It meant not breaking with global capitalism but joining it.

In the view of many on the left, this was a tragic lost opportunity. For Marxist scholar Francisco de Oliveira, it was as if Caesar had decided not to cross the Rubicon or Lenin had called off the October revolution:

> Contrary to Lenin, who perceived the breakdown of the dominant political order and pushed it further along the same path, leading the movement to socialist revolution, Lula *restored* the political order that the cyclone generated by Cardoso's deregulation and capitalist globalization had blown to pieces.

[50] Alfredo Saad-Filho, "Neoliberalism, Democracy and Economic Policy in Brazil," in Philip Arestis and Alfredo Saad-Filho, eds, *Political Economy of Brazil*, New York: Palgrave, 2007, p. 14.

To the absence of hegemony the Workers' Party's only response is to retreat back across the Rubicon, surrendering to the Rome of the dollar, situated somewhere between Avenida Paulista [*São Paulo's financial center*] and Wall Street. In the worst tradition of the Brazilian patronage system, the Workers' Party has tried to monopolize the state machine, on all levels, as well as the directorships of the remaining — but hugely important — state enterprises and quasi-state organs such as the pension funds, staffing them with its own party loyalists …

It would all verge on the theater of the absurd … were it not an ex-worker and ex-trade unionist who, as president, had turned back from the Rubicon to cross, instead, the threshold of totalitarianism.[11]

But Lula took office in Brazil in 2003, not 1917. The dominant order had not broken down and Cardoso's policies had not caused a "cyclone." Lula commanded no Roman legions. He took power through a democratic election, not a revolution. He was able to win the election only because he explicitly promised not to upset the capitalist apple cart. To default on the nation's debts would have triggered an immediate financial crisis similar to the one caused by Argentina's default in 2001. That crisis was disastrous for the poor and hard on everyone else. Radicals sometimes argue that you can't make an omelet without breaking eggs. But voters are not forgiving of leaders who break too many eggs on their watch. Argentine president Fernando de la Rúa had to be extracted from his office by a military helicopter and was sent into exile. If the Brazilian economy had crashed on Cardoso's watch as Argentina's did on de la Rúa's, Lula might have had an opening to move substantially to the left. But it hadn't, and Lula was not about to let it crash on his watch.

The *Letter to the Brazilian People* promised changes in the economic model, but it also promised that the changes would be carefully crafted so as not to upset the progress the country had already made, especially in controlling inflation. This meant crafting political compromises. As Workers' Party leader José Genoino later observed:

When one is in opposition, one expresses the 'poetry' of politics. When one is in power, the 'bloody' side of politics emerges. This side involves constricted choices and is, to some degree, disillusioning and frustrating. Politics cannot survive without dreams, without utopia, without

[11] Fernando de Oliveira, "O Momento Lenin," *Novos estudos* 75 (2006): 23-47. English translation by Neil Larsen, "The Lenin Moment," *Mediations*, Volume 23, No 1. http://www.mediationsjournal.org/articles/the-lenin-moment.

humanism, without revolutionary ideals. But power is a hard reality. It is cold and rational.[52]

Lula put it more simply:

When one is in opposition, one can make idle promises [*bravatas*], because you don't have to carry anything out. When you are in power, you have to actually do things, so you can't make idle promises. It is better to count to ten and rethink what you have to do, than to make mistakes and have to retract them.[53]

Many of the changes Lula actually made were pro-business. Speaking at the inauguration of a new president of the São Paulo Chamber of Commerce, Lula let the businessmen and business women know he shared their concerns about the need to streamline the bureaucracy to make it easier to start businesses and to close businesses that were no longer profitable. He spoke about the need to cut excessive social security payments to federal employees. He said he would have to do this even though it would mean stirring up the unionists who were his base of support because he had to think of the long-term needs of the country.

The first thing he had to do was to stabilize the financial system and prevent an international run on Brazilian securities and a major economic meltdown. He had to send clear signals to the international financial markets. To do this, one of Lula's first acts as president was to appoint Henrique Meirelles as head of the Central Bank. Meirelles had worked as a top executive with BankBoston in both the United States and Brazil, and he had excellent connections on Wall Street. He had also just been elected a deputy to the Brazilian Congress by the opposition Social Democratic Party. Leftists complained that appointing him was like putting a fox in charge of the hen house. That was exactly Lula's point. He reinforced this decision by keeping the other directors of the Central Bank from the Cardoso government.

Many on the left hoped that this was just a temporary transition period, to reestablish stability, and that Lula would implement more radical changes once the economy settled down. And changes did

---

[52] José Genoino. *Entre o Sonho e o Poder*. Edited by Denise Paraná. São Paulo: Geração, 2006, p. 167.
[53] Lula da Silva, Discurso na cerimônia de posse do presidente da Associação Comercial de São Paulo, March 27, 2003.
http://www.info.planalto.gov.br/static/inf_briefdiscusos.htm.

come, gradually and incrementally. But one thing that did not change was Lula's determination to pay the nation's debts. This was more than just a temporary expediency; Lula said it was based on a fundamental sense of responsibility.

Every time I lost an election, we got together a group of economists: Aloízio Mercadante, Paul Singer, Eduardo Suplicy, Paulo Nogueira Batista and so many others that I can't go on listing their names. Maria da Conceição Tavares. And we talked and talked. The discussion was about the International Monetary Fund, about the external debt, about "I don't know how much." Today, what are we proving? First, we are proving the following: we have to learn the lesson of the house. What is the lesson of the house? We have commitments? We have to keep our commitments. They are international commitments, they are commitments made by previous governments. And when you marry the widow you have to inherit the children as well. A person can't want to stay with the woman and not take on the children as well; or a woman with the husband and not the children. We have to marry the package, the happiness and the problems as well.[54]

Lula intended to meet his responsibilities in his new role as his country's symbolic father, just as he did as a husband and father in his personal life and as a union leader responsible for his comrades' lives. He would not walk away from his responsibilities as his own father had done.

He chose a finance minister who shared these priorities. Antônio Palocci was a physician, not an economist, but Lula trusted his loyalty and judgment. Palocci had coordinated the Workers' Party platform committee when it shifted from the abrasive rhetoric of 1998 to the "Lula-lite" of 2002. Lula thought it would be "better to put a good politician in the finance job, someone who gets along well with everybody, instead of an economist, who would just fight with the other economists in the party, because they never agree."[55]

Dr. Palocci thought his patient was doing well under Fernando Henrique Cardoso's treatment plan, but that "one of the most common errors in the treatment of serious illnesses is to interrupt treat-

[54] Lula da Silva, "Discurso na cerimônia de abertura da I Conferência Nacional de Economia Solidária – "Economia Solidária como Estratégia e Política de Desenvolvimento" June 27, 2006.
http://www.info.planalto.gov.br/static/inf_briefdiscusos.htm.
[55] Ricardo Kotscho, *Do Golpe ao Planalto*, São Paulo: Companhia das Letras, 2006, p. 239.

ment at the halfway point, at the first sign of recovery of the patient. When you do that, the illness recurs with more force."[56] Palocci had a good bedside manner and got along as well with business people. His first goal was to convince business leaders that the Lula government was firmly committed to fiscal conservatism and that the policies would be stable for the long term. He thought that "to the extent that important sectors of the economy doubt that the policies we have adopted are for the long term, inflationary expectations and high market interest rates will not subside, prolonging the grave difficulties we are going through."[57]

At its first meetings after the inauguration, the Central Bank raised the prime interest rates, making it clear that controlling inflation would trump social spending or measures to stimulate economic growth. Lula's first budget was more austere than Cardoso's last budget had been. The primary surplus – the money available to service debts – was 4.3 percent. This was higher than the 3.87 percent target specified in the agreement with the International Monetary Fund. Lula announced that he supported legislation, proposed under Cardoso, to make the Central Bank more independent.

Throughout the Lula government, as in all Brazilian governments, there were tensions between the need for financial stability and pressures to spend more on social programs. These tensions often played out as disagreements between his key advisors. As Finance Minister, Palocci had the primary responsibility for maintaining fiscal stability. Lula's Chief of Staff, José Dirceu, had the task of working with Congress and interest groups. Because of the nature of his job, Dirceu was more likely to advocate spending increases. Palocci viewed this difference between himself and Dirceu as a natural consequence of their different responsibilities. He said, "Zé Dirceu tended to defend the expansion of programs and projects and the relaxation of monetary policy. Nothing is more natural."[58]

Since money was scarce, Palocci's insistence on spending cuts often won the day. Lula felt this was necessary:

> When we took over the government, on the first of January, we had to make a budget cut of 14 billion *reais*. Why did we make this cut? Be-

[56] Antonio Palocci Filho, "A Nova Política Econômica," in João Paulo dos Reis Velloso, ed, *Governo Lula: Novas Prioridades e Desenvolvimento Sustentado*, Rio de Janeiro: José Olympio Editora, p. 56.
[57] Palocci, ibid., p. 57.
[58] Antônio Palocci. *Sobre Formigas e Cigarras*. Rio de Janeiro: Objectiva, 2007, p. 78.

cause they had made a budget but didn't have the money. And you can't go on inventing money in your accounts ...
We had to make a decision. Either we do what has historically been done in this country, we pretend to be administering seriously while we go on bailing out the boat and inventing budgets, or we say: "We don't have the money. We won't spend it. We won't spend it and that's it ..." If it is possible, in this country, for a worker with 240 *reais* to support a family, it is possible for each minister to measure, in a cautious and careful way, how to better spend the money that he has. [59]

It was far from certain that these measures would be successful in generating economic growth. Resistance was strong from the left of the Workers' Party itself. In May, 2003, thirty Workers' Party deputies, about a third of the delegation issued a manifesto called "Choose the Path toward Growth Now!" The manifesto argued:

The number is increasing who perceive the impossibility of combining conservative political economics with progressive social policy. The economic fragility of the country comes from the fact of it having become an importer of capital. Submitting itself to the logic of financial capital, Brazil has become stuck in a recessive trap, unable to escape ... The consequences of this policy are disastrous for our nation and our people. Recession threatens, unemployment increases and income falls ... It is time to lower interest rates, invest in production, attack the infrastructure bottlenecks that impede the resumption of growth, open credit for medium, small and micro-enterprises nationwide, generate employment and redistribute income. [60]

Lula would have been glad to spend money on all the good things the dissident deputies wanted. But he didn't have the money and he wasn't willing to risk going back to the years of high inflation when the Brazilian government habitually spent more than it took in and made up the difference by printing money. The *Real Plan* and the fiscal responsibility laws imposed on state governments had forced Brazil to give up that habit, but it did not solve the underlying problem of political pressures to spend more without raising taxes. The Cardoso government had struggled with this problem throughout its eight years, with only limited success. It often resorted to filling the budgetary gap with borrowing that drove up interest rates.

[59] Lula da Silva, "Entrevista à TV Bandeirantes," November 30, 2003. http://www.info.planalto.gov.br/static/inf_briefdiscusos.htm.
[60] Direito Penal, "Tomar o Rumo de Crescimento Ja!" June 14, 2003. http://www.mail-archive.com/penal@grupos.com.br/msg01279.html.

The Lula government hoped to resolve some of these problems quickly in its first term, during his "honeymoon" period. As soon as the economy was stabilized, Lula revived two reforms that had largely stalled under the Cardoso government: social security and tax reform. Economists generally believed that these reforms were essential for increasing the rate of economic growth. They were little mentioned in the campaign because they had been priorities of the Cardoso government and because they had proved very difficult to get through Congress.

At a national forum on the priorities of the Lula government, in May 2003, the coordinator observed that "expenses for Social Security and Assistance are the principal cause of the virtual fiscal blockade that exists in the federal government."[61] Social security costs had increased slowly but steadily as a percentage of the country's gross national product. And demographic projections showed that they would increase even more rapidly in the future if changes were not made.[62]

The Cardoso government had made some reforms in the social security system, but most of its efforts had been blocked in Congress. One of the main reasons was strong pressure from the public employee unions and the Workers' Party. The Workers' Party receives much of its support from unionized government employees and when it was in the opposition, the Workers' Party consistently supported the employees' demands. Now that it was responsible for paying the bills, it changed its tune. Lula's allies in Congress asked the Social Democratic Party to join them in passing some of the reforms the Workers' Party had always opposed. The Social Demo-

[61] João Paulo dos Reis Velloso, "Introdução: Novo governo, novas prioridades e crescimento sustentado: os pontos básicos do XV Fórum Nacional, in Velloso, ed, Governo Lula: Novas Prioridades e Desenvolvimento Sustentado, Rio de Janeiro: José Olympio Editora, p 20.

[62] Raul Belloso, "Desafios do governo Lula na área fiscal," in Governo Lula: Novas Prioridades e Desenvolvimento Sustentado, Rio de Janeiro: José Olympio Editora, pp. 105-129. Hélio Zylberstajn & Luís Eduardo Afonso & André Portela Souza, Reforma Da Previdência Social E Custo De Transição: Simulando Um Sistema Universal Para O Brasil, http://ideas.repec.org/p/anp/en2005/052.html. Tony Smith, "Pension Overhaul Wins Key Vote in Brazil," New York Times, August 7, 2003. Ugo Braga and Luiz Cláudio Cunha, "Longe do Pessimismo: Apesar do protesto das galerias, governo aprova reforma da Previdência e já anuncia um crescimento sustentável," ISTOÉ, December 3, 2003. http://www.terra.com.br/istoe/. André Portela Souza, et al, "Fiscal Effects of Social Security Reform in Brazil, http://www.anpec.org.br/encontro2004/artigos/A04A138.pdf.

crats did the responsible thing and continued to support reform even though Lula would get most of the credit. The Workers' Party leader in the Senate acknowledged their help in his memoir:

> I recognize that we inherited many positive initiatives from the government that preceded us, and that we benefited at various times from the mature attitude of responsible segments of the opposition in the National Congress, and especially in the Senate of the Republic.[63]

The reaction from the state employees was bitter. As they saw it, they had finally elected a Workers' Party government and it had turned on them. Twenty thousand public employees rallied outside Congress in Brasília to oppose the reforms. A few were so angry they smashed windows in the Congress building.

Despite the strong opposition, Lula had some notable legislative success. At the end of 2003, the Congress passed a reform that placed limits on retirement income, imposed taxes on highly paid retirees and increased retirement ages. The new pension legislation made the rules for new public sector workers the same as those for private sector workers. The retirement age for public workers was extended for seven years, to 60 for men and 55 for women, with incentives for those who continue working. Pensions were to be calculated based on average salaries, not on the last or highest salary, at least for new workers. Retired state and municipal workers were to pay an 11 percent tax on pensions above R$1,200 a month.

The Lula government also tackled the very difficult issue of tax reform. Again, this followed up on initiatives the Cardoso government had been unable to complete. In 1997, the Cardoso government had proposed consolidating a number of state and federal taxes into more efficient national value-added taxes.[64] But other priorities intervened and little was done.

The Lula government moved quickly on the issue, calling a two-day conference of governors in Brasília in February 2003 to discuss both social security and tax reform. In two months of intensive negotiations, they managed to reach significant consensus on a proposal that rationalized value-added taxation by state governments, making them all consistent. But there was no consensus on how the

---

[63] Aloizio Mercadante, *Brasil: Primeiro Tempo*. São Paulo: Planeta, 2006, p. 219.

[64] Rogério L.F. Werneck, "An Evaluation of the 2003 Tax Reform Effort in Brazil," Economics Department, Pontifical Catholic University of Rio de Janeiro, June 2004, http://www.econ.puc-rio.br/pdf/td488.pdf.

revenues would be distributed between federal, state and local governments. The state governments hoped to relax some of the constraints that the Cardoso government had imposed on their spending. Finally, in September 2003, the government gave in to these demands and promised the sub-national governments a fourth of the revenue. They also agreed to extend the free tax zone in the Amazon for ten years.

These concessions were not enough to win quick passage in Congress where every interest group took the opportunity to articulate its special needs. Finally Congress passed a modified version of the reforms that included a supplemental value-added tax surcharge of 9.25 percent. Many sectors of the economy, however, were given temporary exemptions from the tax increases.

None of these measures were revolutionary; they continued a gradual process of reform from the Cardoso government. Neither the tax reform nor the social security reform was enough to solve the budgetary problems, but they could at least help to slow the rate at which things were getting worse. Much depended on economic growth taking off and generating more tax revenues. When journalists asked Lula why the reforms were less than he had hoped for and less than Brazil needed, Lula was defensive:

> Lula: Why haven't other governments done what we have done? Why didn't they send the National Congress the social security reform and the tax reform already voted in the House?
>
> Journalist Fernando Mitre: Mr. President, excuse me, but the previous government sent the social security reform to the Congress and the Workers' Party was against it.
>
> Lula: Ah, Mitre, from you? For the love of God, Mitre!
>
> Mitre: But this is true.
>
> Lula: Mitre, the Workers' Party had 50 deputies. To say that the Workers' Party sunk the vote is, at the least, a joke in bad taste. The Workers' Party now has only 100 deputies and we haven't lost any votes yet. You know why, Mitre? Because whoever wants to do politics has to have patience, he has to converse, he has to articulate and that is what we are doing, my friend ... The fact is we have done what many people have been trying to do for twenty years in this country without success. And we did it....
>
> I am aware that if we don't make the reforms Brazil needs, no one will. Do you know why? Because it is hard. To make the reforms I had to resolve a fight with my own people, or let's say, with my base of support in the social movements. And I told them, we are going to do

this because it has to be done. We are going to do it so that thirty years from now my grandson, and your grandson, will be able to have a retirement. [65]

Lula's actions in his first year in office outraged many of his supporters. Heloísa Helena, a fiery Workers' Party senator from the state of Alagoas, protested that:

> Everything that we condemned with vehemence during our long party militancy, they have put into practice as if they were students of the International Monetary Fund and the World Bank. They have not just continued the economic policies of the Fernando Henrique Cardoso government; they have deepened the commitment to the neoliberal project. [66]

Heloísa stuck to her guns and voted against Lula's reforms in Congress. She was expelled from the Workers' Party.

Many of Lula's left-wing critics focused on the concept of "neoliberalism" which the left had used for years to criticize preceding governments. Luciana Genro, a leader of a leftist tendency within the Workers' Party, argued that "what the Lula government is doing today is to implement a political economy of continuity with the neoliberal model of Fernando Henrique Cardoso."[67] João Siscu argued that instead of switching from Plan A to Plan B, Lula had selected Plan A+, a plan even more "neoliberal" than his predecessor's, at least with regard to international financial commitments.[68]

But Marilena Chaui, a philosopher and founding member of the Workers' Party, objected that:

> Speaking of the neoliberalism of the Lula government is just a slogan. This government did not privatize the public sector or cut back on the state. On the contrary, it sought to restructure it in such a way as to move away from the neoliberal conception of politics as technical and

[65] Lula da Silva, "Entrevista à TV Bandeirantes, November 30, 2003. http://www.info.planalto.gov.br/static/inf_briefdiscusos.htm.

[66] Heloísa Helena, "Pronunciamento de Heloísa Helena na Reunião do Dório Nacional," 14 December 2003, in Luciana Genro & Roberto Robaina, *A Falência do PT: e a Atualidade da Luta Socialista,* Porto Alegre: L&PM Editores, p. 151.

[67] Luciana Genro, in Felipe Demier, ed., *As Transformações do PT e os Rumos da Esquerda no Brasil,* Rio de Janeiro: Bom Texto, 2003, p. 21.

[68] João Sicsú, "Rumos e definições da política econômica brasileira: do Plano A de FHC para o Plano A+ de Lula," in João Antonio de Paulo, ed, *A Economia Política da Mudança,* Belo Horizonte: Autentica, 2003.

administrative management of the public sector, and not as the government of society.[69]

She argued that the Lula government "is not a government of the left, but neither is it a neoliberal government." César Benjamin sought a middle ground in this argument, asserting that even if Lula was not continuing the privatizations, he was "legitimating the neoliberal inheritance" because he was not challenging the privatizations that had taken place in the past.[70]

This debate is confusing because "neoliberalism" is a fuzzy concept and it is possible for a government to be neoliberal in some ways and not in others. But the critics certainly had a point. It would be difficult to argue that Lula's government in 2003 was any less "neoliberal" than Fernando Henrique Cardoso's in 2002. It could be called neoliberalism with a human face.

In their memoirs published later on, the key members of Lula's economic team made it clear that they kept many of Cardoso's so-called "neoliberal" policies because they believed they were the right ones for the country. Workers' Party economist and newly elected Senator from São Paulo Aloizio Mercadante stated that it would have been irresponsible to "discontinue good policy initiatives from the past for petty political reasons, instead of perfecting and deepening them."[71] He and Lula's other economic advisors believed that much had been accomplished by the preceding governments and should be retained.[72] Finance Minister Antônio Palocci made this quite explicit:

It is worth emphasizing that the gains obtained by Brazil beginning in 2003 were based on advances achieved by previous governments and which produced, in general terms, important contributions to economic stability.[73]

[69] Marilena Chaui, in *Leituras da Crise*. São Paulo: Editora Fundação Perseu Abramo, 2006, p. 38, 40.
[70] César Benjamin in Felibe Demier, editor, *As Transformações do PT e os Rumos da Esquerda no Brasil*, Rio de Janeiro: Bom Texto, 2003, p. 35.
[71] Aloizio Mercadante, *Brasil: Primeiro Tempo*. São Paulo: Editora Planeta, p. 14.
[72] Aloizio Mercadante, interview in Guido Mantega and José Marcio Rego, editors, *Conversas com Economistas Brasileiros II*. São Paulo: Editora 34, 1999, pp. 355-382. See also the interviews with Paul Israel Singer and Francisco de Oliveria in the same volume.
[73] Antônio Palocci, *Sobre Formigas e Cigarras*. Rio de Janeiro: Objectiva, 2007, p. 100-101.

This point seems so obvious it hardly needs repetition. But in election campaigns, Workers' Party candidates, including Lula himself, often made the opposite claim. They claimed that they made a fundamental change in Fernando Henrique Cardoso's economic model. The facts are that in the first year Lula's team kept the economy afloat by continuing to pay the government's debts and the bureaucrats' salaries and by controlling inflation. They counted on increasing Brazil's exports to get the revenue to pay the bills, to fund educational, social and health programs, to build the country's infrastructure and finance expansion of domestic industries. These were the same strategies the Cardoso government had followed. The only Cardoso policy they did not talk about continuing was privatizing state-owned companies. But there were few good prospects for privatization left in any event, and they were not above privatizing state banks when they got into trouble.

The mainstream economists and the business community were reassured by the continuity in Brazil's fundamental economic model. Investment in the Brazilian economy resumed and economic indicators stabilized. The ship had weathered another storm, the seas were calm and the voyage was back on course. Lula made the most of it. When journalists asked him about his accomplishments in the first year, he said:

> I think the greatest happiness I've had in government is to reach the end of the year and to be certain that we managed to keep the ship from sinking. When we won the elections we had a country without external credibility to finance its exports ... Eleven months later we have record monthly levels of exports. After many years, we are registering, for the first time, a surplus in the deficit of our current accounts. We have almost four billion in surplus. And we are seeing the Brazilian economy returning to growth.[74]

---

[74] Lula da Silva, "Entrevista Concedida à TV Bandeirantes," http://www.info.planalto.gov.br/static/inf_briefdiscusos.htm.

CHAPTER SIX
VOTE-BUYING AND
CORRUPTION SCANDALS

Corruption is so deeply rooted in Brazilian society that one common saying is "the system isn't corrupt, corruption is the system." But the Workers' Party was supposed to be different. It was a party of idealists who made a point of denouncing corruption by its opponents. Fernando Collor had been impeached for corruption, and throughout the Fernando Henrique Cardoso administration the press was full of stories denouncing corruption. In the 2002 election, the Workers' Party collected all these stories and published them in a campaign book, not mentioning that many of the stories had been definitively refuted.[75] The stream of unproved denunciations made the population cynical and by 2002 even Lula said that he was "fed up with denunciations."[76] Corruption was generally accepted as a fact of life, not as something an election might change.

Corruption was hardly mentioned by any of the candidates in the 2002 election and the Lula campaign's position paper was brief and superficial.[77] But Lula did sign an agreement with *Transparência Brasil* to work with them on an anti-corruption plan after he was elected. *Transparência* recommended setting up a central agency to coordinate strategies to prevent corruption instead of waiting for scandals to break out. After the election, however, *Transparência's* staff members kept getting put off when they tried to meet with Lula's staff to implement a plan. After they pursued Lula's chief of staff, José Dirceu, for about a year he brushed them off with a statement that "the Workers' Party government does not steal and it does not allow others to steal." Dirceu seemed pleased with this sound bite and repeated it over and over in his speeches until a series of corruption scandals forced him to resign. *Transparência* concluded that "Lula and the

[75] Larissa Bortoni and Ronaldo de Moura, *O mapa da corrupção no governo FHC*, São Paulo: Editora Fundção Perseu Abramo, 2002. Eduardo Graeff, *Libro Branco: Combate à Corrupção e Denuncismo na era FHC*, Brasília, October 2002. http://www.psdb.org.br/biblioteca/publicacoes/livroBranco.pdf.
[76] Graeff, op cit, frontspiece.
[77] Coligação Lula Presidente 2002, "Combate à Corrupção: Compromiso com a Ética," http://www.pt.org.br.

former hard core of the government thought that they could deal with the issue with just rhetoric."[78]

José Dirceu was done in by a new technology: mini video cameras that can be hidden in offices to record bribes being given and illegal discussions taking place. These are sometimes used by disappointed lobbyists who believe their competitors have won unfairly with bribes. The recordings are then leaked to the press or turned over to the police.

The first corruption scandal of Lula's administration broke out in February, 2004, when one of Brazil's largest television networks broadcast a video showing Waldomiro Diniz, a direct subordinate of José Dirceu, taking kickback money from Carlos Cachoeira, a lottery, gaming and electronic bingo operator.[79] The video had been made in 2002 when Diniz was head of the state lottery in the state of Rio de Janeiro under Workers' Party governor Benedita da Silva. He was asking for illegal cash contributions to fund election campaigns in Rio de Janeiro and in Brasília. These "off-the-books" funds (called *caixa dois* or "second cash-box" in Portuguese) are illegal but widely used by Brazilian political parties. It wasn't corruption for personal enrichment; it was illegal fund raising for partisan purposes.

By the time the video was released, Waldomiro Diniz had been appointed head of the Congressional Relations Office in the Lula government. Faced with the video evidence, José Dirceu had to fire Diniz immediately. There were calls for Dirceu to resign as well, but Lula kept him and gave him a slightly less visible role. Lula knew this was risky, and told his press secretary "this week I made the biggest political error of my life."[80] Much later, Dirceu also said that not leaving the government sooner was his biggest political error.

The opposition was reluctant to make too much of the "second cash-box" scandal because their own candidates often used the same mechanism. Later on, Social Democratic Senator Eduardo Azevedo was accused of having used a second cash-box in his 1998 senate campaign. He was the president of the Social Democratic Party until October, 2005. The Social Democrats defended Azeve-

[78] Claudo Weber Abramo, "Lula e a corrupção," Política Democrática n° 12 (Fundação Astrojildo Pereira, do PPS), http://www.transparencia.org.br/docs/astrojildo.pdf.
[79] Adhemar Alteri. "Brazil's `Waldogate' Affair: The Shoe's on the Other Foot," *InfoBrazil Website.* February 21, 2004. http://www.infobrazil.com/.
[80] Ricardo Kotscho, *Do Golpe ao Planalto,* São Paulo: Companhia de Letras, 2006, p. 275.

do while attacking the Workers' Party, destroying their credibility on the issue.[81]

The Vote-Buying Scandal. A much bigger scandal erupted on May 14, 2005, when *Veja*, Brazil's biggest news magazine, broadcast a video showing Maurício Marinho, the head of the Post Office Department of Contracts and Administration, taking a R$3000 "tip" from a contractor.[82] The video was taken by a marketing consultant, Joel Santos Filho, working for a bidder who was angry about losing a contract.[83] The video was shown on television, and became an instant sensation. It can be seen in streaming video on the Internet.[84] The voices recorded on the video implicated Roberto Jefferson, a federal deputy from Rio de Janeiro and the national president of the Brazilian Labor Party. The Brazilian Labor Party was an important part of Lula's government coalition.

When a major story about corruption appears in the press, the opposition often demands a Parliamentary Commission of Inquiry. A Parliamentary Commission had led to President Fernando Collor's resignation under threat of impeachment and the Workers' Party repeatedly demanded such commissions during Cardoso's presidency. Now that the tables were reversed, the Workers' Party desperately fought to prevent the appointment of a Parliamentary Commission. They gave the same reason Cardoso always gave, the commissions take up so much of Congress's time and attention that little other business can be done.

It is a good point, but Parliamentary Commissions of Inquiry are also the best mechanism the Brazilian government has to respond quickly to a corruption crisis. Judicial processes drag on for years. In this case the video evidence was too stunning to ignore and the Commission of Inquiry was established over Lula's objections. Roberto Jefferson decided not to go down alone and gave an interview to the *Folha de São Paulo*, Brazil's largest newspaper,

---

[81] Fernando Henrique Cardoso, "Carta aos Eleitores do PSDB," http://www.psdb.org.br/diario/htm/diario_numero724.htm#2.
[82] For references on these scandals see Peter Flynn, "Brazil and Lula, 2005," *Third World Quarterly* 26: 1121-1267and David Fleischer, "The Political Corruption Scandals in 2003-2005," unpublished paper. More detail is available, and updated, at http://pt.wikipedia.org/.
[83] Fernando Jaspar, "Após um ano, autor de gravação que denunciou o mensalão quebra silêncio," *Gazeta do Povo*, August 2, 2006. http://www.deunojornal.org.br/materia.asp?mat=117607&pl=Antonio%20Palocci.
[84] The video of Marinho taking a bribe is at: http://www.umbrasilmelhor.com.br/txt/VIDEOPROPINA.html.

claiming that the Lula government had been giving a monthly pay-off or *mensalão* to congressmen from the Liberal Party and Progressive Party, two parties in Lula's coalition. He said that Delúbio Soares, the treasurer of the Workers' Party, ran the scheme and that he and others had been told about it by José Dirceu, Lula's chief of staff.

On June 14, Jefferson testified for six hours before the Parliamentary Commission of Inquiry, accusing José Dirceu and other top Workers' Party officers, but stating that Lula himself did not know about the scheme. The testimony was televised, and business all over the country stopped while everyone watched the hearings. Many stores put televisions in their windows facing the streets so passing shoppers could watch.

Lula put the best face on the events that he could, claiming that so much dirt was being uncovered because his government was doing a vigorous job of cleaning house:

My friends,
Today I want to speak to you about a very serious matter: corruption. It is a topic that for many years has been a great weight on the Brazilian government, and an embarrassment for the Brazilian people.
I want to begin by saying two things.
First: corrupt individuals should always be punished, and always in an exemplary manner. No matter who it is, where he came from, be he ally or adversary. As we all know, corruption is an old ailment. But there is much we can do against this cancer that corrodes our country.
Second: if there has ever been a government that has been implacable in fighting corruption, since the first day, it is my government. Never has Brazil seen so many important and powerful people being arrested for corruption and fraud against the public coffers as now businessmen, judges, legislators, politicians, police officers and high public officials who had acted with impunity for years, even for decades.
This can give the false impression that corruption has increased when, in truth, what has increased, and a great deal, is the struggle against corruption, and as a result of this, there has been a natural increase in the number of arrests and actions by the federal police, which are reported almost every day on television and in the newspapers ...
I have stated before that the struggle against corruption is like a house that has not been cleaned well for a long time, and where a lot of

dirt has accumulated. When you start to clean, what you find is more trash, behind the door, under the furniture, inside the closets. This government has not swept the dirt under the rug.[85]

This argument had some truth to it, but it is impossible to say how much because there is no objective measure of how much corruption goes on in a given year. The Federal Police, especially, were becoming more vigorous in pursuing corruption. This was a result of ongoing modernization efforts. Their equipment and training had steadily improved, and they were doing their job. In an interview on November 4, 2006, a reporter asked Attorney General Antonio Fernando de Souza, "has corruption in the public service increased in the past few years, or has it simply stopped being swept under the carpet, as the president claims?" Souza replied:

> In order to make a statement as to whether it increased or decreased, one would need precise data about past behavior. We have suspicions that there were suspect cases that were not properly investigated. It is important to say that, in the last four years, with regard to the Public Ministry, we have been much more incisive in researching the data needed to process cases of misdeeds or corruption.[86]

But even if more cases were being uncovered because of improved policing, the cases that were being uncovered were hard to ignore. As the evidence of corruption reached people closer and closer to Lula, it got harder and harder to brush it off as housecleaning. Duda Mendonça, the political consultant who crafted Lula's 2002 campaign, testified that R$10 million of his R$25 million fee had come from off-the-books funds supplied by foreign banks and by businessman Marcos Valério. Mendonça said that he was told to open an account in the Bahamas under the name "Düsseldorf."[87]

On March 30, 2006, the federal attorney general formally accused 40 congressmen of participation in the monthly payoff scheme and named José Dirceu as the leader of a criminal conspiracy. This was a quite remarkable action, demonstrating that the attorney gen-

[85] Lula da Silva, "Pronunciamento à nação do presidente da República, Luiz Inácio Lula da Silva, em cadeia de rádio e tv, sobre medidas do governo para o combate à corrupção," June 23, 2005, http://www.presidencia.gov.br/noticias/discursos/.
[86] Fánio Guibu, "Procurador-geral vê maior combate à corrupção sob Lula," *Folha de São Paulo*, Nov 4, 2006,
http://www1.folha.uol.com.br/fsp/brasil/fco411200620.htm.
[87] Peter Flynn, "Brazil and Lula, 2005," *Third World Quarterly* 26: 1121-1267.

eral's office was truly acting independently of the presidency, as it is supposed to do. The attorney general also indicted the Workers' Party's treasurer, Delúbio Soares, and its president, José Genoino.[88] The attorney general's report on the monthly payoff scheme was a rigorously researched, carefully documented 136-page legal document. It stated that:

> The evidence in the current inquiry demonstrates the presence of a sophisticated criminal organization, divided into active sectors, that was professionally structured to practice crimes such as embezzlement, money laundering, active corruption, fraudulent administration, as well as diverse forms of fraud.[89]

At first, Lula tried claiming that the accusations were a conspiracy by "elites" that were out to get him. But few believed that. The video recordings and the evidence given under oath were too convincing. Besides that, everyone knew that the business elites were happy enough with his government and had no reason to cause political instability. Finally, Lula apologized to the public, claimed that he had been betrayed by his party, and promised to clean things up. His remarks were taken to refer to José Dirceu and other high Workers' Party officials, but he never named those he said had betrayed him. On subsequent occasions he went on to praise the same individuals. He said:

> I helped to create this party [*the Workers' Party*] and, you know, I lost three presidential elections and won the fourth, always being faithful to its ideals, as faithful as I am today. I want to say to you, with all frankness, that I feel betrayed. Betrayed by unacceptable practices that I knew nothing about. I am indignant about the accusations that appear every day, and that are offending the country. The Workers' Party was created precisely to strengthen ethics in politics and to fight at the side of the poor people and the middle classes of our country. I have never changed, and I am certain that the same indignation that I feel is shared by the great majority of all those who have accompanied us on this journey.[90]

---

[88] Procuradoria Geral da República, "Mensalão: PGR denuncia 40 pessoas," http://www.pgr.mpf.gov.br/pgr/imprensa/iw/nmp/public.php?publ=6890.

[89] Antonio Fernando Barros e Silva de Souza, Procurador-geral Da República, Denúncia no Inquérito n° 2245, March 30, 2006., page 11. http://www.pgr.mpf.gov.br/pgr/asscom/mensalao.pdf

[90] Wikinoticias, "Lula se diz traído e pede desculpas ao povo brasileiro," August 12, 2005.

The attorney general's report moved the case beyond denunciations and political posturing. Delúbio Soares and José Genoino resigned their party posts. Dirceu resigned from the government and returned to the Chamber of Deputies, protesting his innocence. On November 30, he was expelled from the Congress and prohibited from holding public office until 2015. He returned to the private sector, working as a lobbyist. His influence in the Lula government, and particularly in state-owned companies, was reputed to remain high.

Of course, an indictment is not a conviction and José Genoino insisted that "the Workers' Party never mounted a criminal organization, and I never participated in a criminal organization."[91] Genoino insists that the payments to legislators were campaign contributions, not bribes. These arguments could only be resolved in a court of law with proper rules of evidence and legal protections, a process which takes years.

The business community was reassured that Antônio Palocci, the finance minister, was still running the economy. But then he was threatened by unrelated corruption allegations. Palocci held on until March 27, 2006, when he was forced to resign because of evidence that he or someone close to him violated bank secrecy laws to get information about a young man who was testifying about Palocci's visits to a disreputable house maintained in Brasília by associates from the time when he was mayor of Riberão Preto. The young man, a watchman, had received an unusual sum of money, but it turned out to be a legitimate payment by his natural father. After resigning, Palocci declared his candidacy for the Chamber of Deputies in the 2006 election, and was re-elected with 152,000 votes. José Genoino was also elected to the Chamber of Deputies in 2006, by a very large vote, and continued to be a leader of the Workers' Party.

There was no evidence that Lula or his close associates were enriching themselves personally, at least not substantially. Brazilian law requires candidates for office to file statements disclosing all their assets. Lula's statement showed ownership of three apartments in São Bernardo do Campo, the industrial suburb of São Paulo where he lives, and a few bank and investment accounts. His net worth in his 2006 declaration was R$839,033 or US$384,000, compared with

http://pt.wikinews.org/wiki/Lula_se_diz_tra%C3%ADdo_e_pede_desculpas_ao_p
ovo_brasileiro.
[91] José Genoino, *Entre o Sonho e o Poder*, op cit, p. 176.

R$422,900 in 2002. It is generally believed that his apartment was a gift from a company with which his union was doing business.

Lula's son, Fábio Luiz Lula da Silva, was remarkably successful in winning contracts from state enterprises for his Gamecorp television company.[92] One Workers' Party official was found to be driving a new sports utility vehicle contributed by a Petrobras contractor. When cash payments are made under the table, it is generally assumed that a certain amount sticks to the hands of the messengers. But the known accumulations of wealth by Workers' Party associates are modest compared to those attributed to many other Brazilian politicians.

Antônio Palocci's reported net worth in 2006 was only R$295,196 or US$136,000, according to his form filed with the Supreme Electoral Tribunal, including his cars, his home, a few investments and the value of the telephone lines to his house. José Dirceu was not allowed to run for office in 2006, so his net worth was not available. But he was not accused of significant personal enrichment while in office. Of course, Brazilian politicians often hide assets with front men known as *laranjas*. But hidden assets are vulnerable to being discovered by Brazil's vigorous investigative reporters. After leaving office, Palocci started a consultancy which enabled him to accumulate substantial wealth. This was discovered by a journalist in 2011 after Lula's successor had reappointed Palocci as chief of staff. He was once again forced to resign the office.

Brushing Off the Vote-Buying Scandals. When the monthly payoff scandal broke, Lula's critics blamed him for it. Fernando Henrique Cardoso urged Lula to apologize to the nation and announce that he would not run for re-election on the grounds that "the fault is not with those who are chosen, but with those who do the choosing."[93] There was talk of impeachment, but the opposition was afraid to introduce an impeachment resolution because Lula's base of popular support continued to be very strong. The head of the Supreme Federal Tribunal, Nelson Jobim, reportedly told politicians that any attempt to impeach Lula could lead to a profound period of social unrest.[94]

---

[92] Folha de São Paulo, "Publicidade oficial ajuda a bancar TV de filho de Lula," Nov 28, 2006. http://www1.folha.uol.com.br/fsp/inde28112006.shl.
[93] Epaminodas Dedo, "FHC rebate petista e chama Lula de "demônio", *Folha Online* September 25, 2006.
http://www1.folha.uol.com.br/folha/brasil/ult96u83815.shtml.
[94] Diogo Mainardi, *Lula é Minha Anta*. Rio de Janeiro: Editora Record, 2008, p. 25.

Lula's supporters insisted he was off the hook because no smoking gun had been found. Deputy Osmar Serraglio, of the Democratic Movement Party, argued that "no objective responsibility can be placed on the top leader of the nation simply because he occupies the position at the top of the executive power. This would mean assigning responsibility without any scientific evidence."[95] For Lula, the buck stopped with José Dirceu. Dirceu claimed to be "a victim of unfounded allegations" but he accepted his fate and insisted that Lula knew nothing.[96] In an interview with American diplomat William Perry, later revealed as part of WikiLeaks, Dirceu admitted that he had maintained a second cash-box in all his campaigns, as he said all Brazilian politicians do. He said that Lula, "who doesn't do much on his own initiative," should have paid more attention to finding legitimate sources of funding for the party.[97] He described the vote-buying scheme as "crazy and perverse" but denied any personal knowledge of it, a denial that the American diplomat thought unconvincing. He cast aspersions on Congressman José Genoino and Governor-elect of the state of Rio Grande do Sul, Tarso Genro. He said Lula was depressed about the events and didn't think he would run for re-election, or that he would win if he did.

But Lula's depression was short-lived because popular concern with the scandals soon abated. Many of Lula's supporters brushed off the scandals, viewing them as unimportant, unproven or just politics as usual. Wagner Tiso, one of Brazil's top musical arrangers and composers, was overheard by reporters saying, "I am not worried about the ethics of the Workers' Party or any kind of ethics. For me, this is of no interest. I believe the Workers' Party played the game you have to play to govern the country." His companion, the actor Paulo Betti, replied, "Yes, politics does not exist without dirty hands. You can't do it without sticking your hands in the shit."[98] Cristovam Buarque, the former Workers' Party governor of the Federal District, quipped that Lula's slogan should be "he steals but he is

[95] Osmar Serraglio quoted in "A guerra batalha por batalha," Forum, Publicaao da Editora Publisher Brasil, November 2006, p. 22.
[96] "Trajetoria," blog de Zé Dirceu, http://blogdodirceu.blig.ig.com.br/.
[97] Tatiana Farah, "Dirceu diz que mensalão foi esquema 'louco e perverso'," O Globo, December 20, 2010. http://clippingmp.planejamento.gov.br/cadastros/noticias/2010/12/20/dirceu-diz-que-mensalao-foi-esquema-louco-e-perverso.
[98] Josias de Souza, Folha de São Paulo, Sept 3, 2006.

one of ours." Buarque left the Workers' Party and ran under a different label in the 2006 elections.[99]

The publicity had only a brief impact on Lula's ratings in the opinion polls. The percent rating the Lula government "poor" peaked at 29 percent in December 2005, just exceeding the 28 percent rating it "good." But even more respondents, 41 percent, rated it as "regular" or average. For these respondents, the corruption problems apparently meant that the Workers' Party was just like the others. Even more striking is how quickly the government's popularity recovered. Lula's apology and sacking of his key aides seemed to satisfy most people. The Workers' Party lost some of its prestige among middle-class voters, but its support continued to grow among the poor and less educated, especially in the northeast.

Many of Lula's supporters accepted the arguments that his government's housekeeping efforts were getting out more dirt or that Lula was under assault by his political opponents. In a 2006 survey commissioned by the Workers' Party, a strong majority, 69 percent, agreed with the statement that "there is corruption in the majority of governments, sometimes even more in governments other than Lula's," while only one in five thought the Lula government was more corrupt than others. Only 2 percent volunteered that they did not believe that the Workers' Party gave money to deputies. Most of the respondents who were Workers' Party supporters said they believed Lula did not know about the bribes. Most of the supporters of other parties believed that he did.[100]

Corruption for Campaign Fund Raising. When Lula wanted to win the 2002 presidential election, he thought he needed a coalition to do so. He did not want a coalition with just a few minor leftist parties as he had had before; he wanted a mainstream party that would bring him respectability and votes from moderates. Forming an alliance with a mainstream party would make it clear that he was not an extremist. Fernando Henrique Cardoso had defeated him twice with just such a coalition.

[99] Wilson Tosta, "Cristovam não descarta apoiar Lula num eventual 2º turno," *estadao.com.br*, August 28, 2006,
http://www.estadao.com.br/ultimas/nacional/eleicoes2006/noticias/2006/ago/28/310.htm.
[100] Núcleo de Opinião Pública da Fundação Perseu Abramo. 2006. *Imagen Partidária e Cultura*
http://www2.fpa.org.br/portal/modules/wfdownloads/viewcat.php?cid=51.

Brazilian electoral coalitions are often fluid until the last minute when slates must be registered with the Supreme Electoral Tribunal. Just before this deadline in 2002, Lula, Dirceu and other Workers' Party leaders met in the Brasília apartment of Congressman Paulo Rocha with José Alencar and representatives of Alencar's Liberal Party. The Liberal Party is a center-right party linked to the Universal Church of the Kingdom of God, an evangelical Protestant church. Alencar was an entrepreneur from Minas Gerais, and Lula thought he would make a good vice presidential candidate. From an ideological point of view, an alliance between a left-wing "socialist" party and a pro-business "liberal" party made little sense.[101] But it made sense politically as a means of "balancing the ticket" and appealing to voters and lobbyists who distrust ideology and wanted reassurance that Lula was a pragmatic politician.

Dozens of journalists had heard about the meeting and were waiting for an announcement. If he couldn't get Alencar, Lula would probably just nominate a Workers' Party leader for vice president. According to Lula's press secretary, "it was clear to everyone that the impasse was over the question of the amount of financial aid the Liberal Party wanted from the Workers' Party to finance its campaign." Three years later, when the scandals broke out, the press secretary learned that the amount was 10 million *reais*.[102]

There is no way the Workers' Party could have provided this money from legal campaign funds; it had to come from the off-the-books kickbacks from contractors. This statement, from Lula's press secretary Ricardo Kotscho, is the closest thing to a "smoking gun" proving that Lula knew about corrupt practices. Lula just says that these off-the-books funds are common practice in Brazil, and neither admits nor denies using them.

Buying Support in Congress. It is understandable why a candidate would feel the need to use off-the-books funding to win a hotly contested campaign. But why should an immensely popular president, just elected with 62.5 percent of the popular vote, resort to buying votes in Congress? The bribes (or off-the-books campaign contributions if you prefer) were expensive; one early estimate was $136 million *reais* a year. This money could only come from illegal

[101] Claudio Weber Abramo, "Nada sera impossível," *Observatório da Imprensa*, November 28, 2001, http://observatorio.ultimosegundo.ig.com.br/artigos/fd281120011.htm.
[102] Richard Kotscho, *Do Golpe ao Planalto*, São Paulo: Companhia das Letras, 2006, p. 223.

kickbacks or misuse of government funds, either of which put Lula or his subordinates in danger of criminal prosecution. Why run such a risk and compromise one's widely proclaimed principles? The answer may be found in a constitutional structure that makes it difficult for even a very popular president to govern effectively. Despite Lula's landslide presidential victory, his coattails were not strong enough to give him a majority in Congress. Parties belonging to Lula's coalition had elected only 42.5 percent of the representatives in the Chamber of Deputies. This is not something unique to Lula or the Worker's Party; it is inherent in the country's proportional representation system. Fernando Henrique Cardoso was elected by a similarly large margin and had the same kinds of problems. The problem is with the 1988 constitution, enacted to protect the country's transition from military authoritarianism by constraining the president's power. The public expects the president to get results, and gives him credit or blame for the outcome, but the system makes it very difficult to put together a congressional coalition to pass a president's program.

To be effective, a president must find a way to persuade deputies from other parties to join his coalition or at least support his legislative initiatives. Lula did that. When the Chamber of Deputies was sworn in on February 1, 2003, the number of deputies in his coalition was 42.5 percent. By June, two major parties had joined the coalition and the coalition had 72.1 percent of the deputies.[103] Party switching and coalition shifting are normal in Brazil, but there is always a price to be paid. Typically, political parties negotiate to see how many ministries they can get for joining a coalition. A small party gets a small ministry such as Sports or Culture with a small budget. A big party gets a big ministry such as Transportation or Social Security with a big budget. The parties use these ministries to provide patronage jobs and contracts for their supporters. This may be viewed as "corruption" but most of it is technically legal.

Lula changed the usual practice, largely in an effort to provide more jobs for Workers' Party activists. He broke with the tradition of the "single door" whereby each ministry was controlled by a single party and all "positions of confidence" (non civil-service jobs) in the ministry were filled by people chosen by that party. He appointed

[103] David Fleischer, "The Political Corruption Scandals in 2003-2005," paper presented at the 26th International Congress of the Latin American Studies Association.

Workers' Party people and people from allied parties to positions in each of the ministries. This led to conflict, some of which led directly to leaks to the press about corruption. **Jobs for Party Loyalists.** Finding jobs for all the Workers' Party leaders who felt they deserved them cut into the resources Lula had to offer deputies from other parties in exchange for their loyalties and votes. His commitment to maintaining a primary fiscal surplus so as to pay off the country's debts cut into his resources for pork barrel spending. The monthly payoff was a relatively inexpensive way of buying loyalty from these deputies, many of whom switched not to the Workers' Party itself but to one of the other coalition parties.

The Workers' Party always had idealists and revolutionaries, but its core was union members more concerned with economic issues. Over the years, more and more of its support came from public employee unions. Its meetings came to be dominated by people making careers in politics and public administration. By winning power, the party won control of thousands of jobs for its members. Many Workers' Party stalwarts had careers that provided only modest incomes, so getting a government job meant a large increase in income. As Wendy Hunter observed in her history of the Workers' Party, "ideological considerations aside, party militants felt also that their dedication to the PT [Workers' Party] deserved to be rewarded with jobs in the federal administration."[104] This was complicated by the fact that there were many factions in the Workers' Party and jobs had to be allocated to each faction. Once the top jobs were allocated to the leaders of the faction, those leaders could hire supporters for lesser positions.

The Brazilian government has a very large number of jobs that are filled at the discretion of the president. At the end of the Cardoso administration, there were by one estimate approximately 21,000 such posts in the federal government. According Cardoso, most of these were low-level jobs that were filled by people recruited from within the bureaucracy. In his estimate, the really important jobs probably number around 2,000, which he acknowledged is still a significant number of people.[105] A precise count by the *Folha de São Paulo* in February 2007, found that there were 19,802 positions of confidence in the federal government with salaries ranging from R$1,232

---

[104] Wendy Hunter. *The Transformation of the Workers' Party in Brazil: 1989-2009*. New York: Cambridge University Press, 2010, p. 162.
[105] Personal correspondence from Fernando Henrique Cardoso.

to R$7,595 a month. Of these, 3,884 were elite jobs with salaries of R$4,898 a month or more, supplemented with a housing allowance of approximately R$1,800.[106] This is roughly comparable to the number of positions the president of the United States is estimated to control, about 4,000, but in the United States many of these must be confirmed by Congress.

In November 2006, the Workers' Party quoted statistics showing that it had filled only 2,499 positions of confidence by July 2005 and another 1,566 by May 2006.[107] This probably refers to the elite positions that are normally given to party activists. In Lula's first term, the Workers' Party maintained control of the key positions in almost all the ministries, even those with a minister from another party. This was a cause of internal conflicts within the ministries, some of which leaked out to the press in the form of corruption accusations. In the second term, Lula returned to the traditional "closed door" practice in which the positions of confidence in each ministry are given to one party. As a result, the Workers' Party was anticipating losing as many as 1,200 positions of confidence in Lula's second term.[108]

There are also many positions of confidence in each of Brazil's state governments; indeed, the number in the São Paulo state government rivals that in the federal government. These positions are very important to activists from all political parties, but especially to those from left parties and working-class backgrounds who have less attractive alternatives in the private sector.

Sociologist Francisco de Oliveira resigned from the Workers' Party, of which he had been a founder, soon after Lula da Silva was elected. He was disappointed that the Lula government was not living up to its socialist ideals. He worried that people would suspect he was feeling slighted because he was not offered a job in the new administration. Eager to show that this was not the case, he reported that, even before the Lula government took power, he received a visit from a representative of the transition team who told him that:

[106] Eduardo Scolese and Pedro Dias Leite, PT teme perder 1.200 cargos com reforma," *Folha de São Paulo*, February 17, 2007.
http://www1.folha.uol.com.br/folha/brasil/ult96u89638.shtml
[107] Data provided by José Genoino's office from a Workers' Party data base, the Sistema de Arrecadação de Contribuições Estatutárias,
http://www.pt.org.br/site/secretarias_def/secretarias_int.asp?cod=5084&cod_sis=19&cat=169.
[108] Ibid.

The top positions in the new government have to be negotiated, but for any second level position, in my area of competence and preference, I had only to make my choice and I would have the right of first refusal. He then pulled out a giant organizational chart of the Brazilian government to look for positions or functions I might choose ...[109]

Rewarding supporters and allies with government jobs in this way is a Brazilian tradition, and while it is sometimes viewed as "corruption," it is not illegal. It can be used to reward loyalty in congressional votes, but it is a subtle process. Jobs are not often given out for specific votes. Paying congressmen directly for their votes is much less common, and is illegal. These kinds of payments have sometimes been made by private individuals and interest groups. The Workers' Party is the first in Brazilian history to have used the party organization itself to systematically organize such payments. This may have been done because it was viewed as less expensive and more efficient than giving out leadership positions or reaching compromises with other parties. As Roberto Jefferson explained the thinking:

It is cheaper to pay a mercenary army than to share power. It is easier to hire a deputy than to discuss a project of government. ... He who is paid does not think.[110]

It may seem easier, but only if you get away with it. The corruption scandals were a turning point in the Lula government because they cost him many of his key advisors and forced him to look more seriously beyond the Workers' Party for congressional support. In his first two years, his government was thought to be dominated by three key advisors: Luiz Gushiken, his minister of communication, José Dirceu, his chief of staff, and Antonio Palocci, his minister of finance. All three were lost to the corruption scandals. For the remaining six years of his presidency, Lula often appointed people who were less well known and more dependent on him. His eventual successor, Dilma Rousseff, was one of these people. He also relied more heavily on the traditional practice of allocating control of ministries to leading politicians of allied parties as a means of ensuring support

---

[109] Francisco de Oliveira, " Tudo que é sólido se desmancha em... cargos," *Folha de São Paulo,* 14 December 2003. http://www.consciencia.net/2003/12/12/oliveira-pt.html.
[110] Peter Flynn, op cit, p. 1232.

in congress. His government became less a Workers' Party government, more definitively a Lula government.

CHAPTER SEVEN
ENDING HUNGER WITH FAMILY ALLOWANCES

Lula used his first public statement after his election to highlight a key priority: "The principal objective of my government is to combat hunger and misery. I will feel that my life is complete when all Brazilians can eat three times a day." The speech was enthusiastically received. Columnist Alberto Amadei called it "the most important declaration by a Latin American head of state since Salvador Allende in 1973." Amadei recognized that it was not a new idea, but he felt that "it was more because it was less. It was grandiose for its obviousness."[111]

The Zero Hunger program was not a spur-of-the-moment inspiration. The Citizenship Institute, a non-profit organization associated with the Workers' Party did extensive field research, held hearings around the country, and prepared an impressive 118-page document called *The Zero Hunger Project: A Proposal for a Food Security Policy for Brazil*.[112] The concept of "food security" had been advanced by European governments to justify protecting their farms from competition by countries with warmer climates and cheaper labor. Countries like Brazil. The Europeans did not want to be completely dependent on foreign countries for their food and they wanted to protect their scenic countryside.

But Brazil's problems were different. Brazil is the world's fourth largest food producer and the Zero Hunger advocates knew that "our agriculture is strong enough to meet all of our domestic needs and still generate foreign currency through exports." Except for remote backland areas, there is no shortage of restaurants and grocery stores. Brazil's problem is poverty, not food shortages. The Zero Hunger program argued that "poverty is not bad luck, but the result

[111] Alberto Amadei, "Tres vêzes ao dia," Iberoamérica, November 21, 2002, http://www.lainsignia.org/2002/noviembre/ibc_120.htm.
[112] Instituto Cidadania, "Projeto Zero Fome: Uma Proposta de Política de Segurança Alimentar para o Brasil," http://www.pt.org.br.

of a perverse development model that produces ever greater concentration of income and employment."[113]

The more radical Zero Hunger advocates hoped to use the food security issue as a wedge to challenge neoliberal capitalism. If the poor were going hungry in the midst of plenty, the economy should be reoriented to produce healthy foodstuffs for local use instead of export crops. Critics argued that it would be simpler and more efficient to just give the poor money and let them buy their own food. But many of the activists were profoundly suspicious of the capitalist food industry's involvement with multinational corporations. They were concerned that people would waste their money on junk food promoted by mass advertising. They wanted to build a people's alternative food system.

Lula didn't try to mediate between the different philosophies for ending hunger. He decided to give them all a chance, creating a very complex program with multiple components based on different theories about the causes of hunger. He made this decision explicit in his speech inaugurating the program:

> The Zero Hunger program is complex, as complex as the enemy it proposes to combat. It unites a package of simultaneous actions that will be developed during the four years of the government. It is composed of emergency measures and structural measures which are permanent and will definitively resolve the problem.
>
> Zero Hunger involves practically all the ministries, the state governments, the municipal governorships, social organizations, businesses and the population. All will have a role to play in his historic challenge. And everyone, at the right time, will be called upon to help in our war. Today we are taking a great step. And I know that it will be a long road before we achieve our goal. The victory against hunger will require much effort, much persistence, much courage, and the dedication of all of us during the next four years.
>
> I know that many, before me, have tried to confront the hunger program in Brazil in one way or another. And if they did not solve it, it is because the problem did not receive the priority it deserves, or because it could not count on the indispensable mobilization of society.[114]

---

[113] Zero Hunger Program, Brazil's Food Security Policy, no date. http://www.fomezero.gov.br.

[114] "Discurso do presidente da República, Luiz Inácio Lula da Silva, na cerimônia de lançamento institucional do programa Fome Zero e instalação do Consea – Conselho Nacional de Segurança Alimentar, January 30, 2003. http://www.info.planalto.gov.br/static/inf_briefdiscusos.htm.

Lula was trying to mobilize a social movement, not just organize a human-service program. He wanted to please everybody, not get into a debate about which program was best. So the plans for Zero Hunger incorporated 41 programs including agrarian reform, support for family farms, nutritional education programs, nutritious food at low prices in popular restaurants, programs to teach fishing, micro-credit programs for rural enterprises, literacy projects, support for cooperatives and programs to collect and distribute food around the country.[115] Lula's goal was to bring new energy to these programs by generating mass enthusiasm.

However, many of these programs confronted substantial obstacles and, even if successful, would take a long time to work. Lula insisted that hunger could not wait for a lengthy process of institution building. People had to eat right away. He wanted to teach people to fish, but he also wanted to give them fish while they were learning. The Zero Hunger activists proposed to solve the immediate problem by issuing a Food Security Card, modeled, surprisingly, on the food stamp program in the United States. The card would allow the holder to buy a certain amount of approved foods from approved providers. The food security program was to be organized and implemented by committees of activists on the federal, state and local level. Local committees would decide who would get a Food Security Card, how much they would get and also help them get the educational and social services they needed to improve their lives.

Critics argued that this would be an administrative nightmare and that it would be better to give people money and let them decide for themselves how to spend it.[116] If a family had food from its own garden, for example, they could spend the money on transportation or schoolbooks or medicine or something else they needed. From the beginning there was a tension in Zero Hunger between these two organizational models. One saw it as a movement of volunteers and community activists to transform society and eliminate the root

[115] Instituto Cidadania, Ibid. Vânia Rodrigues e Nilo Bairros, "Entrevista com José Graziano," *Iberoamérica*, January 30, 2003, http://www.lainsignia.org/2003/enero/ibe_113.htm. Lula da Silva, "A integra do discurso de Lula no lançamento do Fome Zero," *Revista Epoca*, http://revistaepoca.globo.com/Epoca/0,6993,EPT478324-1659,00.html.
[116] Ricardo Paes de Barro, "Miséria Zero, deve ser a próxima etapa," *O Estado de São Paulo*, 16 January 2005. Maya Takagi, A Implantação da Política de Segurança Alimentar e Nutricional no Brasil: seus limites e desafios, doctoral dissertation, Universidade Estadual de Campinas, 2006.

causes of hunger. The other saw it as a government program to provide food for hungry people who needed it right away. A social
movement depends on mass enthusiasm and energy and cannot wait
for bureaucrats. A government entitlement program, such as the
Mexican program to which Zero Hunger was often compared, requires months of planning and implementation work.[117] Lula decided
to mobilize both kinds of efforts at once, hoping they could rein-
force each other.

José Graziano da Silva, a professor of agricultural economics at
the University of Campinas, was appointed to a new extraordinary
Cabinet position as Minister of Food Security and the Struggle
Against Hunger. Graziano was a key member of the team that had
done the planning for Zero Hunger. Food and agriculture reform
were his life work, as they had been for his father, José Gomes da
Silva, who had worked on a similar plan in 1991.[118]

Frei Betto was appointed special counselor to the president in
charge of social mobilization for the Zero Hunger program. Frei
Betto is a personal friend of Lula's, and in the beginning he had an
office in the presidential palace. He teamed up with Oded Grajew, a
businessman who had helped found the World Social Forum.

Zero Hunger was coordinated by a Council on Food and Nutritional Security with thousands of volunteers. It had three thematic
divisions: one for economics, production and distribution; one for
nutritional health and one to discuss organizational monitoring. It
also had working groups devoted each of the following topics: harvest planning, genetically modified food, the mass movement against
hunger, the Second National Conference on Food Security, zero
hunger and racial equality, living with drought and the Program on
Nutrition for Workers. Each of these groups had a minimal budget
and relied heavily on volunteers. Each overlapped in multiple ways
with established government bureaucracies in the ministries of agriculture, health, and education. Organizationally, it was a mess.

---

[117] Walter Belik and Mauro Del Grossi. "O Programa Fome Zero no Contexto das
Políticas Sociais no Brasil," Texto preparado para o Congresso da SOBER em Juiz
de Fora, 2003.
http://www.fomezero.gov.br/download/O%20Fome%20Zero%20no%20contexto
%20das%20politicas%20sociais%20Walter%20Belik_Del%20Grossi.pdf.
[118] Maya Takagi, A Implantação da Política de Segurança Alimentar e Nutricional no
Brasil: seus limites e desafios, doctoral dissertation, Universidade Estadual de
Campinas, 2006, p. 23.

Frei Betto was eager to mobilize Zero Hunger as a tool for social change. He said: "Zero Hunger is not a welfare program. The distribution of food is the least important thing. If the government gives money instead of food, the family can spend in local businesses and stimulate the local economy. What we want is to generate employment, income and independence."[119]

José Graziano agreed with these long-term goals, but his responsibilities focused on more immediate food relief measures. Frei Betto wanted to mobilize a nationwide movement of volunteers to teach literacy and social consciousness, following Paulo Freire's theory of the pedagogy of the oppressed. He wanted local committees of volunteers to have control over who got money and who did not so as to make sure people were being helped to change their lives, not just put on the dole. Frei Betto recalls that José Graziano said, "He never expected a program of such magnitude. He imagined that his work would be to provide the Food Security Card to the poor families, and that the rest would be taken care of by the machinery of the federal government."[120]

José Graziano does not remember it that way. He says he always supported the management committees, and that the Food Security Card was simply an emergency measure to be combined with other policies. Graziano says:

> Frei Betto was in charge of a vague project of social mobilization that had a small interface with Zero Hunger through the management committees which I always supported. I believe it is early to reach any judgment about him and his team, but if it is true that they helped in some things such as the defense of the management committees, they also confused things a lot because they never became part of the government, limiting themselves to making suggestions and trying to develop quasi-clandestine parallel structures (in the sense that nobody knew what they were doing) from inside the presidential palace.[121]

At first, the Brazilian middle class responded to the social movement with enthusiasm. Supermodel Giselle Bündchen contributed $15,000 raised at a January 2003, fashion show. People in affluent neighborhoods took up collections, corporations offered free telephone and office support. But no one was prepared to convert

---

[119] Frei Betto, *Calendário do Poder.* Rio de Janeiro: Rocco, 2007, 107.
[120] Frei Betto, op cit., 108.
[121] Personal correspondence from José Graziano, September 2007.

this enthusiasm into a functioning, effective social program. Lula insisted that hunger was urgent; it could not wait like other reforms. In March the press reported that Bündchen's check had not yet been cashed. The only visible sign of Zero Hunger in action was two pilot programs in towns in the northeast. Newspapers ran headlines such as "Bureaucracy 10, Hunger 0" and "Amateurism 1, Hunger 0."[122]

José Graziano says that the problem with Bündchen's check was a transitory glitch that was resolved and that the press gave too much attention to these organizational problems. The negative press coverage did, however, have a significant impact on public opinion, drawing attention away from many things that were accomplished. Graziano points out that one of the first things Zero Hunger did was to increase the value of the food allowance for children under six, something which had not been done since 1991. It also increased nursery-school programs and set up literacy projects and a program to build wells in towns without reliable water supplies.

From the beginning, Frei Betto was frustrated by a lack of funds for his office.[123] He waited months for an appointment with José Dirceu to discuss funds, but it was well into the second year before anything materialized. Many government programs received less money than was budgeted because finance minister Antonio Palocci was holding money back to make debt payments. Palocci favored distributing financial aid as efficiently as possible, not spending money on organizing programs. Frei Betto and Oded Grajew were expected to raise money from corporations and private citizens for their volunteer efforts. The state oil company, Petrobras, promised a big contribution, but that money didn't materialize either.

At Frei Betto's invitation, theologian Ivo Poletto took two years out of his life to volunteer with Zero Hunger because he believed Lula was committed to revolutionizing society. Poletto saw this as an opportunity to "implement a new kind of economy based on cooperation and participation, on solidarity between human beings and with the environment." He knew this sounded utopian, but he thought Lula would put the full weight of the government behind it and he wanted to be part of it. Thousands of other idealistic Brazilians felt the same way.

[122] Larry Rohter, "Brazil's War on Hunger Off to a Slow Start," *New York Times*, March 30, 2003.
[123] Frei Betto. *Calendário do Poder.* Rio de Janeiro: Rocco, 2007.

The organization Poletto found himself in had little budget and no legal clout. It could only make recommendations to elected officials and bureaucrats. He ended up writing a bitter book about the "illusion of governmental power of a group that took nine months just to get the funding released for its own work. It was a group which depended, until now, 100 percent on the good will of other entities and persons to carry out its goals."[124]

Setting up a new bureaucracy to administer Food Security Cards did not go smoothly either. Reporters continued to file stories about abuses and mix-ups having to do with the local committees that supervised the distribution of funds. In some cases, Zero Hunger funds were channeled to government employees or political favorites rather than to the truly hungry.[125] There was no convincing argument why a new card and a new bureaucracy were needed when the country already had programs for funneling money to the poor. These existing programs had their limitations; they tended to focus on limited groups within the population. So the government decided that the best policy was to correct these deficiencies and set up a single registry program. Instead of a new Food Security Card there would be a Family Allowance Card dispensing money recipients could spend as they wished.

The difficulty in getting Zero Hunger established was repeated in many other programs. As an opposition candidate for many years, Lula was accustomed to spending much of his time advocating for his ideals. As president, he found that having the right ideals was not enough. He had to spend much of his time getting around bureaucratic roadblocks to get programs implemented. He later recalled that:

> In the public sphere, municipal, state or federal, you have a very competent bureaucracy and an historical bureaucracy. Sometimes I feel as if I was a train. The train is the government and the station is the machine. One train goes by, it makes noise, breaks down, goes off the track, and the station just ignores it. It can't be bothered and waits until the train moves along. Then along comes another train with more noise, more smoke, more whistle, more passengers, and the machine is still there.

[124] Ivo Poletto, Brasil: *Oportunidades Perdidas: Meus dois anos no governo Lula*, Rio de Janeiro: Garamond, 2005, pp. 108, 115.
[125] Larry Rohter, "Effort to Reduce Poverty and Hunger in Brazil Falls Short of Its Goals," *New York Times*, May 29, 2005.

We learned, after a lot of time, that there is only one way to make things happen in the government, to put Toyota-ism into place, that is, to get all the people involved. If there are ten people who have to sign a document, you have to make the ten sit around a table until a decision is taken right there. Because if you follow the usual practice of the machine, a paper leaves my desk, goes to Fernando Haddad, who turns it over to the head of his office, who gives it to the president of Capes, who passes it on to the heads of I don't know how many offices, who will return it I don't know how many times. With all the comings and goings, this citizen will lose three kilograms walking from table to table. It isn't anyone's fault, it is the fault of the system, it is the structure that functions this way, for the protection of the structure itself, even more so today.

We are living in a very serious time of collective hypocrisy in this country. Any public functionary today … is going to count to ten a thousand times before signing anything.[126]

In the case of the food security programs, resolving the bureaucratic problems required a reorganization to concentrate responsibility in the hands of a skilled administrator. In January 2004, the Special Ministry for Food Security was replaced with a Ministry of Social Development and Combat Against Hunger. This Ministry also incorporated programs from the Ministry of Social Assistance that ran the Family Allowances program. To run the new Ministry, Lula appointed Patrus Ananias de Sousa, then a federal deputy and formerly the mayor of Belo Horizonte.[127] Ananias was a former law professor and candidate for governor of Belo Horizonte. He brought political and administrative skills to the position, not special expertise on food issues.

José Graziano says he left the directorship in part because he was concerned that the local management committees were not part of the new structure. But he continued to be an enthusiastic advocate of combining food security programs with complementary programs to provide education, employment and income. He later took a position with a United Nations program based in Santiago, Chile, that

[126] Lula da Silva, "Discurso na cerimônia de comemoração dos 60 anos da Sociedade Brasileira para o Progresso da Ciência," October 21, 2008. http://www.info.planalto.gov.br/static/inf_briefdiscusos.htm.
[127] Maya Takagi, A Implantação da Política de Segurança Alimentar e Nutricional no Brasil: seus limites e desafios, doctoral dissertation, Universidade Estadual de Campinas, 2006, pp 132-133.

promotes similar programs throughout Latin America. Frei Betto recalls the reasons he left the program as follows:

> Fundamentally, the Zero Hunger program was made up of 60 public policies to benefit 11 million families, 44 million very poor people. In a year and a half these people were supposed to be able to leave the program and go forward on their own. In summary, it was supposed to be a liberating program. In 2003, it went very well and I was very excited. In 2004, Lula fired the minister in charge of the program and named another. The program changed radically: there are families who entered in 2003 who are still there; of the 60 public policies there is only one — the Family Allowance — that aims to give a sum of money to each family every month.
>
> Why did they change it? Because they discovered that the program was a fantastic source of votes. Every family that received these subsidies voted for Lula and for his guys, above all in the northeast.
>
> At first, there was a committee of civil society representatives that decided which families would go in and which would leave. Later they were substituted with mayors and bureaucrats, even knowing the high level of corruption with them. In fact, they began to enter their relatives, nephews, etcetera, into the program.
>
> Summing up, the program changed completely with respect to the beginning and I wasn't in agreement. So I left. I told Lula that I didn't want to continue with the program. It was December 2004 and no one knew about the serious corruption cases yet. [128]

Of course, the reason the Family Allowance program won votes is that it reached millions of families quickly. The program Betto was organizing was unable to do that, although it might have done better with more resources. The Zero Hunger program recruited many activists who were disappointed by Lula's other economic and social policies. It gave supporters around the world something to talk about. It provided jobs, or at least volunteer positions, for thousands of idealistic supporters. But the Lula government never put serious money into the social movement part of the program. When the movement did not generate results quickly enough, and got a lot of negative publicity, the government shifted attention to the Family Allowances program which was administratively efficient and provided immediate benefits for millions of people.

---

[128] Paolo Moira, "Lula's government: Interview with Frei Betto," latinamericapress. October 31, 2008. http://www.latinamericapress.org/articles.asp?art=5737.

José Graziano insists that combining benefits programs was always part of the planning for Zero Hunger.[129] In a paper presented in 2006, he and his co-authors emphasized that "the primary axis of the Food Security Program is the integration of structural policies to generate employment and income." They argued that achieving food security in Brazil required "an economic model that privileged economic growth with redistribution of income."[130]

The bottom line is that hunger did decrease, albeit at about the same rate that it had been decreasing under the previous government. The best data on hunger are collected when the Brazilian National Health Service sends community health workers to visit families in their homes. The home-health workers focus especially on the needs of infants and children. The reports of these workers provide the best direct measure of the nutritional needs of the population. The percentage of children under one year of age who were malnourished declined steadily from 1998 to 2007.[131] The figures show steady improvement from 7.8 percent malnourished in 1998 down to 1.6 percent in July, 2007. There is no way to determine how much of this decline is due to economic growth and income redistribution versus programs specifically focused on hunger. A comprehensive review by Maya Tagaki suggests that targeted programs have been most effective in remote communities in the semi-arid northeast.[132]

The Family Allowances are the culmination of a fundamental philosophical shift in Brazilian social programs. Until recent years, Brazil had espoused the philosophy that social programs should be universal, for everyone, not focused on the poor. Programs that limited benefits to the poor, and required the poor to do something in exchange, were suspect because they had been pioneered by the military dictatorship in Chile and "neoliberal" Mexican governments and

[129] Remarks by José Graziano at the Latin American Studies Conference, Montreal, September 2007.
[130] Maya Takagi, Mauro Eduardo de Grossi and José Graziano, "O Programa Fome Zero dois anos depois," paper presented at the 2006 meetings of the Latin American Studies Association, San Juan, Puerto Rico.
[131] These data are from the Sistema de Informação da Atenção Básica, using figures for December of each year and July, 2007 data.
http://tabnet.datasus.gov.br/cgi/deftohtm.exe?siab/cnv/SIABSBR.DEF.
[132] Maya Takagi, A Implantação da Política de Segurança Alimentar e Nutricional no Brasil: seus limites e desafios, doctoral dissertation, Universidade Estadual de Campinas, 2006.

were favored by the World Bank.[133] Brazil historically had tried to offer benefits for everyone as a right, not "welfare-ist" benefits given only to those in need. In practice, however, these benefits were very costly and often went mostly to those with formal employment and documents. They were paid for with inflationary spending, which was hardest on the poor. The programs did not concentrate the country's limited resources where they were most needed.

The end of hyperinflation in 1994 boosted the real incomes of the poor, but there was little progress after that. Beginning in 1995, two Brazilian states experimented with "conditional transfer" programs that gave poor mothers money on the condition that they make sure their children attended school regularly. These programs were effective, so in 2000 the federal government initiated a comprehensive program called the School Allowance *(Bolsa Escola)*. It was part of an initiative to eradicate child labor. Mothers were required to make sure their children attended school at least 85 percent of the days. In return, they received a plastic bank card to withdraw a small monthly stipend. The program was very popular and effective.[134] The improvement was most significant in the rural areas.

This plan was pioneered by Magalhães Texeira, a Social Democratic mayor of Campinas, then adopted and publicized by Cristovam Buarque when he was the Workers' Party governor of the Federal District. The Lula government's Family Allowance program was an expansion and reorganization of these existing programs. It combined several existing programs, including the ill-fated Food Security Card program and a program that helped the poor with energy bills. It covered pre-school children on the condition that the mothers take them in to health clinics for checkups. Both the health and schooling conditions depend on schools and clinics being available, so these requirements could not have been imposed fifteen or twenty years earlier in many of the less-developed rural areas.

The Family Allowance is a popular, efficient, large-scale program that helps reduce poverty and inequality. It made a real national impact quickly, meeting the urgent need Lula promised to address. There is concern that combining all the programs in one package means families will have less contact with social workers and that the behavioral goals of specific programs may be lost. Too many munic-

---

[133] Tina Rosenberg, "A Payoff Out of Poverty?" *New York Times Magazine*, December 19, 2008.
[134] Sônia Miriam Draibe, "Brasil Bolsa-Escola y Bolsa Familia," forthcoming in a book to be published by Flacso-Chile.

ipalities report that all of their children attend school 100 percent of the time. The organizers of the program are concerned about these problems and are using micro-credit programs and other mechanisms to provide recipients alternatives to staying on the dole. The idea for the Family Allowance originated in the professional human-service community; it did not come from social movements or participatory budgeting groups. It does not empower social movements to give out money; the municipal governments register families and determine who qualifies for the benefit. It is a market-oriented program in that it gives people money to spend as they choose, and it stimulates the retail economy, especially in poor rural areas. It is popular with the World Bank and other multinational organizations, and it does not transform commercial agriculture or food processing industries in any way. But it meets urgent human needs and it is immensely popular with the poor so no one denounces it as "neoliberal." For Lula, the philosophical debates about welfare-ism versus social transformation are a waste of time:

> When I was founding the Workers' Party and I would talk with the most ideological persons, who came from the political militancy of the past, what would irritate me deeply is when someone would ask: is it tactical or is it strategic? I knew that whether it was strategic or tactical, what I wanted was a party.
> In this case, I could not care less whether the program is welfare-ist or not. What concerns me is knowing whether the children of this country are having breakfast, lunch and dinner. This is what concerns me.
> Our role is not to discuss philosophy. Our problem is to discuss the following: is the program serving, in a categorical form, the people we wish to serve? Are the mothers who receive the Family Allowance putting their children in school? Are the women who are pregnant getting the examinations they need? Are the young children getting vaccinated? And what's more, we are going to have a Smiling Brazil because now the children will have their teeth well treated as well.
> It is this that will count in the history of this Program. If we enter into a scholastic debate, if it is welfare-ist or not, if it is structuralizing or not, we will not accomplish anything. [135]

---

[135] Lula da Silva, "Discurso na cerimônia de abertura do Seminário Internacional Bolsa Família," October 20, 2005.
http://www.info.planalto.gov.br/static/inf_briefdiscusos.htm.

CHAPTER EIGHT
RURAL DEVELOPMENT, LAND REFORM, AND THE ENVIRONMENT

While Brazil is not overpopulated, there is a great concentration of land ownership and a large impoverished rural population. Very large rain forests and other important ecosystems, especially in the Amazon basin, are in danger of deforestation and environmental degradation. Some of these forests are inhabited by native peoples whose way of life is fragile and threatened by the incursion of modern society.

Environmentalists around the world want to preserve the Amazon rain forest as part of the fight against global warming and to protect endangered species. But Brazilians often resent any suggestion that Brazil should forego developing its resources because of problems because of concerns of those in wealthy countries. Faced with what many people see as irreconcilable conflicts, Lula insisted that Brazil could have it all. He pointed out that the Amazon is not just a nature reserve; it is home to 25 million people who deserve all the good things of life. He insisted that Brazil has enough land for commercial agriculture and sensible land reform. And he insisted that both can be done with sustainable environmental practices.

Land Reform. Unlike Mexico and Bolivia, Brazil did not have a land reform in the twentieth century. The military governments tried creating agricultural settlements in remote areas, but they were poorly supported and generally did not succeed. Before the *real* plan stabilized Brazil's currency, people with extra money often bought land as a hedge against inflation. Sometimes this land was left unused for periods of time while hungry people who wanted to farm it were landless.

After the restoration of democracy, the government began to appropriate unproductive land to distribute to needy farmers. But this was a very slow bureaucratic process and a movement was organized to pressure for faster action. The most powerful movement organization, the *Movimento Sem Terra (MST)* or Landless Farmer's Movement, was organized largely by Catholic leftists. It sought more than distributing land; it wanted a radical transformation of society away from corporate capitalism.[136] It wanted autonomous communities where the "poor and destitute learn how to transform relations of exploitation and oppression into relations of solidarity and liberation."[137]

In the early 1990s, the MST developed the tactic of invading unproductive land and demanding that the government give it to the invading settlers. This tactic was successful in arousing public opinion and sometimes getting the bureaucracy to move. But it was risky because the landowners often organized against the invasions, sometimes going so far as to hire gunmen to kill leaders or groups of settlers. This repression backfired politically because the mass media was sympathetic and the urban public responded to the press coverage. In response, the Fernando Henrique Cardoso government greatly increased the rate of settlement of families.

As time passed, though, the middle-class public began to become disillusioned with the MST. In part, this was because of the high cost of settling families. José Graziano, Brazil's best known expert on the subject, estimates the cost of settling a family on legally appropriated land at R$46,000 and on purchased land at R$76,000.[138] This is a great deal of money to spend on a single family in a country with tens of millions of poor people. As Graziano points out, if this money were just invested in a savings account it would produce an income greater than the national minimum wage. Worst of all, this money was sometimes wasted when the settlements failed economically, even with continued government subsidies. Critics began to call the settlements rural shantytowns.

Advocates promote land reform as a moral imperative. Poor rural people need land, they say. Brazil has lots of land, so the government should give them some, and the sooner the better. But the reality just giving away land doesn't work. Making a decent living on a small plot of land in today's world requires a lot of investment. Often it involves specialized skills and activities beyond just growing food. Critics argue that the movement wants to turn the clock back to a 19th century world of small family farms, but with the govern-

[136] Angus Wright and Wendy Wolford, *To Inherit the Earth: The Landless Movement and the Struggle for a New Brazil.* Oakland, Ca: Food First Books, 2003.

[137] Wilder Robles, "The Landless Rural Workers Movement (MST) in Brazil," *Journal of Peasant Studies,* 28, 2001, 147.

[138] José Graziano, "A Reforma Agrária no Brasil do século XXI," unpublished draft provided by author. Jose.GrazianoDaSilva@fao.org.

ment guaranteeing everyone a 21ˢᵗ century standard of living. Sociologist Souza Martins articulated this criticism:

> Globalization is a fact of life. Today the world market provides an outlet for Brazil's cash crops, cultivated by the big farmers, and new farming techniques mean that a handful of efficient commercial farmers can provide food for the cities. There is no longer a pressing need for agrarian reform ... the only possible form of agrarian reform today is the market-oriented type ... which allows family farms to fit into market niches left by the big capitalist farms ... the MST is doing a disservice to the cause of agrarian reform by its radical opposition to the only possible form of agrarian reform. [139]

The movement's leaders understood these arguments, but argued that the solution was a social revolution that would pull Brazil out of the world capitalist system. When the pressures peaked during the first Fernando Henrique Cardoso administration, Cardoso made it clear that he thought of agrarian reform as a program to help poor families who had limited skills and opportunities, not as an assault on productive commercial agriculture. He clamped down on land invasions by passing regulations stating that no land would be redistributed after it was illegally invaded and that no person convicted of an illegal invasion would be allowed to receive land anywhere for at least two years. This dampened the enthusiasm for invasions and the movement began to emphasize political actions including sit-ins in banks and government offices.

Lula's rhetoric encouraged activists to hope that he would be different. During the 1994 election campaign, he promised a rally of landless farmers at Pontal do Paranapanema in the state of São Paulo that "with one stroke of the pen I will give you so much land you won't even be able to occupy it." [140] As the reality of taking power got closer, he backed away from these promises.

When the 2002 election approached, the landless farmers' movement was divided. Some activists wanted to keep things quiet so as not to turn the middle class against Lula and lose the election. Others wanted to heat things up to pressure Lula to publicly commit to live up to his promises. On March 23, 2002, one of the more radi-

---

[139] José de Souza Martins, *O Poder de Atraso*, São Paulo: Editora Hucitec, 1994. Quoted in English in Sue Branford and Jan Rocha, *Cutting the Wire: The story of the landless movement in Brazil*, London: Latin American Bureau, 2002, p. 281.
[140] Eduardo Scolese, *A Reforma Agrária*, São Paulo: Publifolha, 2005, p. 86.

cal groups took center stage by occupying a farm in Buritis, Minas Gerais, owned by Fernando Henrique Cardoso's adult children. They draped the farm with red flags and were shown on television drinking from the Cardosos' glasses and sprawling on their furniture. The middle-class public was horrified. The militants were seen as lawless and disrespectful of authority. There was no legal justification for occupying this land because it was being actively farmed, not held for speculative purposes. The Cardosos reacted cautiously, filing a complaint with the local authorities for redress and waiting a long time before finally calling in federal forces to have the occupiers evicted. Lula was forced to use one of his campaign telecasts to reassure the nation that the Workers' Party would respect the rights of anyone who used their land productively.

In 1994 the Workers' Party campaign had promised to settle 500,000 families, in 1998 it had promised 1,000,000. Early 2002 campaign planning documents had included a number of 500,000, but in the end no number was promised. Lula refused to say whether he would continue to enforce Cardoso's "anti-invasion" rules. Two years before, the Workers' Party had joined a lawsuit trying to overthrow them.

Once Lula was elected, there was a rush of land invasions by people who hoped that he would greatly increase land distributions. In December 2002, there were 60,000 families camped out waiting for land; by October 2003, there were more than 200,000 (with the average family estimated to have 4.2 children).[141] The Lula government had no plans to exempt these families from the rules and regulations that make getting land for a settlement a long and arduous process. Sociologist Zander Navarro opined that "the government's action has been scandalously irresponsible because it encouraged land occupations, but did not have any strategy for dealing with the reaction of the landowners."[142]

Lula responded to the pressure from the MST and other movement organizations with ambiguous rhetoric, hoping to avoid upsetting any of the interests involved. On July 2, 2003, he received a delegation from the MST, accepted a basket of gifts, and allowed himself to be photographed wearing the movement's trademark red

---

[141] Scolese, op cit, pp. 86-87.
[142] In the *Folha de São Paulo*, September 22, 2003, quoted in Scolese, op cit., p. 92.

baseball cap for three seconds.[143] This was enough to provoke outraged protests from farm lobbyists and pressure groups.

The meeting with the MST might have been ignored if it were not for the movement's anti-capitalist rhetoric and Lula's fuzziness in responding to it. The MST regularly marched with portraits of Lenin, Castro and Ché Guevara, and signs calling for socialist revolution. Sympathizers argue that this is a sort of political theater that should be taken with a grain of salt. But when the president enthusiastically received a group carrying a sign saying "Agrarian Reform: for a Brazil Without Large Farms," the owners of those large farms could hardly help but respond.

Powerful landowner lobbies pressured Congress to protect property rights. A Joint Parliamentary Commission of Inquiry was established, and the Lula government made it clear that it was not going to turn Brazil's highly productive commercial farms over to the landless. In its 2005 review of social policies, the National Institute for Applied Economic Research summarized the problems as follows:

> The current political situations suggests that the process of agrarian reform will continue to confront difficulties in several fronts: in the Federal Executive power itself, in the continuing resistance from states and municipalities, in the judiciary, in the legislature, in the conflict with rural dwellers, and in the intransigent defense of agricultural business by a significant part of the government.[144]

The annual number of settlements of families had peaked in 1997 before the Cardoso government clamped down on occupations. Settlements declined substantially by 2002 and continued to be low in the first years of Lula's presidency. This outraged the landless farmers' movement, who felt betrayed by Lula. Close to 12,000 MST supporters expressed their disappointment with a 17-day march from Goiânia to Brasília in 2005.

In 2006, a splinter group from the MST, the Movement for the Liberation of the Landless Farmers Movement, invaded the Chamber of Deputies in Brasília armed with sticks, stones and blocks of cement. The activists caused R$150,000 in damage to glass doors, windows, computer terminals and other equipment. They were pro-

[143] *ISTOÉ,* July 9, 2003.
[144] Instituto de Pesquisa Econômica Aplicada, *Políticas Sociais: Acompanhamento e Análise* 11, Agosto 2005, p. 149.

testing the measure prohibiting the land reform agency from legalizing the occupation of illegally seized land. The police recovered a videotape showing leaders of the organization planning the invasion two months in advance. The leader of the invasion was Bruno Maranhão, former national secretary for social movements of the Workers' Party. The MLST had received R$9 million in funding from the Lula government, and the land reform agency claimed that it had been involved in kickback arrangements with landowners who arranged to have activists invade unproductive lands so they could get compensated for them by the government.[145]

Lula had little choice but to approve the decision of President of the Chamber Aldo Rebelo, to have the police arrest the activists. The police arrested 537 people, and 41 were reported injured. Maranhão ended up spending 38 days in jail. He had no hard feelings, however, and after his release from jail he announced that he wanted his job with the Workers' Party back so he could campaign for Lula's re-election.[146]

The Lula campaign toned down its rhetoric in the 2006 campaign, promising only to "maintain the continuity of the Agrarian Reform Program, giving priority to creating quality settlements and recuperating existing settlements."[147] Surprisingly, this time the government actually delivered more than expected. In 2005 the number of families resettled increased sharply to 127,000 and in 2006 it reached 155,000 according to the official figures. In 2007, 67,535 families were settled and R$1.4 billion was spent on purchasing land. The emphasis was on making settlements more effective rather than just increasing the number of families settled. Lula's annual report to Congress for 2008 states that the government is "developing new forms of credit and technical assistance and searching for a new model of settlement, based on economic viability and environmental sustainability."[148]

In recent years, more than half of the families have been settled in the states of Pará, Maranhão, Matto Grosso, Bahia and Rondônia, states which "are still in the process of consolidating their agricultural frontier, with the availability of land not yet developed or with

[145] *ISTOÉ*, June 14, 2006.
[146] *Folha de São Paulo*, July 27, 2006.
[147] *Lula Presidente: Programa de Governo 2007/2010*, p. 15.
http://www.lulapresidente.org.br/download/PlanoGoverno.zip.
[148] Lula da Silva, *Mensagem ao Congresso Nacional*, 2008, p. 68

poorly defined ownership."[149] As José Graziano explains, "the agrarian reform question in Brazil is no longer a national problem, but a regional problem." Today's land reform program is focused on the "millions of extremely poor families who have no other escape." It is in the semi-arid northeast, in rural areas and in the peripheries of urban areas, in enclaves of poverty where "we find the greatest concentrations of misery and hunger in the country."[150]

In the more productive central and southern regions of the country, there is simply very little "unproductive" land to be appropriated. With currency stabilization in 1994, wealthy people have no longer needed to own land as a hedge against inflation. Global food prices have increased and Brazil's farmland is used profitably by commercial farmers. Land prices are increased steadily, and the land reform contributes to the increase in land prices when it purchases land, at high market prices, to give to landless settlers.

José Graziano says that "the various landless farmers' groups that exist today in the country no longer fight for 'agrarian reform,' in general. They fight for preferential settlement for 'our families' that are camped out waiting for land."[151] They have become more like unions, agitating for public funds for their members. And the Lula government has responded to these pressures.

Brazil's land reform has, at great expense, helped many desperately poor people who lacked the skills to integrate into the modern economy. It has not, however, fundamentally transformed Brazilian agriculture. João Pedro Stedile, the best known leader of the Landless Farmer's Movement, was frustrated with the Lula government, which he considered to have a "neoliberal project." He took pride in the fact that the movement survived and continued the struggle. He argued that:

> We had hoped that the electoral victory [of Lula] could unleash a new rise of the movement of masses and that the agrarian reform would have a larger impetus behind its implementation. There has been no agrarian reform under the Lula government. On the contrary, the forces of financial and international capital, through their multinational corporations, have increased their control over Brazilian agriculture.

---

[149] Instituto de Pesquisa Economica Aplicada, *Políticas Sociais: acompanhamento e análise* 13, 2007, p. 342 p. 342.
[150] José Graziano, "A Reforma Agrária no Brasil do século XXI," unpublished draft provided by author.
[151] Ibid.

Today, the greater part of our riches, the production and distribution of agricultural commodities, are under the control of transnational corporations. They have allied themselves with capitalist landowners and produced the agri-business model of exploitation. [152]

It is certainly true that commercial agribusiness dominates Brazilian agriculture, as João Pedro Stedile states. Lula, however, doesn't see this as a problem; he takes pride in agribusinesses' accomplishments. In his report to Congress he brags that:

Agribusiness accounts for 25% of the production of the economy, and in the last five years, the country's agriculture was the sector that grew most in exports, with an annual growth rate of 16.3%. ... Brazil's rural producers are efficiently fulfilling the role of supplying the country with agricultural products of good quality at accessible prices. In addition to providing for the … normal internal supplies, the surplus production reveals the competitive capacity of the country, which has become the world's primary producer of beef and chicken, sugar, coffee and orange juice, and the world's second largest exporter of grains. [153]

Environmental Issues. Lula started strong by appointing Marina Silva as minister of the environment. Marina was a colleague of Chico Mendes, the world-renowned rubber trapper organizer murdered in 1988 by ranchers who were illegally logging the rainforest to make room for cattle. Before becoming minister, Marina was a senator from the state of Acre, in the Amazon basin. No one doubted her competence or commitments, but she was just one minister and she had to work with other ministers with powerful constituencies. This included the minister of agriculture and ministers with responsibilities for economic and infrastructure development.

Marina lost the struggle against genetically modified seed to Minister of Agriculture João Roberto Rodrigues, who represented a very powerful constituency. She had a long dispute with the chief of staff, Dilma Rousseff, over building a hydroelectric dam on the Madeira River, the Amazon's longest tributary. Brazil relies on hydroelectric dams for much of its power, and there were significant power shortages when the rainfall was less than average. Marina Silva lost the job of coordinator of the development plan for the Amazon to head of the Nucleus for Long-Range Planning, Roberto Mangabeira Un-

---

[152] João Pedro Stedile, "MST: 25 Years of Stubbornness," *MRzine*, January 24, 2009. Original published in *Caros Amigos*, January 29.
[153] Lula da Silva, Mensagem ao Congresso Nacional 2008, p. 34.

ger.[154] This last bureaucratic defeat was especially galling because Long Range Planning has not traditionally been a major power center.

The leader of Brazil's Green Party, Rio de Janeiro Congressman Fernando Gabeira, joined forces with the Workers' Party in 2000 in the hope of building a "red/green" alliance. He was encouraged when the Workers' Party adopted a strong environmental platform for the 2002 elections. But Gabeira quickly became disillusioned with the government's implementation of its promises. On October 14, 2003, Gabeira told Congress he was leaving the Workers' Party, explaining that:

> When I entered the Workers' Party and encouraged the Greens to unite with the Workers' Party, I was thinking along European lines. I thought that the Workers' Party could develop a role similar to that of the European Social Democrats. But now that the Workers' Party has come into power, I see that their perspective is similar to that of the Eastern European communists, a strict productivist vision, with no understanding of environmental variables.[155]

From the beginning, Lula insisted on the compatibility of development and environmental goals. At a national environmental conference in 2003, he told Marina Silva and other leaders that:

> There still exists, on the part of many people, some out of innocence and some out of bad faith, the idea for society that whoever defends the environment is against development, as if development was just the destruction of that which we have inherited from nature to put something else in its place. And, thank God, there are people like you ... many of them anonymous, who have demonstrated, with much sacrifice, and it is true – some have died for this – that it is possible to create a good development policy without destroying nature. Using, most of all, the riches which we can extract for development from the regions in which our forests, our rivers and our wildlife are still preserved.[156]

[154] *The Economist*, "Marina Marches Off," May 15, 2008.
[155] Fernando Gabeira, "Leaving the Workers' Party," in *Navegação na Neblina*, Porto Alegre: L&PM, 2006, p. 37.
[156] Lula da Silva, "Discurso na cerimônia de lançamento da Conferência Nacional do Meio Ambiente," June 5, 2003.
http://www.info.planalto.gov.br/static/inf_briefdiscusos.htm.

Marina Silva was in agreement with this in principle, indeed the rubber trappers of Acre were as much interested in sustainable economic development as they were in preserving the environment. And Brazil had strong environmental legislation that protected native peoples in remote regions and strictly limited the amount of land that could be cleared for commercial ranching and agriculture. But enforcement of this legislation was spotty at best, sometimes because state governments were corrupt, sometimes simply because of the weakness of police and legal institutions in remote areas of a very large and sparsely populated country. The assassination of Dorothy Stang, on February 12, 2005, dramatized these problems. Stang was a 74-year-old American-born nun who immigrated to Brazil in the early 1970s and devoted her life to helping poor farmers in state of Pará in the Amazon region. She was apparently murdered by gunmen hired by a land developer. She reportedly tried nonviolence, quoting the Biblical passage, "Blessed are the peacemakers, for they shall be called the children of God" to the gunmen. But they shot her, in front of witnesses, seemingly confident in their impunity from arrest or punishment.

The worldwide publicity about the killing highlighted the failure of the Lula government to stop the deforestation of the Amazon. It dramatized the inability of the legal system to properly record titles to land, and the corruption and malfeasance in the criminal justice system. The land reform agency had no computers or updated maps and was understaffed. It was no match for speculators with false documents and hired guns and corrupt judges to back them up. A worker for the pastoral land commission said "the notary public offices are controlled by judges, who either choose not to see what is going on or participate themselves in the land schemes. The *grileiros* (document forgers) are always close friends of mayors, judges, police delegates, town council members and state legislators, so none of the local authorities want to take action against them."[157]

Prompted by the publicity, Lula took personal charge of federal government intervention to find and prosecute the killers, not just of Stang but of other activists in the region. In his February "Coffee with the President" radio program, the interviewer included a question about the killings:

[157] Larry Rohter, "Brazil's Lofty Promises after Nun's Killing Prove Hollow," *New York Times*, September 23, 2005.

Luís Fara Monteiro: Mr. President, you are personally taking charge of the federal government action in the state of Pará. Agrarian conflicts continue to generate violent actions, such as the deaths in recent days of the missionary Dorothy Stang, the farmer Adalberto Xavier Leal, the community leader Cláudio Matogrosso and the labor organizer Daniel Soares da Costa Filho.

President Lula da Silva: I think it is abominable that people still think that a .38 revolver is the solution for a conflict, no matter how serious it may be. So we will not rest until we arrest the killers. And more than this, we will arrest those who sent them, to show the people, clearly, that our government does not allow impunity, that the Amazon is ours, and that we are going to take care of our territory with sovereignty, without vacillation.

These things have inconvenienced some reactionaries, some conservatives in the wood growing areas, because the good wood harvesters are working in accord with the government, they are making agreements with Minister Marina [Silva]. Now, in the same way that we give a concession to exploit gas, to exploit water, to exploit petroleum, we have to have the authority to give authority to the wood harvesters to cut down a tree, a tree that at times took 400 years to grow, the citizen can't just go there and cut it down, believing that he has no responsibility to future generations.[158]

Dorothy Stang's assassins and their alleged employer were arrested and prosecuted, but they filed appeals and the legal process dragged on for years.[159] Despite Lula's intervention, the underlying problem was not solved. By September 2005, a local settlement leader in the community where Dorothy Stang had worked reported that "we have no security and no support here. For us, nothing has changed. There are gunmen all over the place, we're being threatened again, and when we ask the government for help, nobody comes."[160]

Finally, in May 2008, Marina Silva resigned as environmental minister and returned to her seat in the Senate. She said her resignation was designed to "shake up" Brazilian environmental policy that she said had accomplished too little, especially in Lula's second term.[161] Lula's major emphasis was clearly on economic development

[158] Lula da Silva, "Programa de rádio "Café com o Presidente," February 21, 2005. http://www.info.planalto.gov.br/static/inf_briefdiscusos.htm.
[159] Alexei Barrionuevo, "Brazil Orders New Trial in Nun's Death," *New York Times*, April 7, 2009.
[160] Larry Rohter, "Brazil's Lofty Promises after Nun's Killing Prove Hollow," *New York Times*, September 23, 2005.
[161] Estadao.com. "Atuação foi pífia neste mandato," May 18, 2008.

during the second term, but he praised Marina effusively and quickly appointed another prominent environmentalist, Carlos Minc, to take her place. Minc's views on protecting the Amazon are just as strong as Marina Silva's. [162] He wore a necktie with the words "Deforesting the Amazon is Prohibited" printed on it to his inauguration ceremony.

Lula was concerned, though, that the press would insist on portraying the change of ministers as an ideological shift. He spent much of his speech at Minc's inauguration ceremony praising Marina Silva, recalling how the press had insisted on portraying the endless discussions between her and Chief of Staff Dilma Rousseff as an ideological struggle between an "environmentalist" and a "developmentalist." He said that he was present at the discussions and never recognized the accounts he read in the papers the next day. He said he sometimes suspected that there was a dwarf hiding under the table who was making up stories about what had gone on. He said he knew the torments Minc would go through because:

> For the first thing, they are going to try to sell the following idea: Marina is leaving because she is an environmentalist and Minc is entering because he is a developmentalist. A woman is leaving who wants to save the Amazon, a woman from [the state of] Acre, and a man is entering who is from Rio de Janeiro and wants to destroy the Amazon. I, who has known both of you for 30 years, know that neither of the two versions is true. Neither is Minc one who wants to cut down the Amazon, nor is Marina one who failed to take seriously, as she did in the Sustainable Amazon plan, the possibilities of developing the region, to improve the life of the rubber tappers, of the traditional gatherers and cultivators, of the fishermen, to improve the lives of the farmers, and to allow that even the lumbering industry can survive by doing things correctly as they should be done. [163]

Nothing symbolized Lula's ties to commercial agriculture more than his friendly relationship with Blairo Maggi, the governor of Mato Grosso and one of Brazil's wealthiest ranchers. His firm is the

http://www.estadao.com.br/estadaodehoje/20080518/not_imp174493,0.php.
[162] Carlos Minc, "Five Challenges," Our Planet: The Future of Forests. September 2008, pp. 4-5. http://new.unep.org/PDF/ourplanet/2008/sept/en/OP-2008-09-en-ARTICLE1.pdf.
[163] Lula da Silva, "Discurso na cerimônia de posse do novo ministro do Meio Ambiente, Carlos Minc, ´ May 27, 2008.
http://www.info.planalto.gov.br/static/inf_briefdiscusos.htm.

biggest soy producer in the world, and it has cleared huge tracts of *cerrado* scrublands on the edge of the Amazon forests. Greenpeace tried to present him with a "golden chainsaw" award at a school ceremony, but he escaped through a side door.[164]

But Blairo Maggi is far from a crude developmentalist with no sensitivity to environmental values. He makes a sophisticated, well-reasoned argument that the best way to protect Brazil's environment is to have the land managed by responsible landowners who can be held responsible for following environmental legislation. At a panel discussion in Washington, D.C., in 2008, he joined representatives of the Environmental Defense Fund and other leaders in supporting efforts to use carbon offsets to control global warming.[165]

In December 2008, Lula announced that the government had formed a committee of 17 ministries to develop the embryo of a plan to deal with climate change. He recognized that the plan needed work, but he said Brazil was ahead of China or India, and certainly ahead of countries [such as the United States] that had not yet signed the Kyoto Protocol on climate change. He stressed, however, that:

> It is not enough to have a plan, all the decrees a president can make are not enough. We have to have a process of raising the consciousness of Brazilian society of the comparative advantages that a society like Brazil has, in preserving its nature, in correctly taking care of its forests, because this will end up being a gain for the country, instead of prejudicing it as some thought a few years ago.[166]

Fernando Gabeira's fear that the Workers' Party had a "strict productivist vision with no understanding of environmental variables" was an overreaction, as subsequent posts on his Web site have recognized.[167] Lula certainly understands the environmental issues. He told a conference on the ethics of development that "in Brazil we know well the costs of development at any price: economic vulnera-

---

[164] Richard Bourne, *Lula of Brazil: The Story So Far.* Berkeley, University of California Press, 2008, p. 141.

[165] Blairo Maggi, "Agribusiness and Sustainability: Farming in Matto Grosso, the Border of the Amazon." Remarks at Brazil Institute, Wilson Center for Scholars, December 5, 2008. http://www.wilsoncenter.org.

[166] Lula da Silva, "Discurso do Presidente da República, Luiz Inácio Lula da Silva, durante reunião do Fórum Brasileiro de Mudanças Climáticas," December 1, 2008. http://www.info.planalto.gov.br/static/inf_briefdiscusos.htm.

[167] Fernando Gabeira, "Leaving the Workers' Party," in *Navegação na Neblina*, Porto Alegre: L&PM, 2006, p. 37.

bility, social exclusion, environmental degradation, and the degradation of moral values.[168] And he appointed Marina Silva and Carlos Minc to advocate for environmental concerns in the policy process. Compromises on many difficult issues were less than the environmental activists would have liked, but better than nothing. Marina Silva recognized that hydroelectric dams had to be built in the Amazon, and she managed to delay approval until the environmental impacts were minimized with state-of-the-art technology.

In August 2009, Marina Silva left the Workers' Party, after three decades of active membership. She praised Lula as a "living hero" for making progress on the environment, but thought that she could keep the pressure up more effectively from outside the party. She joined the Green Party and became its candidate for the presidency in 2010.[169]

[168] Lula da Silva, "Speech at the Opening of the International Conference on the Ethics of Development," July 3, 2003.
http://www.info.planalto.gov.br/exec/inf_discursosdata.cfm
[169] Barrioneuvo, Alexei. 2009. "A Child of the Amazon Shakes up a Nation's Politics, *New York Times*, August 28.
http://www.nytimes.com/2009/08/29/world/americas/29silva.html?pagewanted=1&sq=Barrionuevo%20amazon&st=cse&scp=1

CHAPTER NINE
FROM PARTICIPATORY BUDGETING TO ADVISORY COUNCILS

Participatory budgeting was a Workers' Party innovation that many hoped would cut through elitism and bureaucracy to build a true participatory democracy.[170] It developed out of radical thinking that criticized representative democracy as responsive to elitist interest groups and sought to replace or supplement it with direct democratic forms.[171] It had some success in Workers' Party governments on the state and local level, especially in the city of Porto Alegre in the southern state of Rio Grande do Sul. By the time of Lula's 2002 campaign, however, it had run into so many problems on the state level that it was seldom mentioned. Olívio Dutra, who had made participatory budgeting a theme of his Workers' Party governorship in Rio Grande do Sul, lost his bid for re-election in 2002 despite the Lula landslide.

Participatory budgeting, as practiced in Rio Grande do Sul and other states, involved open public assemblies where thousands of citizens met at the local, regional or state level to establish spending priorities. These meetings were open to all citizens, not limited to representatives of organized groups. Activist organizations sometimes mobilized large number of participants and tended to dominate the discussions. This came to be resented by representatives of groups that had different styles of participation, and by political parties with ties to those groups. Because of its close association with the Workers' Party, participatory budgeting was resented by leaders of competing parties, including several that had strong roots in the labor movement and working class constituencies. As Goldfrank and Schneider observe:

Several PDT (Democratic Labor Party) and PMDB (Brazilian Democratic Movement Party) leaders considered participatory budgeting to be an affront not only to representative democracy and es-

[170] William R. Nylen, *Participatory Democracy versus Elitist Democracy: Lessons from Brazil*. New York: Palgrave, 2003.
[171] Clovis Bueno de Azevedo, *A Estrela Partida ao Meio: Ambigüidades de Pensamento Petista*, São Paulo: Entrelinhas, 1995.

pecially to elected city councilors, but also to the elements of organized civil society, such as legally recognized neighborhood, business, and professional associations. Participatory budgeting, in this view, was unconstitutional and, with its open format, allowed PT (Workers' Party) activists to dominate the assemblies and manipulate the decisions.[172]

The competing parties organized their own participatory groups, known as regional development councils or popular consultation forums. These were often made up of representatives of organized groups. When they won elections, they ended the participatory budgeting meetings and relied on these alternative groups for advice and support.

Participatory budgeting could also be frustrating for the participants because there was never enough money to fund all the good ideas. Hard decisions had to be made about priorities, and ultimately the elected officials had the authority and responsibility to make them. Participatory budgeting is a mechanism, like a New England town meeting, that works better on a community level than in an entire state because of the numbers of people involved. The only way it could work for the country as a whole would be for local meetings to elect delegates to regional and national meetings, a process that would reinvent representative democracy.

As an alternative to participatory budgeting on the federal level, the Lula government adopted an idea that had been developed in Spain: creating Economic and Social Development Councils.[173] These councils have been adopted in many countries, including most of the western European countries. The members of Brazil's council are appointed by the President for two-year terms, with the possibility of reappointment. They are representatives of important groups in society. In the European model, the custom has been to have one third business people, one third labor, and one third from "civil society." In the Brazilian case, the first council included 41 business representatives, 13 trade unionists, and 36 representatives from other

[172] Benjamin Goldfrank and Aaron Schneider, "Competitive Institution Building: The PT and Participatory Budgeting in Rio Grande do Sul,," *Latin American Politics and Society* 48: 1-32, 2006.
[173] Romerio Jair Kunrath, CDES: O Conselho do Desenvolvimento Econômico e Social do Brasil, doctoral dissertation, Universidade Federal do Rio Grande do Sul, 2005. http://www.cdes.gov.br.

groups.[174] The heavy representation of business was chosen because of concern that the business leadership would feel neglected or threatened by a leftist government. Lula viewed these councils as a means of building broad consensus for his programs:

> I am the president of all the Brazilian people and not just of those who voted for me. We are building a new social contract in which all the forces of Brazilian society will be represented and will be heard. Therefore, I seek interchange with all the sectors that will be united in the Council for Economic and Social Development. I am going to seek contacts and points of support for our projects to change society, wherever they may come from. The change, which we seek, is not for one social, political or ideological group. It will most benefit the unprotected, the humiliated, the offended and those who, now, see the possibility of personal and collective redemption. It is the cause of all. It is universal *par excellence*.[175]

In addition to the federal Council on Social and Economic Development, known as the Big Council, chaired by Lula himself, there are specialized councils working with different ministries and government agencies. The consultations on the budget involved representatives of 70 non-governmental organizations from all 27 states, all of them invited by the government.[176]

The number of members from each sector of society on a council is not critical because the norm is for the councils to reach consensus before making recommendations. The Council on Social and Economic Development did, in fact, reach consensus on a National Development Agenda.[177] The resulting document avoids controversial issues such as whether the tax burden is too high, as business believes, or whether more taxes are needed to fund social programs. It focuses on points where there is widespread agreement. It does, however, establish an important national priority, "to make Brazilian society more equal, without racial or gender disparities, and with in-

[174] Rudá Ricci, "O Plano Plurianual Federal: a outra face do governo Lula," Revista Espaço Academico, Year 3, No 26, July 2003. http://www.espacoacademico.com.br/026/26ricci.htm.

[175] Lula da Silva, "Discurso no XXXIII Fórum Econômico Mundial," January 26, 2003. http://www.info.planalto.gov.br/exec/inf_discursostitulo8.cfm.

[176] Rudá Ricci, "O Plano Plurianual Federal: a outra face do governo Lula," Revista Espaço Academico, Year 3, No 26, July 2003. http://www.espacoacademico.com.br/026/26ricci.htm.

[177] Conselho de Desenvolvimento Econômico e Social, *Agenda Nacional de Desenvolvimento*, Brasília 2006. http://www.cdes.gov.br/.

come and wealth well distributed and vigorous upward social mobility." It insists that equity should be the first priority in judging social and economic policies. The focus of the document is on goals, not on the specific means to achieve them. The goals, however, have more substance than might appear at first glance. Making reducing inequality the first priority is quite different from making economic growth the first priority and waiting for the fruits to "trickle down" to the poor. The goals are given more teeth by the establishment of an "Equity Observatory" with a technical staff that monitors progress toward achieving the goals and issues reports its findings.[178]

This is not participatory budgeting in the sense that it was originally conceived. The participants are selected by the government, they represent organized groups and they do not make actual budgetary decisions. The council argues, however, that its National Development Agenda was "a product of participatory democracy, of the integration of society and government."[179] Angela Cotta Ferreira Gomes, a deputy secretary for the council, says that "participatory budgeting works better on the municipal level, but not so well on the state or federal level. The Lula government's early efforts to use it were not productive. But the council adopted many procedures and practices learned from the experience with participatory budgeting."[180] Important lessons included the need for a technical staff to support the council's work and the importance of seeking consensus.

[178] Conselho de Desenvolvimento Econômico e Social, *Observatório da Eqüidade, Relatório de Observação* No. 1, 2006. http://www.cdes.gov.br/.
[179] Ibid., p. 5.
[180] Presentation at the Bildner Center, City University of New York, Sept 27, 2007.

CHAPTER TEN
BUILDING NATIONAL SELF-ESTEEM
WITH FOREIGN POLICY

One of Lula's first acts as president of Brazil was to fly to Porto Alegre, Brazil's southernmost city, to address 100,000 anti-globalization activists at the third gathering of the World Social Forum. The forum was created, in Porto Alegre in 2001, as a counter to the World Economic Forum, a conclave of top corporate and political leaders who usually meet in Davos, Switzerland. The World Social Forum was closely associated with the Workers' Party in Porto Alegre and it drew tens of thousands of participants from all over the world. They shared their experiences in the struggle against neoliberal capitalism and their commitment to the principle that "another world is possible."

Lula's appearance at the World Social Forum would have been a triumphant moment except for several uncomfortable facts. The Workers' Party had lost the governorship of the state of Rio Grande do Sul, of which Porto Alegre is the capital, in part because residents feared that the radical rhetoric was scaring away foreign investors. Lula had promised, in his *Letter to the Brazilian People*, to honor agreements with the International Monetary Fund, the World Social Forum's arch-nemesis. And, to add insult to injury, Lula had announced that immediately after his appearance at the World Social Forum, he would fly to Davos to address the World Economic Forum. World Social Forum activists wanted to smash the World Economic Forum, not court it.

Consistent with his general philosophy of leadership, Lula sought to please both groups. He insisted that he would deliver the same message at both places, and he did. The message was that economic growth was not enough, that it had to be accompanied by action against hunger and misery. The corporate leaders couldn't have agreed more.

The activists at the World Social Forum understood that Lula could not have been elected on an anti-capitalist platform. But they hoped that once elected he would distance Brazil from ties to multinational corporations and favor smaller, locally owned companies and cooperatives. They had some basis for these hopes in the Workers' Party's rhetoric. The Workers' Party position paper on foreign policy for the 2002 elections focused on Brazil's subordinate position to the United States in international affairs. It advocated an "alternative model of economic development" which would be less vulnerable to foreign markets, develop closer integration with South America and forge new links with countries such as India, China and Russia. It said that Brazil should be "very careful" about joining a Free Trade Area of the Americas with the United States. It also stressed that the United States should drop its non-tariff barriers to free trade, and urged Brazil to develop advanced exports instead of going back to its old policies of protectionism.

The proposals were modest, especially the proposal to think carefully about a Free Trade Area of the Americas rather than oppose it outright. There was none of the anti-American rhetoric used by leaders such as Hugo Chávez of Venezuela and Evo Morales of Bolivia. But it set a tone that was more assertive about Brazilian independence than the previous administration.

Throughout Fernando Henrique Cardoso's presidency, the Workers' Party complained about his frequent trips abroad. They insisted he should stay home and work on domestic concerns. Cardoso had been foreign minister, he was fluent in English, Spanish and French, and he enjoyed meeting important people around the world. His opponents accused him of being more interested in hobnobbing with the rich and powerful than in solving Brazil's problems.

Lula speaks no foreign languages and had very little international experience before becoming president. He was generally expected to spend more time at home. To everyone's surprise, he proved just as eager to travel abroad as Fernando Henrique Cardoso had been. His first trips were to the places Brazilian presidents frequently visit: neighboring Latin American countries, North America and Europe. After meeting George Bush in Washington, he flew to Havana to see Fidel Castro. He got along well with everybody, and seemed especially comfortable with George W. Bush's informal style, despite the latter's lack of interest in Brazil.

In addition to these expected courtesy calls, Lula added visits to a number of African countries that had never before seen a Brazilian president. These were countries where Brazil had few existing economic or other interests and critics argued that his time could have been better spent at home. But he was looking to the future, to a world that would be less centered on the great powers of today. And even in today's world, he thought there might be opportunities for more trade between nations of the global south and for taking more independent initiatives in multilateral organizations. Lula was not just interested in foreign policy as an end in itself; he wanted to use it to help build a culture of transformation by strengthening the country's national self-esteem.[181] As he said in a 2003 speech:

> Brazil must understand that the most important goal we have, at this point in time, is to rebuild our self-esteem, to believe in ourselves, to believe that we are competitive, and to discover where we can become competitive in confronting this world which is ever more globalized.[182]

Self-esteem means taking responsibility for one's own fate and taking active initiatives to realize it. As Sean Burgess explains, "the importance of *auto-estima* [self-esteem] is that it is a signal that a people are making decisions on their own terms to address their needs as they see them."[183] There is a critical difference between Lula's approach and that of Latin American leaders whose rhetoric is heavily anti-American. In Lula's view, blaming other nations for a Brazil's problems would be a symptom of a national inferiority complex. He made this explicit in a speech to the Council on Foreign Relations in New York on September 25, 2003:

> I have made a commitment that it was necessary to recover the self-esteem of the Brazilian people, to recover our credibility before our own people and the world... I have often criticized my friends in and outside of Brazil who address the rich countries as if they were responsible for our misery. I have made it a point to say, in every forum in which I participate, that it is our own fault, in America and in Brazil, for not having resolved our own problems. It is not the fault of the United States, or of the European Union, or of Japan, or even of God. It is our own fault, that of our own elite, that we did not make the deci-

---

[181] Sean Burges, "Auto-estima in Brazil: The logic of Lula's north-south policy," *International Journal*, Autumn 2005, p. 1140.
http://www.colombiainternacional.org/Doc%20PDF/EU-The-logic-Lula's-south-south-foreign%20p.pdf.
[182] Lula da Silva, "Discurso na Solenidade de Abertura do Seminário Brasil - China: 'Um Salto Necessário'," April 30, 2003.
http://www.mre.gov.br/portugues/politica_externa/discursos/discurso_detalhe.as p?ID_DISCURSO=2095.
[183] Burgess, op cit, p. 1135.

sions we should have made fifty years ago. We did not resolve the problem of illiteracy, we did not make an agrarian reform when the rest of the world did, and we did not redistribute income, even when the Brazilian economy was the fastest growing in the world. [184]

Of course, winning a dispute is great for self-esteem, and Brazilians were proud of winning a dispute in the World Trade Organization with the United States over tariffs. Even if you can't win, just being taken seriously can be a boost to self-esteem. Lula made this point with a parable:

An elephant is so large that the elephant's trunk is as big as ten mice, but put a mouse close to an elephant and watch how that animal shakes with fear. I think what we did is say to the Americans, "We respect you. We want you as our privileged partners. But we also want to be respected. [185]

In June, 2004, the Lula government sent a force of 1,100 troops to Haiti to lead a multilateral peace-keeping force. They replaced troops from the United States as the leader in the multilateral effort. The stated purpose of the mission was to aid the United Nations Security Council and to help the Haitian people, but many commentators noted that it also gave Brazil a more prominent role on the world stage. [186] Brazil's effort was welcomed by the United States, but that wasn't a problem for Lula. His goal was not to thumb his nose at the United States, but to assert Brazil's national maturity and capabilities.

Building self-esteem also meant taking pride in the country's accomplishments and in its ability to help others. Lula informed the Secretary General of the United Nations that Brazil would not need help from a newly created anti-hunger fund because it had its own

[184] Lula da Silva, Discurso no Conselho de Relações Internacionais (Council on Foreign Relations)," September 25, 2003.
http://www.mre.gov.br/portugues/politica_externa/discursos/discurso_detalhe.as p?ID_DISCURSO=2158.
[185] Luiza Damé, "Lula compara EUA a um elefante que se 'borra' de medo de rato," O Globo, September 8, 2010.
http://oglobo.globo.com/economia/mat/2010/09/08/lula-compara-eua-um-elefante-que-se-borra-de-medo-de-rato-917581119.asp.
[186] Anna Ioakimedes, "Brazil's Peacekeeping Mission in Haiti: Doing God's or Washington's Work?," Council on Hemispheric Affairs, December 6, 2004.
http://www.coha.org/NEW_PRESS_RELEASES/New_Press_Releases_2004/04.
91%20Brazil%20in%20Haiti%20the%20one.htm.

resources. He offered to help South Africa, Namibia, Mozambique and São Tomé and Príncipe with their fight against AIDS, taking pride in Brazil's well-known success in this area. Lula also found occasions to provoke "Brazilian entrepreneurs, telling them that they should not be afraid to become multinationals."[187]

He also bought a new $56.7 million dollar Airbus A-319 to replace the aged Boeing 707 that was the official presidential plane (although Cardoso had usually chartered planes for his trips abroad). His opponents criticized this as an unnecessary luxury; the press dubbed it the "AeroLula". But the plane suited Brazil's image as an emerging global power. Why shouldn't the president of Brazil have a plane as good as those used by other heads of state?

Expressing independent views on global issues was another way of expressing national autonomy. The Lula government opposed the United States' invasion of Iraq, along with many other countries, and suffered no reprisal from the George W. Bush administration. Brazil also took the United States and Western Europe to task for protecting their steel and agricultural industries against Brazilian competition. This criticism drew attention to the wealthy countries' failure to live up to their own rhetoric about free trade.

In the ongoing negotiations about the proposed Free Trade Area of the Americas, the United States emphasized protections for intellectual property, while Brazil emphasized freer access for Brazilian agricultural products in the United States markets. Cuba, Venezuela and Bolivia were strongly against the proposal on principle, and Venezuela organized a Bolivarian Alliance for the Americas in an attempt to unite the region against the United States and Canada. Brazil declined to join the Bolivarian alliance, but neither did it push hard to see if it could negotiate a Free Trade Area of the Americas treaty that would have advanced its interests. The United States did not make a big push for an agreement either, perhaps because its primary concern in Latin America is with Mexico which is already in the North American Free Trade Association. The Mexicans were not especially eager to have more competition from Brazil. So the issue languished and a treaty was never completed, leaving Brazil and the United to negotiate more specific agreements on each issue.

---

[187] Lula da Silva, "Palavras no Encontro com Estudantes Brasileiros," Havana, September 27, 2003.
http://www.mre.gov.br/portugues/politica_externa/discursos/discurso_detalhe.as p?ID_DISCURSO=2167.

Much the same thing happened in the World Trade Organization where there were ongoing negotiations to try to lower trade barriers between the developed and developing countries. These meetings began with a series of conferences in Doha, Quatar, so they became known as the "Doha Round." This effort failed largely because of the unwillingness of the United States and Europe to lessen agricultural and other subsidies for their domestic producers. Lula was disappointed because he thought the goals of the Doha Round were sound and would be in the interests of the poor nations of the world. He used his personal rapport with President George W. Bush to urge him to make completing the negotiations a priority, but he failed. In a speech to the World Social Forum in Caracas in 2009, he said:

> I can tell you that a little while ago I called President Bush, and I said, Bush, what legacy do you want to have when you leave government? The war in Iraq? Or do you want to make the Doha Round? Brazil doesn't need to gain anything, the rich countries don't need to gain anything, but the poor must gain, most of all in the African continent, which cannot continue being the miserable continent in the twenty-first century as it was in the nineteenth. So I said, Bush why don't you add the Doha Round to your biography? But because he had a small difference with India, he didn't do it. So he left government with the legacy of the war in Iraq, the legacy of no commercial accord, and the legacy of the worst economic crisis that we are now going through. Simply because these people don't have any sensibility.[188]

Brazil usually has few conflicts with neighboring nations. One exception during Lula's presidency was a conflict with Bolivia over natural gas. Bolivia has large natural gas fields, which have been exploited by foreign companies, by far the largest of which is the Brazilian national energy company Petrobras. The largest markets for Bolivian natural gas are in Brazil and Argentina, and Petrobras has built pipelines to move the gas to São Paulo. This has placed Brazil in the unusual position of being the attacked as an imperialist power exploiting an impoverished third-world nation.

The Lula government responded to Evo Morales's' move to nationalize the natural gas with restraint and moderation, caving in to

---

[188] Lula da Silva, "Discurso durante o encontro com participantes do Fórum Social Mundial 2009: painel "América Latina e o Desafio da Crise Internacional," January 29, 2009. http://www.info.planalto.gov.br/cxcc/inf_discursosdata.cfm.

his demands for more money.[189] This reflected both sympathy for the Bolivian people and the fact that, for the short-term, Brazil's industrial heartland in São Paulo was dependent on Bolivian natural gas. Brazil and Argentina started paying more for Bolivian gas, reflecting generally higher world energy prices. In the longer-term, Petrobras will shift more of its investment into developing Brazilian gas fields, including offshore, even if the costs may be higher.

Occasionally Lula made off-the-cuff remarks that could have caused problems if taken seriously, such as suggesting that Brazil might decide to build atomic weapons and might not let international authorities inspect its reactors. Lula had no intentions of starting a nuclear arms race with Argentina, and had no other use for nuclear weapons, so he let this issue drop. He did authorize building a nuclear-powered submarine for the Brazilian navy, arguing that it would help to protect Brazil's substantial offshore oil reserves.

Building a military alliance between the countries of the southern tip of South America was another of Lula's trial balloons that made little sense. The southern tip countries have no history of fighting wars except against each other, and no common enemy.

A clear example of putting symbolism ahead of economic interests was Brazil's decision to fingerprint all Americans entering the country. This was not something thought up by Lula's government, it was started by a court order from an eccentric judge in retribution for an American policy of fingerprinting visitors from many countries, including Brazil. But the American finger printing was done efficiently with modern digital equipment. The Brazilian response to the judge's order resulted in lines as long as eight hours in Rio de Janeiro for a few days as the police used antiquated paper and ink methods.

Many Brazilians were amused to see Americans suffer some of the indignity imposed on Brazilians and others entering the United States. Frei Betto reports that foreign minister Celso Amorim "smiled from ear to ear with the discomfort of the American government."[190] The lines died down when the Brazilians imported modern German digital fingerprinting equipment and there seemed little point in collecting information they had no plans to use. Finally, they gave the whole thing up to avoid a negative impact on the tour-

---

[189] Patrícia Zimmerman and Paula Ribeiro, "Brasil aceita pagar US$ 100 milhões a mais por gás boliviano," *Folha Online*, Feb 15, 2007.
http://www1.folha.uol.com.br/folha/dinheiro/ult91u114550.shtml.
[190] Frei Betto, *Calendário do Poder*, Rio de Janeiro: Rocco, 2007, p. 286.

ism industry. Although the American policy applied to many countries that are quite hostile to the United States, no other country reacted as Brazil did.

When his second term began, in January 2007, Lula put symbolism on the back burner for a while and focused on economic growth. This meant focusing on Brazil's relationships with the countries that still control the major markets and sources of investment capital in the global economy. He skipped the 2007 World Social Forum meeting in Nairobi, Kenya, and went directly to the World Economic Forum meeting in Davos. His message there was one the World Social Forum activists would not have welcomed: "I have told the Latin American leaders we have to stop traveling around the world whining about our misery and blaming others for our disgrace. Many times, the responsibility is our own." He also said that "it is necessary to stop the practice of the rich countries giving money to governments that at times do not apply it correctly. The money must go to development projects that generate employment, wealth and improvements in the quality of life."[191]

Lula was turning away from anti-American rhetoric at a time when Venezuela's Hugo Chávez, Bolivia's Evo Morales and Ecuador's newly elected president Rafael Correa were heating it up. Brazil was joining Mexico, Chile, Colombia and Uruguay in this regard. Lula hosted United States President George W. Bush and first lady Laura Bush in March 2007, when they visited social projects in São Paulo and announced an initiative to increase ethanol production. Bush's Latin American trip was seen as a counter to Hugo Chávez's attempt to rally Latin American nations with anti-American rhetoric. Chávez paralleled Bush's Brazil visit with a dramatic visit to Buenos Aires, Argentina, where he denounced US imperialism. Chávez and Fidel Castro have denounced ethanol production for taking agricultural land away from producing food for the poor. Lula insisted that Brazil could produce both food and ethanol, and studiously ignored Chávez's anti-American blandishments.

Fueling its own automobiles with ethanol produced from sugar cane has been one of Brazil's success stories, dramatically cutting its dependency on imported oil. By 2007, Brazil was the world's only major ethanol-exporting nation. The United States could provide a

191 Adriana Stock, "Lula pede que países pobres parem de "chorar a miséria," *Folha Online*, January 26, 2007.
http://www1.folha.uol.com.br/folha/bbc/ult272u60365.shtml.

major market if it were not for the subsidies the United States gives to its own ethanol-producing corn farmers, and the 54-cent-a-gallon tax the United States imposes on Brazilian ethanol. The decline in global oil prices after the financial crisis of 2008, however, made ethanol much less competitive financially, at least for a time.

Brazilian exports to the United States were stagnant during Lula's first term, and he wanted to take advantage of the fact that George Bush seemed to be developing some interest in Latin America. He scheduled a formal meeting with Bush at his Camp David, Maryland, retreat, in April 2007. Marcos Azambuja, a former Brazilian undersecretary of state, remarked "it finally dawned on Lula that better relations with the US, besides opening up opportunities in trade with the biggest market in the world, will help Brazil play a more important role in the global political arena."[192]

The constitutional crisis in Honduras in 2009 provided an opportunity for the Brazilian Foreign Ministry to demonstrate its new importance by moving into an area that has historically been within the sphere of interest of the United States. President Manuel Zelaya, a close ally of Hugo Chávez, decided to promote a "non-binding referendum" to call a constituent assembly that might modify the constitution so that he could run for a third term as president. The Honduran Constitution specifically prohibited even raising such an issue, but provided no clear mechanism for impeaching a president who might try to do so. The military removed him from office at the request of the Supreme Court of Honduras. Power was given to Roberto Micheletti, a member of the Honduran Congress from the same party as Zelaya.

At first, the global reaction was highly negative, with most countries viewing the events as an illegal *coup d'état*, although some Republicans in the United States argued that there was constitutional justification for the military's action. The Obama government in the United States opposed the military action and called for restoring Zelaya to office. Brazilian Foreign Minister Celso Amorim decided that Brazil should take the initiative in organizing diplomatic support for Manuel Zelaya's return. He thought that the overwhelming response from the world's governments would quickly force the Honduran government to concede. On July 6, 2009, he told the press that:

---

[192] Fabio Alves, "Brazil's Lula, Cooling to Chávez, Heads to Camp David," *Net News*, March 31, 2007. http://www.caribbeannetnews.com/news-754--12-12--.html.

Without the economic help of the World Bank and the Interamerican Development Bank, without petroleum and with its economic relationships with the United States suspended, the illegal [*golpista*] regime will not resist very long. We won't see results within 24 hours, but neither will it take a month, only a few days or weeks. [193]

But things did not work out as Amorim expected. The Honduran military was resolute in the face of half-hearted pressures from the United States and other countries, and negotiations in Costa Rica dragged on with no clear resolution. As more details became known about the legal and constitutional situation in Honduras, it became less clear that it was completely unjustified, even in the reported view of one United Nations consulting committee. [194] Finally, Zelaya succeeded in re-entering the country clandestinely but was unable to generate a mass uprising and ended up taking refuge in the Brazilian embassy. The government managed to stall until the date of the next scheduled elections and the United States and other countries accepted the results. It became clear that Brazil had no significant ability to influence events in Honduras, but its impotence was matched by that of the United States, Venezuela and other countries closer to the scene.

Having failed to resolve a minor conflict in a Central American banana republic, Lula decided to take on one of the planet's most difficult and seemingly intractable problems. He traveled to Israel to share his message of dialog as the solution to conflict. On March 15, 2010, he told the Knesset:

> In my personal trajectory – as union leader and political leader – I have experienced conditions of high conflict. I didn't flee from conflicts; I tried to resolve them through dialog, even when it seemed an ingenuous exercise, an impossible task. In the opposition, I sought dialog. I arrived at the Presidency through dialog, I governed by dialog. I bet on

[193] Agência Brasil, "Celso Amorim desacredita golpe em Honduras," *Diário Popular,* July 6, 2009.
http://www.diariopopular.com.br/site/content/noticias/detalhe.php?id=5&noticia
=345.
[194] UOL Notícias, "ONU desmente imprensa e reitera condenação a golpe em Honduras," October 14, 2009.
http://noticias.uol.com.br/ultnot/internacional/2009/10/14/ult6817u4721.jhtm.

democracy, even when it seemed impossibly far off. With these sentiments, we have reiterated the historical positions of our diplomacy.[195]

It was a particularly inauspicious time to deliver this message. The Israeli government had just embarrassed another visitor, United States Vice President Joseph Biden, by announcing plans to build housing for Jewish Israelis in Jerusalem just as indirect talks between the Israelis and Palestinians were set to begin. Lula completed his trip without problems, visiting the Holocaust museum, meeting with entrepreneurs, and encouraging social and economic links between Brazil and Israel, but without further homilies on the virtues of dialog.

Support for Dictatorships. The respected Spanish newspaper *El País* published an op-ed essay by Moisés Naím titled "Lula: The Good, the Bad and the Ugly."[196] The good was his domestic policy. The bad was not sharing the credit with Fernando Henrique Cardoso. The ugly? His support for despots in neighboring countries and around the world. Naím concludes that "Lula will pass into history as a very good president for his people, and a very bad neighbor for the lovers of liberty."

Lula arrived in Cuba in March 2010, just after dissident Orlando Zapata Tamayo died as the result of a hunger strike. Supporters of Cuban dissidents had written asking him to express support for political prisoners held in Cuba, but he said he never received the messages. When questioned by an Associated Press reporter about the Cuban hunger strikers, Lula responded:

> Look, I think hunger strikes should not be used as a human rights pretext to free people. Imagine if all the bandits who are in prison in São Paulo went on hunger strike and demanded to be free. Now, look, we have to respect the determination of the justice system and the Cuban government to arrest people in accord with Cuban legislation just as I expect them to respect Brazil, as I want to respect what the United States does, following the law. Beginning with that, if a citizen does a hunger strike until he dies … I did a hunger strike once, and I'd never do it again, I'd never do it again. I think it is an insanity to mistreat

[195] Lula da Silva, "Discurso do Presidente da República, Luiz Inácio Lula da Silva, durante sessão plenária especial do parlamento israelense (Knesset)," March 15, 2010. http://www.info.planalto.gov.br/static/inf_briefdiscusos.htm.
[196] Moisés Naím, "Lula: lo Bueno, lo Malo y lo Feo," *El País*, May 9, 2010. http://www.elpais.com/articulo/internacional/Lula/bueno/malo/feo/elpepiint/20 100509elpepiint_9/Tes.

your own body. But it is not only in Cuba that people die of hunger strikes. Everyone remembers in Ireland when IRA people died of hunger strikes. I see that everyone criticizes the Cuban government because of the deaths, but no one talks about the IRA deaths. I wish it hadn't happened, but I can't question the reasons why people are arrested in Cuba, any more than I want Cuba to question me about why people are arrested in Brazil.[197]

The opposition criticized Lula's remarks in the press and the legislature, but foreign minister Celso Amorim came to Lula's defense saying, "it is one thing to defend democracy, human rights, and the right to free speech. It is another thing to be supporting everything that is dissident in the world. That is not our role."[198] He suggested that people concerned about democracy in Cuba should focus on ending the US embargo against Cuba.

Mauricio Rands, a federal deputy for the Workers' Party said, "The president expressed himself poorly or he was misunderstood. We don't accept that somebody can be detained just because they have disagreements with the government. The president is well aware of the difference between a political prisoner and an ordinary prisoner."[199] Lula's apparent lack of concern for the plight of political prisoners, in Cuba or elsewhere, is surprising in light of his and his brother Frei Chico's experiences. A computer search of his speeches found only one instance of the phrase "preso político," a reference to his own status as a former political prisoner.[200]

A reporter questioned him about this during a press conference in Havana in May 2010:

Reporter: Mr. President, doesn't it bother you, given your history, when a political prisoner dies in prison because of a hunger strike? Doesn't it move you to want to intervene in the situation?

Lula da Silva: No, but let's see. You have to intervene when you are asked to intervene. Let's take my example. Let's take the kidnappers of

[197] Lula da Silva, "Entrevista exclusiva concedida à agência Associated Press," March 9, 2010. http://www.info.planalto.gov.br/static/inf_briefdiscusos.htm.
[198] Newsroom, "Lula Irks Friends and Foes by Comparing Cuban Dissidents to Criminals," Brazzil.com, March 12, 2010. http://www.brazzilmag.com/component/content/article/83-march-2010/11961-lula-irks-friends-and-foes-by-comparing-cuban-dissidents-to-criminals.html.
[199] Ibid.
[200] Speeches searched on May 22, 2010 for both "preso politico" and "prisioneiro politico" at http://www.info.planalto.gov.br/static/inf_briefdiscusos.htm.

Abílio Diniz. You are all very young, but you know this history. The kidnappers of Abílio Diniz … went on a dry hunger strike, without water, which would lead to certain death. In 2001 I personally called President Fernando Henrique Cardoso. I went to the prison to speak to the kidnappers and I persuaded them not to do on a hunger strike without water, and once Christmas was over, we negotiated their release … In these situations, one can only help when one is asked to help … I have never refused to help any person, in any part of the world, if I am asked to help. [201]

Abílio Diniz was a Brazilian supermarket entrepreneur who was kidnapped and held for six days in 1989 by supporters of a Chilean revolutionary group, the *Movimiento de Izquierda Revolucionária*. His kidnappers were captured and sentenced to prison terms of 26 to 28 years. [202] Lula reports that he was asked to help them, after they had served ten years in prison. When the reporters pushed him about why he didn't do the same for the Cuban prisoners, he insisted that they should have contacted him through the Brazilian embassy or the Ministry of Foreign Relations, insisting that:

> What I can't do is arrive in a country and be presented with people who say they contacted me, when they didn't contact me. It isn't the right way to ask for solidarity. Anyone who knows me knows that my soul may be anything but that a person who doesn't give solidarity. This is part of my life, and therefore I don't fail to discuss these matters in any part of the world, as long as I am asked. [203]

Lula's claim that he would have spoken up for the Cuban political prisoners if only they had asked him through proper channels was not convincing. Their supporters made repeated efforts to solicit his support through all available channels, before and after this incident, to no avail.

Lula's reaction to the protests after the contested election in Iran in 2009 was strikingly unsympathetic to the protestors. He had al-

[201] Lula da Silva, "Entrevista coletiva concedida antes da partida para o Palácio da Revolução para encontro com o Presidente de Cuba, Raúl Castro," Havana, February 24, 2010.
[202] *Folha Online*, "Sequestro de Abilio Diniz também teve participação de estrangeiros," February 3, 2002.
http://www1.folha.uol.com.br/folha/cotidiano/ult95u45205.shtml.
[203] Lula da Silva, "Entrevista coletiva concedida antes da partida para o Palácio da Revolução para encontro com o Presidente de Cuba, Raúl Castro," Havana, February 24, 2010.

ready extended an invitation to Mahmoud Ahmadinejad to visit Brazil, and was eager to develop closer diplomatic and economic ties with Iran. The protests which questioned Ahmadinejad's legitimacy and highlighted the oppressive nature of the Iranian regime were inconvenient for Lula's plans. He responded that:

> I am very far from Iran, and certainly our ambassadors will soon be giving us information about what is happening there. But my impression is that this is a demonstration of losers … This is not the first country to have an election in which someone wins and the losers protested. In Brazil, this is becoming the fashion. The people who win lose in the courts, and the opposition takes power … Now look, Ahmadinejad got 61% or 62% of the vote. It is a very large vote for anyone to imagine that there was fraud … In Brazil we have already had this experience. I myself have participated in a demonstration of those who lost. I protested.[204]

Lula met with Ahmadinejad in New York in September 2009, and said that "I am not constrained in my meeting with Ahmadinejad; I don't care what other presidents think."[205] He said that Ahmadinejad has assured him that Iran's nuclear program was for public purposes, and that the United Nations had not proven otherwise. He also defended the Iranian election, saying that he had lost three times and didn't complain. He noted that Iran was a major oil producing nation, and that Brazil and Iran had much to discuss. Lula welcomed Ahmadinejad to Brazil in November 2009, and visited Iran in May 2010, where he and Turkish premier Recep Tayyip Erdogan negotiated an agreement to process Iranian uranium in Turkey. At no time did Lula raise the issue of political prisoners or repression of opposition movements in Iran.

Iranian dissident Akbar Ganji objected that "we know that Lula is following his economic and political interests. But for us the important thing is democracy. The president should take the green [democracy] movement seriously… The Brazilian government's sup-

[204] Jamil Chade, "Para Lula, protesto é choro de "perdedores"", *Estado de São Paulo*, June 16, 2009.
http://www.estadao.com.br/estadaodehoje/20090616/not_imp387944,0.php.
[205] Marília Martins, "O Brasil tem muito a conversar com o Irã', diz Lula," *O Globo*, 24 September 2009. http://oglobo.globo.com/mundo/mat/2009/09/24/brasil-tem-muito-conversar-com-ira-diz-lula-767750051.asp.

port for the Iranian regime will hurt it in the long run because the Iranian people know that this is a criminal regime."[206] New York Times columnist and best-selling author Thomas Friedman said that when he saw the picture of:

> Iran's President, Mahmoud Ahmadinejad, joining his Brazilian counterpart Luiz Inácio Lula da Silva, and the Turkish prime minister, Recep Tayyip Erdogan, with raised arms — after their signing of a putative deal to defuse the crisis over Iran's nuclear weapons program — all I could think of was: Is there anything uglier than watching democrats sell out other democrats to a Holocaust-denying, vote-stealing Iranian thug just to tweak the US and show that they, too, can play at the big power table?
> No, that's about as ugly as it gets. [207]

Lula's trip to Iran was intended to raise Brazil's international profile, but it may have backfired. The agreement Lula and Erdogan negotiated with Ahmadinejad was ignored by the United States and the major powers that went ahead with their efforts to strengthen sanctions against Iran as if nothing had happened. The Brazilian and Turkish proposal was widely viewed as containing loopholes that would permit Iran to continue developing nuclear weapons.[208] Iran announced that it would continue to enrich weapons-grade uranium itself as well as sending some to Turkey. Many Brazilian commentators thought the intervention was naïve and embarrassing, undercutting Brazil's prestige.[209] The Rio de Janeiro newspaper *O Globo* opined that "the reckless diplomatic operation undertaken by the Lula government to save the world ended as a episode in a story

[206] Reinaldo Azevedo, ""Brasil não pode ignorar drama de dissidentes no Irã," *Veja*, 11 May 2010. http://veja.abril.com.br/blog/reinaldo/geral/brasil-nao-pode-ignorar-drama-de-dissidentes-no-ira/.

[207] Thomas L. Friedman, "As Ugly as it Gets," *New York Times*, May 25, 2010. http://www.nytimes.com/2010/05/26/opinion/26friedman.html?scp=2&sq=friedman&st=Search.

[208] *O Globo*, "Anatomia do fracasso da política externa," May 20, 2010. http://oglobo.globo.com/opiniao/mat/2010/05/20/anatomia-do-fracasso-da-politica-externa-916639608.asp.

[209] Alexei Barrionuevo, "Iran Deal Seen as Spot on Brazilian Leader's Legacy," *New York Times*, May 24, 2004. http://www.nytimes.com/2010/05/25/world/americas/25brazil.html?scp=4&sq=brazil&st=cse. *O Globo*, "Anatomia do fracasso da política externa, 24 May 2010. http://oglobo.globo.com/opiniao/mat/2010/05/20/anatomia-do-fracasso-da-politica-externa-916639608.asp.

where magic carpets fly and genies fly out of bottles to solve the world's problems: only to disappear in a cloud of smoke."[210] Political analyst Amaury de Souza said, "the most charitable interpretation is that we were naïve ... in a game like this, being labeled naïve just shows you have a third rate diplomacy."[211]

But the influential newspaper *O Estado de São Paulo* thought the US should have waited to see if the Brazilian initiative would work, since it didn't really believe that sanctions would work. It thought the American, Russian, British, French and Chinese reaction was saying to Brazil and Turkey, "All right, now get out of the sandbox so we big kids can play."[212] The *Estado* pointed out that the sanctions proposed by the United States were generally viewed as unlikely to work either, so there was little harm in giving the Brazilian/Turkish approach a try.

To balance its editorial pages, *O Globo* published a comment by Arlindo Chingalia, a congressman from the Workers' Party and head of the chamber of deputies. Chingalia asserted that the agreement was "an extraordinary accomplishment by Brazilian diplomacy," and that there was no justification for escalating the sanctions.[213] He criticized the Brazilian opposition and media for discounting the agreement and argued that it was now up to the United States to either negotiate peacefully or use the nuclear issue as an excuse to destabilize the Iranian regime. He pointed out that he had discussed his initiative with US president Barack Obama, and the foreign ministry released a letter in which Obama encouraged him.[214] Lula agreed, arguing that the countries that insisted on sanctions for Iran were countries that "do not know how to do politics without an enemy."

[210] *O Globo*, "Nossa Opinião: Suicídio diplomatic," 24 May 2010. http://oglobo.globo.com/opiniao/mat/2010/05/24/nossa-opiniao-suicidio-diplomatico-916670739.asp.

[211] Barrionuevo, op cit.

[212] O Estado de Sao Paulo, "A reposta Americana," May 20, 2010. http://www.estadao.com.br/estadaodehoje/20100520/not_imp554128,0.php.

[213] Arlindo Chinaglia, "UTRA OPINIÃO: Um acerto para a paz," *O Globo*, May 24, 2010. http://oglobo.globo.com/opiniao/mat/2010/05/24/outra-opiniao-um-acerto-para-paz-916670878.asp.

[214] Natuza Nery, "Obama disse em carta a Lula que acordo com Irã criaria confiança," *O Globo*, May 21, 2010. http://oglobo.globo.com/mundo/mat/2010/05/21/obama-disse-em-carta-lula-que-acordo-com-ira-criaria-confianca-916646345.asp.

He said that the Brazilian newspapers who criticized his efforts had an "inferiority complex:"

> I am sad because we have an inferiority complex in many people's heads. A part of our political elite which writes columns saying, 'Why did Brazil get involved in this? It isn't our business.' Brazil doesn't have to get permission from anyone to talk with anyone it likes.[215]

Conclusions. Foreign policy is not usually an important focus of Brazilian politics. Brazilians usually prefer to leave foreign affairs to the professionals in the Ministry of Foreign Relations. Brazil has few conflicts with its South American neighbors, and has not traditionally sought to intervene in conflicts between major powers. Lula sought to expand Brazil's diplomatic role, in part because its global economic interests were growing, in part because he saw it as a means of building national self-esteem.

Some foreign policy analysts were concerned that the Lula administration pursued symbolic, psychological goals at the expense of important economic interests. Writing in 2006, Professor Eiiti Sato of the University of Brasília argued that Brazilian foreign policy under Lula overemphasized two somewhat contradictory ideas. First, the idea that Brazil is threatened by avaricious designs of other countries, principally the United States. Second, an exaggerated belief in the role that the country can play in the world. Sato argued that "the international community is not so avid to exploit the riches which Brazil presumably possesses, nor is the role which Brazil can play on the international scene so outstanding, considering the resources the country can deploy."[216]

Sato was concerned that fear of American designs on Brazil's wealth might explain why the proposal to create a Free Trade Area of the Americas was allowed to languish. The Lula government preferred to focus on the Doha Rounds, which were global rather than regional, but it failed in bringing these to a successful conclusion.[217] Opposing the Free Trade Agreement was popular with much of the

[215] *O Globo*, "Para Lula, países que defendem sanções contra Irã buscam 'inimigo,'" May 20, 2010, http://oglobo.globo.com/pais/mat/2010/05/20/para-lula-paises-que-defendem-sancoes-contra-ira-buscam-inimigo-916642638.asp.
[216] Eiiti Sato, "A Política Brasileira e sua Coerência com a Ordem Internacional," Instituto de Relações Internacionais da Universidade de Brasília, 2006.
[217] *O Globo*, "NOSSA OPINIÃO: Suicídio diplomatic," May 24, 2010. http://oglobo.globo.com/opiniao/mat/2010/05/24/nossa-opiniao-suicidio-diplomatico-916670739.asp.

Brazilian public who were suspicious of American intentions. But the economic reality is that access to markets and resources from the United States and Europe are essential to the Brazilian economy as it is structured today.

Economically, Brazil did well under Lula's government, so it is hard to argue that the failure to complete the Doha Round or the Free Trade Area of the Americas were serious impediments. Brazil continued to vigorously pursue bilateral trade agreements and to expand trade with a great many countries.

Lula did seem to have had an exaggerated sense of the influence that Brazil could have in solving problems such as the Israeli/Palestinian and Iranian nuclear disputes, or even in the political crisis in Honduras. Brazil had little to lose in these ventures, and Lula could claim credit for advocating peaceful, nonviolent alternatives, and for asserting Brazil's independence from United States hegemony. He might have played a more constructive and helpful role, however, if he had used his personal prestige and credibility to advocate for democracy and human rights, and especially for freedom for political prisoners.

CHAPTER ELEVEN
WINNING REELECTION IN 2006

Lula's landslide re-election in 2006 was a shock to both to those who thought he was tainted by the corruption scandals and to leftists angry over his orthodox economic policies. At the peak of the corruption scandals in 2005, there had been talk of impeaching Lula by those who wanted to hold him responsible for the actions of top officials who reported directly to him. Others thought it best to leave him in office until the 2006 elections on the theory that he would be a weak candidate for re-election and might bring the rest of the Workers' Party down with him. Both of these opposition scenarios turned out to be wrong. Not only was Lula re-elected, but the Workers' Party held its ground, albeit with a significant shift in its base of support.

Lula's popularity dipped briefly in 2005, at the peak of the scandals, but it recovered in plenty of time for the 2006 elections. He was never weak enough in the polls to make impeachment a possibility in the Brazilian Congress, so the opposition turned its attention to the 2006 elections. José Serra, the Social Democrat Lula had defeated in 2002, ran close to Lula in the opinion polls throughout 2005, and actually pulled ahead of him at the end of the year. In the December 2005 Datafolha poll, 36 percent of the respondents supported Serra, 29 percent supported Lula and one in ten favored Anthony Garotinho, the former governor of Rio de Janeiro.

By February 2006, however, Lula's team had successfully spun the corruption scandals and he regained the lead in the polls. Social Democratic leaders feared that José Serra had peaked, and they started to consider other candidates. There are no primary elections in Brazil, nomination decisions are made by party leaders. The strongest contenders are often the governors of the largest states who are well known and control significant patronage resources.

Brazil's largest and wealthiest state, São Paulo, is the base of the Social Democratic Party, and its governor, Geraldo Alckmin, was an automatic contender for that party's nomination. Alckmin ran weaker than Serra in the early pre-election polling, but may have been because he was simply less well known. His previous campaigns had been remarkable successful. He was first elected to the municipal council of the city of Pindamonhangaba in the state of São Paulo in 1972 when he was nineteen years old and a medical student.[218] He was popular, competent and easy to work with. He became president of the city council at 23, mayor at 23, state legislator at 29 and federal congressman at 33. Mário Covas, a leading São Paulo politician, selected him as running mate in successful governorship elections in 1994 and 1998. He succeeded to the governorship when Covas died in 2001.

As governor of São Paulo, Alckmin invested heavily in expanding subway lines and toll highways administered by private companies. He worked to modernize and reduce the state bureaucracy, reducing taxes and implementing computerized bill paying to minimize corruption. He also expanded social programs, including youth programs, free internet access in low-income areas, loans to small business, and a program offering well-balanced meals to the poor for R$1.00. He cracked down on violent crime, greatly increasing the state's prison population and cutting the homicide rate. The state's economy did well during his governorship. It was a record that could be marketed effectively.

One possible stumbling block was his apparent links to conservative Catholic circles that had been supportive of the military governments. In January 2006, the newsmagazine *Revista Época* published a report that Alckmin was involved with the secretive Catholic order Opus Dei.[219] He denied membership in the organization, although he is a devoted and active Catholic, as was his father. His reported Opus Dei membership was cited repeatedly in Internet blogs and discussion lists as if it were a proven fact, but it did not become an issue with the wider public.

Alckmin was respected for his accomplishments and he presented a reassuring and competent, if unexciting, image on television. He very much wanted to run for president at a time when many experts suspected that Lula would be unbeatable. Commentators suggested that running a losing campaign in 2006 might hurt José Serra's chances in 2010 when Lula would be unable to run under the current constitution. Taking all these things into account, the party leaders decided to nominate Alckmin. Under Brazilian law, he had to resign

[218] Angélica Maria Cortez Cavalheiro, *Geraldo Alckmin: Nome e Imagem. Uma Viagem Cultural pelo Vale do Paraíba*, Aparecida-SP: Editora Santuário, 2004.
[219] Eliane Brum and Ricardo Mendoça, "O governador e a Obra," *Revista Época*, January 16, 2006. http://revistaepoca.globo.com/Epoca/0,6993,EPT1107598-1664,00.html.

the governorship to run for president. José Serra then resigned his post as mayor of the city of São Paulo to run for governor of the state.

Heloísa Helena, the Workers' Party renegade outraged by Lula's economic and social policies, declared for president under the banner of the Party of Socialism and Liberty, a new party started by disillusioned Workers' Party leftists. Cristovam Buarque, another disillusioned former Workers' Party stalwart and a former Minister of Education in the Lula government, declared under the banner of the Democratic Labor Party. Aécio Neves, the Social Democratic governor of the state of Minas Gerais, decided to run for re-election to that post rather than trying for the Social Democratic presidential nomination. He was also considered a possible candidate in 2010, when he would turn 50 years old. Anthony Garotinho of Rio de Janeiro looked at his poll numbers and decided not to run.

One of Brazil's largest and most powerful political parties, the Democratic Movement Party, decided not to launch its own presidential candidate. The Democratic Movement Party is very strong in many Brazilian states, but it often has difficulty uniting around a single candidate for national office. Its politicians often support the presidential candidate they expect to win, regardless of party, in the expectation of getting cabinet positions and other rewards after the election. Lula had formed a loose coalition with them during his first term, and they supported him for re-election in 2006 in the expectation that, with the likely weakness of Workers' Party candidates, Lula would be in even greater need of their support in Congress.

There were also three minor party candidates who used the free television time allocated to each party but who received very little attention. Paid television advertising is strictly limited under Brazilian election laws. Each candidate gets an allocation of free television time proportional to the percentage of the vote the parties supporting him or her received in the previous election, and is allowed to buy paid television spots in the same proportion.

Heloísa Helena launched a vigorous people's campaign, dressing informally and traveling around the country by bus and commercial airliner instead of a chartered jet. Geraldo Alckmin used his substantial television time for positive, constructive proposals, hoping the voters would warm to him once they got to know him. His campaign was hurt, however, by organized crime uprisings in the state of São Paulo in 2005. As governor, he had been responsible for the state's prisons and for maintaining law and order, and it was hard to make the point that the uprising was a reaction by criminals to policies that had brought down the overall homicide rate.

Political marketing is quite sophisticated in Brazil with campaign professionals conducting frequent surveys and focus groups.[220] The result is that candidates often sound much alike as they tell people what they want to hear. Their advertisements show them having their morning coffee in a bakery where they can be filmed mixing with the people. They all have northeastern *forró* music for their campaign jingles because it has been shown to appeal to northeasterners. They all use their first names because the electorate prefers them.

In their initial television broadcasts, Lula and Alckmin presented similar messages. Both promised economic growth, social inclusion, health and education. Both condemned organized crime and moral decadence. If you examined the text of their advertisements without seeing the name of the speaker, it would be difficult to say which was which. Lula used blue, the color of the Social Democratic Party, in most of his advertisements instead of the Workers' Party's trademark red. The Workers' Party's star was minimized and hidden in a corner.

Lula spoke with confidence, compassion and candor. His salt-and-pepper beard, graying hair and impeccably tailored suits gave the impression of a caring, mature father who knew what his people needed and how to get it for them. Alckmin sounded like the friendly physician that he is, giving good advice about health and education directed largely at the mothers in the audience. Heloísa Helena was spirited and angry, expressing frustration with the powers that be, and promising to replace the slick politicians with a working mother's common sense wisdom. Cristovam Buarque sounded intelligent and thoughtful, but failed to generate much enthusiasm from the voters.

The polls show that Lula connected with the people, especially the less affluent and those in the poorer parts of the country. The poor, in particular, liked him because he knew what they were up against and because he gave them a plastic card to withdraw a monthly allowance from the bank.

Most importantly, Lula had brought results in his first term, especially for the poor. Poverty was down, people were eating better.

---

[220] Andréa Leal, Flavio Machado and Guilherme Evelin, "Quem agüenta tanto café?," *Revista Epoca* September 11, 2006.
http://revistaepoca.globo.com/Revista/Epoca/1„EDG75245-6009,00.html.

This was partly due to policies continued from the previous administrations – inflation control and the family allowances – but the beneficiaries were happy to give Lula the credit. They liked his warm, expressive personality and the fact that he grew up in poverty in the northeast and could sympathize with their problems. They could forgive him for bending the rules, especially because he and his colleagues were not lining their own pockets, at least not too much. Some observers said that Lula was like a Santa Claus for the poor.

As the campaign entered its first month, Alckmin's poll numbers seemed perpetually stuck in the twenties. Finally, on September 8, Fernando Henrique Cardoso circulated a long email "letter to the electors of the Social Democratic Party" in which he chastised the party for not emphasizing the corruption issue.[221] Cardoso's letter came very late in the game, and was immediately published in the national press. He frankly admitted that the party had erred in defending its own leader, Eduardo Azevedo, who was implicated in a scandal.

Cardoso's letter was not well received. Columnist Nêumanne Pinto denounced late-game moralizing in a column titled "Shut Your Mouth, Fernando":

> The problem of the Social Democrats is timing and brazenness. Lula has not turned this around because the public is stupid, but because the *tucanos* (Social Democratic leaders) think they are stupid. If the question is ethics, how can the opposition convince us that it is, what is the real difference between the *petistas* (Workers' Party leaders) who expel their leaders who get caught, and these who ... worked scandalously to absolve their then national President Eduardo Azevedo ... who was obviously just as guilty.[222]

Cardoso had no illusions that the public would be persuaded by a late-campaign focus on the corruption issue. He argued that the party had a moral obligation to highlight the issue on principle even if the people weren't yet with them. Everyone expected Lula to coast to an easy first-term re-election victory.

Then, to everyone's surprise, just two weeks before the vote, the corruption issue blew up in Lula's face. In its September 20 issue, the

[221] Fernando Henrique Cardoso, "Carta aos Eleitores do PSDB," http://www.psdb.org.br/diario/htm/diario_numero724.htm#2
[222] José Nêumanne Pinto, "Cala a Boca, Fernando," *Jornal da Paraíba*, September 14, 2006, http://www.neumanne.com/da_jp20.htm.

newsweekly *IstoÉ* published an exposé claiming that José Serra, the Social Democratic candidate in 2002, had been involved in an ambulance overpricing scandal when he was minister of health in the Cardoso government.[223] This was based on a report from Trevisan Vedoin, a businessman who was being investigated for the scheme. Last-minute scandals are sometimes the result of political manipulation by candidates who hope to swing votes in their favor before the accusations can be investigated. Lula had no need for a last-minute scandal, as he repeatedly pointed out in the next few weeks. But other Workers' Party candidates in the state of São Paulo did. São Paulo is Brazil's most important state with a quarter of the country's population, a third of its gross national product, 40 percent of its industry, and almost as many government jobs as the federal government. It generates half of the revenues from major federal taxes.[224] The state also has effective investigatory agencies capable of uncovering and prosecuting corrupt officials and former officials.

São Paulo is the historical base of both the Workers' Party and the Social Democrats, and control of the state government is a very important prize for both parties. Workers' Party Vice-President Marta Suplicy had been elected mayor of the city of São Paulo in 2000, but lost the race for re-election to José Serra of the Social Democrats in 2004. Aloizio Mercadante, a Workers' Party senator, was running against José Serra for governor of São Paulo in the 2006 elections and was trailing badly in the polls.

The last minute *dossier* revealed by *IstoÉ* looked like an attempt to rescue Mercadante's candidacy and win control of the state for the Workers' Party. This seemed likely because three members of the Parliamentary Commission of Inquiry reported that Vedoin had testified that Serra had no involvement in the matter. Sure enough, the Federal Police quickly discovered that Workers' Party operatives had paid R$1.7 million for false documents and doctored videos implicating José Serra and Geraldo Alckmin in the scandal.[225] The newspa-

[223] IstoÉ, "Os Vedoin acusam Serra," September 20, 2006.
http://www.terra.com.br/istoe/.
[224] Marli Moreira, "Serra promete governo eficiente e centrado na ética," Agência Brasil, January 1, 2007.
http://www.agenciabrasil.gov.br/noticias/2007/01/01/materia.2007-01-01.2317636338/view.
[225] Gabriela Gurreiro, "PSDB e PFL protocolam pedido de investigação contra Lula ao TSE," *Folha Online*, Sept 19, 2006.
http://www1.folha.uol.com.br/folha/brasil/ult96u83317.shtml.

pers published photographs of huge piles of money intended for payment of the forged documents. Freud Godoy, a special advisor to Lula's personal secretary, resigned after having been accused of purchasing the documents. Godoy denied any involvement.[226] Aloizio Mercadante said that the *dossiergate* was "unacceptable" and that it had "unquestionably" damaged his candidacy at a point when it was "in a rhythm of growth." He stated that "we cannot accept militants who believe that they can define a campaign through clandestine activity. This is a vestige of the dictatorship that has survived in a part of the left. The rules and the laws must be respected. And whoever does not respect them must accept the consequences."[227] He could not, however, overcome the evidence that it was his own organization that did it.

The corruption issue dominated the last week of political campaigning. Lula said "never has a government investigated and punished corruption as much as this one." He insisted that corruption had not increased, "what has increased is the combat against corruption." Geraldo Alckmin responded, "what kind of president is this who doesn't know anything? A president has the obligation to know what goes on around him." Heloísa Helena said, "it was bad before, and now it is worse." She noted that the ambulance kickback scandal began under the Cardoso regime. Cristovam Buarque said that Brazilian politics "is more corrupt all the time," and that the corrupt politicians "want to make the people believe that all politicians are the same as them."[228]

All this debate took place in the media; there was no debate between Lula and the other candidates in the first round of the election. A debate was scheduled for the Thursday night before the Sunday election and Lula told the television station he was coming, but finally decided not to. The television station was irritated, especially because he gave them only one hour's notice. They set up an empty

---

[226] Epaminondas Neto, "Assessor de Lula pede demissão após caso do dossiê anti-Serra," *Folha Online*, September 18, 2006,
http://www1.folha.uol.com.br/folha/brasil/ult96u83279.shtml.
[227] Andrea Catão, "Mercadante admite que compra do dossiê prejudicou sua candidature," *Folha Online*, September 27, 2006.
http://www1.folha.uol.com.br/folha/brasil/ult96u83957.shtml.
[228] James Cimino, "Dossiê repercute no horário eleitoral; Lula diz estar decepcionado," *Folha de São Paulo*, September 22, 2006.
http://www1.folha.uol.com.br/folha/brasil/ult96u83612.shtml.

chair with his name, and allowed the other candidates to direct questions to him as if he were there.

The other three candidates spent much of their time criticizing Lula for arrogantly refusing to answer the people's questions. Alckmin said that by his absence Lula was sending a message to the Brazilian people that "I am not interested in your opinion. I do not have to account to anyone." Helena said that Lula had an obligation to "come down from his throne of corruption, cowardice and arrogance." Cristovam Buarque asked whether Lula would renounce office if the police investigation showed that he was responsible for the misuse of public resources.[229] Were voters voting for Lula or for his vice president?

On debate night, Lula spoke to a rally of his supporters in his home community of São Bernardo in the industrial suburbs of São Paulo. He attacked the press, Fernando Henrique Cardoso and the "small, biased elite of this country." He claimed that "at root, this is a question of skin color. It was not written that my class would arrive at power."[230] This was an odd observation since Lula's skin color is not very different from that of the other candidates.

The last Datafolha poll, in the two days before the election, showed Lula with half of the valid votes. The margin of error was plus or minus 2 percent. Alckmin had risen to 38 percent, with 9 percent for Helena and 3 percent for other candidates. This made the election a cliff-hanger because Lula needed 50 percent of the valid votes, excluding those who cast blank ballots as a protest, to win on the first round. Voters who were disillusioned had a reason to vote for one of the opposition candidates – it did not matter which one – just to force Lula into a second round when he would have to answer questions.

Brazil's electoral machinery is run by a Superior Electoral Tribunal that is consistent throughout the country. Voters enter their preferences on computerized electronic voting machines, and the results are printed out and faxed to Brasília. Within a few hours of the election, the votes are in and everyone accepts their accuracy. The state of São Paulo, the largest state, is usually the slowest in submitting its results, but they only take an extra hour or two. Within a few hours of the polls closing it was apparent that the São Paulo voters were

---

[229] Josias de Souza blog, Folha de São Paulo,
http://josiasdesouza.folha.blog.uol.com.br/arch2006-09-24_2006-09-
30.html#2006_09-29_02_50_38-10045644-0.
[230] Ibid.

going strongly for Alckmin, and that this would be enough to keep Lula under 50 percent. Lula watched the results from his apartment in São Bernardo with a circle of close friends. As the returns came in, he launched into a bitter attack on the "screwballs" (*alporados*) in his own party who had sabotaged his campaign with their bungled operations. Launching into a racing metaphor he said "someone does fifty rounds around the track, driving carefully, opening up a tremendous lead over the opponents, and then on the last curve, some of our own personnel throw oil on the track. There is a name for this. Sabotage." He speculated that the "stupid" agents of his own party's "intelligence" department had fallen into a trap laid by the opposition.[231]

The final results showed Lula with 48.61percent of the vote, and percentages of his opponents at 41.64 for Alckmin, 6.85 for Helena and 2.64 for Buarque.[232] Geraldo Alckmin's vote was much larger than expected, putting him in a strong position for the second round. Helena's vote was weak, leaving her supporters with no congenial alternative. To make matters worse, former President Fernando Collor de Mello won Helena's Senate seat from the state of Alagoas with 44 percent of the vote, while her party's candidate received only 8.7 percent (Senate elections do not require a 50 percent vote). Collor announced that he would support Lula, and Lula welcomed his support saying he had paid his dues to society.

The vote was very uneven between regions. Lula won 70.9 percent of the vote in the northeastern state of Pernambuco where was born. But Geraldo Alckmin won 54.2 percent of the vote in the largest state, São Paulo, where Lula has lived since childhood. Lula received 49.1 percent in the state of Rio de Janeiro, compared to 28.9 percent for Alckmin and 17.1 percent for Helena, her best showing in any state. In general, Alckmin carried the south central and south of Brazil, the most modern and developed part of the country. Lula carried the north and northeast, the poorer and more traditional states.

The socio-economic differences in the voting patterns were larger than in 2002. Lula was strong among low-income voters and weak

[231] Josias de Silva, "Lula culpa PT for 'derrapagem na última curva," October 7, 2006, *Folha de São Paulo*, http://josiasdesouza.folha.blog.uol.com.br/arch2006-10-01_2006-10-07.html.
[232] David Fleischer, *Brazil Focus: Special Report*, October 2, 2006. http://www.wilsoncenter.org/news/docs/BFDF10022006%20Special%20Report.doc. Official results at: http://www.tse.gov.br/internet/index.html.

among upper income groups. He had more support from men than from women, and more from older voters than from the young. His support was very strong in the northeast, but weak in the south and the southeast. He was ahead because Brazil has so many poor people, and because Brazilian law requires everyone to vote. But he was in danger of becoming the candidate of the poor instead of the consensus candidate he was in 2002.

The results left Lula no choice but to meet Alckmin for at least one face-to-face debate. He still had a very strong base of support, but his trend was down while Alckmin's was up. People knew Lula well and had firm ideas about him. Many still had no strong impression of Alckmin, so the first debate was a make-or-break occasion for him. It was scheduled for Sunday evening, October 7, and drew an enormous audience.

The debate lasted for two and a half hours, with five segments, and it was gripping television all the way.[233] Each segment was chaired by a single journalist who directed questions to the candidates, but also invited the candidates to direct questions to each other. The first question, from journalist Ricardo Boechat, was about how the candidates would stimulate Brazil's economic growth. Alckmin promised to cut spending and corruption, as he did when he was governor of São Paulo. Lula replied "the only thing they know how to do is cut expenses where they should not, with the salaries of the workers."

The real excitement came when it was Alckmin's turn to direct a question to Lula. He stated that the president of Brazil has a great many police and investigative resources at his disposal, and listed many of them. The president should be the best-informed man in the country. He should have the answer to the one question Brazilians are waiting for: where did the 1.7 million *reais* for the forged *dossier* come from?

Lula ducked the question, saying that he was the president, not a police detective, and that he, like everyone else, was waiting for answers from the appropriate authorities. He said he wanted to know what was in the *dossier*, and suggested that the only person who benefited from it was his opponent. In response, Alckmin turned directly to Lula and challenged him to "look the Brazilian people in the eye and tell them where the money came from." Lula responded that

---

[233] Clips of highlights of the debates can be found by searching http://youtube.com. There was extensive summary and commentary in all the Brazilian press.

Alckmin must be nostalgic for the days of the military dictatorship when the police tortured people to get answers in a half an hour. In a democracy, he said, it takes longer. He claimed that no government had done more to expose corruption, and criticized Alckmin for squashing legislative investigations in São Paulo when he was governor.

The remainder of the debate ranged over a variety of issues, although frequently returning to corruption. Lula bragged about the Family Allowance program reaching 11 million families, while claiming that the Social Democrats only know how to privatize industries and raise taxes. Alckmin replied that the Family Allowance was developed by the Cardoso administration, and only had its name changed by the Lula government. He listed the many social programs implemented by the São Paulo government when he was governor.

Alckmin accused Lula of being weak in foreign policy, for not winning a seat for Brazil on the UN Security Council, and failing to stand up to Bolivia when it nationalized Brazilian natural gas investments. Lula defended his conciliatory foreign policy, and expressed sympathy for the Bolivian people who have nothing to sell but their natural gas. When criticized for allowing Chinese consumer goods to flood the Brazilian market, he pointed out how successful Brazil had been in selling airplanes and other things to China.

Lula argued that life had improved for Brazilians during his presidency, and challenged Alckmin to admit it. He challenged Alckmin on the security problems in São Paulo, especially the uprising by organized crime against the police. Alckmin pointed out that this is a national problem, and argued that homicide rates had come down during his administration in São Paulo. Alckmin promised to sell the luxurious new airplane Lula had bought.

Lula accused Alckmin of planning to privatize more government companies. Alckmin protested that his campaign platform clearly stated that he would not privatize Petrobras or major government banks as the Workers' Party was claiming. Lula claimed everyone knows that the Social Democrats and their liberal front allies had sold off the country and asked, "when there is nothing left to sell, what will they sell? The Amazon?"

The corruption issue kept coming up throughout the debate, in questions from the journalists as well as from the candidates. Journalist Franklin Martins asked "What guarantee do we have, in the case that you are re-elected, that there won't be more surprises?" Lula replied, "in past governments, corruption was shoved under the rug. Not in my government! I have lost long-time friends. And I will lose as many as necessary if they continue to make mistakes."

Some commentators complained that the debate did not go through the details of the candidates' positions on the issues. Others said that the point of the debate is for the public to see how the candidates handle themselves as personalities. In this sense, the debate was very successful. Each side of the debate claimed their candidate won, and both did well with many questions. Lula had a hard time with the question about where the money came from, but it was a very hard question to answer. He seemed a bit defensive at times, and in his comments after the debate he complained about Alckmin behaving as if he were a police interrogator. The Social Democrats were delighted with Alckmin's performance, and thought that he had a real chance of winning.

Commentators disagreed about who "won" the debate, but there was no question that Alckmin was the one who needed to win. As the underdog and lesser-known candidate, this was his chance to face Lula on equal terms. Everyone waited eagerly for the national polls to see if the debate would shift any votes.

The first poll results were leaked on Monday night and published by Datafolha on Tuesday. They showed Lula gaining apparently because many voters thought Alckmin was too harsh and not sufficiently respectful of Lula. Lula capitalized on this sentiment by telling the public how surprised and shocked he was by Alckmin's attack.

The outcome of the debate confirmed publicist Duda Mendonça's view that debates are primarily about personality, not issues. Mendonça counseled that debates are theater, and that the candidates' personal style matters much more than issues or accomplishments. In his memoirs he observed that, "what the public wants from a candidate in a debate is a sincere human being, truthful and balanced. If you systematically attack your adversary, you lose sympathy. It gives the impression that you are a radical individual, so full of rancor that you are incapable of presenting proposals and solutions, so you turn to systematically offending and wounding your rival."[234]

Lula responded firmly and confidently even when his position was inherently weak, as it was on the corruption issue. Alckmin did not do so well when he was attacked on the privatization issue. In their post-debate analysis, the Social Democratic leaders thought that

---

[234] Duda Mendonça, *Casos & Coisas*. São Paulo: Globo, 2001, pl. 130.

he acted as if he was ashamed of his party's record. [235] Referring to Drew Westen's theory in *The Political Brain*, columnist Josias de Souza argues that Lula's triumph was due to superior emotional intelligence enhanced by coaching from Duda Mendonça.[236] Alckmin never recovered the initiative after the first debate. The Workers' Party claimed that Alckmin would privatize Petrobras and the Banco do Brasil if he were elected. Alckmin protested that his campaign platform explicitly stated that he would not privatize these companies. Fernando Henrique Cardoso accused the Workers' Party of using "big lie" propaganda tactics.

Workers' Party spokesmen claimed it was fair to attack the Social Democrats for privatization, even though their platform opposed it, because it was "in their genes." This put Alckmin on the defensive as he promised not to privatize anything, while pointing out that the Lula government itself had privatized two banks. At no point was the merit of privatization actually discussed, although many of the privatizations of the Cardoso era had demonstrable benefits. Telephone service, for example, has expanded dramatically since it was privatized over the strong objections of state employees and the Workers' Party. But the Alckmin campaign did not think this argument could be made, and remained on the defensive.

The *dossier* case was largely forgotten since there were no new revelations. Critics raised questions about how the details and pictures of mounds of money had been released to the press so quickly.[237] Workers' Party supporters mounted a media campaign to minimize the corruption allegation by arguing that corruption was just as bad or worse under the Cardoso government. Singer Chico Buarque circulated a letter arguing that "the media says much more about the monthly payoffs than it did about all those stories about Fernando Henrique, the purchase of votes, the privatizations." He argued, "when the opposition says that this is the most corrupt government in Brazilian history ... where is the corrupt-o-meter? We know that corruption is everywhere in Brazil."[238]

---

[235] Josias de Souza, "Blog de Josias," *Folha Online*, August 12, 2007. http://josiasdesouza.folha.blog.uol.com.br/arch2007-08-12_2007-08-18.html.
[236] Ibid. Drew Westen, *The Political Brain*. New York: Public Affairs, 2007.
[237] Raimundo Rodrigues Pereira, "Os Fatos Ocultos," *Carta Capital*, October 18, 2006. http://www.cartacapital.com.br/index.php?funcao=exibirMateria&id_materia=545 7.
[238] "Opinião de Chico Buarque sobre a eleição presidencial, October 8, 2006.

Chico Buarque went on to say that economic policy was not a critical part of his voting decision because he believed that "the economy will not change if a Social Democrat is elected. Things are so tied up that honestly I do not see much difference between the next Lula government and one from the opposition. But the country made an important step in electing Lula." He criticized the criticisms he often heard on the street, that people like Lula are not well enough educated, are not prepared, do not speak foreign languages. He also felt that there might be some opportunities for social investment that would be a higher priority for Lula.

Lula continued to pull ahead in the polls and Alckmin toned down his aggressive criticism of Lula and placed less emphasis on the corruption issue. In the second televised debate, on October 19, he avoided aggressive questioning of Lula and, in the view of some pundits, may have even been too soft spoken. Renato Rabelo, the president of the Communist Party of Brazil, one of Lula's allies, observed that "in the first debate, he was too aggressive, he hit below the belt. In the second, he was, as he said … zen." Rabelo thought Alckmin was "unbalanced, revealing insecurity with erratic behavior."[239]

Marta Suplicy, the former Workers' Party mayor of the city of São Paulo, thought that Alckmin was too rigid in following the advice of his marketing consultants. Instead of answering questions directly, she thought, he changed the topic and offered prepared statements on other topics. She thought that the debate enabled the viewers to learn about the "personality, profile and project" of the candidates and that "this is good for Lula because the Brazilian people, to the extent that they are able, in the second round, to get to know Geraldo Alckmin better, are choosing Lula."[240]

The polling results confirm this observation. In the last two weeks of October Lula's numbers rose sharply while Alckmin's declined. However, this may have been less a rejection of Alckmin than a return to the level of popularity Lula had in the past. Many Brazilians felt more secure sticking with Lula than taking a chance on

Posted in *Carta Capital*, the *Folha de São Paulo*, and at http://phpones.wordpress.com/2006/10/08/.

[239] "Debate SBT: Renato Rabelo faz ironia com 'Alckmin zen'," *Vermelho Online*, October 20, 2006. http://www.vermelho.org.br/base.asp?texto=9042.

[240] Felipe Neves, "Marta Suplicy compara atitude de Alckmin em debate à de Paulo Maluf," *Folha Online*, October 20, 2006.
http://www1.folha.uol.com.br/folha/brasil/ult96u85530.shtml.

Alckmin. Lula's campaign capitalized on this feeling with the slogan "don't change the certain for the doubtful." Columnist Gilberto Dinerstein summarized the election as follows:

> Lula won for a simple reason. He was able to align his past as a migrant from the northeast with the social advances of the four years of his administration. This led the voters, most of whom are poor, to identify strongly with him. It is clear that this identification was stimulated by a continual marketing effort, as if it were always an election year. It is also clear that Lula benefited from a beneficial inheritance from the previous government (low inflation, increasing exports, and better control of costs). But the numbers showed that in the last four years, the poor had a significant increase in income. Brazil is a country where most people are poor, and the poor people felt better off. To understand Lula's victory, everything else, including Alckmin's performance, is secondary. [241]

Lula won 61 percent of the votes in the second round of the 2006 presidential election, the same as his win over José Serra in the second round of the 2002 election. The survey data, however, show that the social composition of the vote was quite different. In 2002, Lula ran stronger among young people and among the higher educated respondents. In 2002, he ran well in all regions of the country, although slightly better in the northeast. In 2006, there was a very strong regional split in the vote, with Lula triumphing in the poorer regions of the north and northeast and doing much worse in the more affluent south and southeast. In 2002, he ran as well with affluent as with low- and modest-income voters. In 2006, Lula lost among Brazilians with a college education or with an income more than ten times the minimum wage. All these social differences were more acute in the first round of the election than in the second, as Lula recaptured many of the voters who were upset by the *dossiergate* scandal and his refusal to participate in the first round of the debates.

In the 2006 poll, Datafolha included a question about the respondents' "declared color." Brazilian pollsters do not routinely use "race" as a variable because racial categories are not sharply defined as they are in the United States. When the census asks about race it includes "brown" (*parda*) as a category. There is also a category of "indigenous" and a "yellow" (Asian) category, but the number of

[241] Gilberto Dimenstein, "Por que Lula venceu," *Folha Online*, http://www1.folha.uol.com.br/folha/pensata/ult508u329.shtml

respondents in these categories was too small for valid results. In the weighted Datafolha sample, 42 percent of the respondents were identified as white, 37 percent as brown, 15 percent as black, 4 percent as indigenous and 3 percent as yellow. The results show a sharp racial division in the vote, with Lula winning very strongly among voters categorizing themselves as "black," and more strongly among "brown" than "white" voters. This statistical result is to be expected since skin color is strongly correlated with income. There was almost no mention of racial issues in the campaigns or the debates.

In 2002, Lula had the luxury of being vague about exactly what he was going to do. In 2006, he ran on his record. The ideological left was angry because his new economic model turned out to be even more "neoliberal" in many respects than his predecessor's. Many among the better educated and more affluent classes were outraged by his party's vote buying and use of forged documents to subvert the electoral process. But these voters were outnumbered by the masses of Brazil's less affluent, less educated voters who were thankful for the benefits they received under Lula's government. Perhaps just as important, they continued to be inspired by Lula's life story and like him as a personality.

Many in the educated classes thought he could have done better. Former president Fernando Henrique Cardoso regretted that a leader who had started out by "standing up against the rottenness of the union movement had turned into an ordinary politician." He thought that Lula had "assassinated the symbol that he represented by his inability to understand his moment in the greatness of history" when he chose to win an election by "equaling the most backward practices in Brazilian politics."[242] For the poor, however, it was enough that Lula had won, even if he had to play the same dirty game the elites had played for decades. No matter his faults, they could not let him lose.

---

[242] Folha online, "FHC defende privatizações e diz que não é contra venda da Petrobras," October 17, 2006.
http://www1.folha.uol.com.br/folha/brasil/ult96u85308.shtml.

CHAPTER TWELVE
MAKING BRAZILIAN CAPITALISM BOOM

Official statistics released at the beginning of 2006 showed that economic growth in Lula's first term had averaged 2.6 percent a year, almost exactly the same as the average of Fernando Henrique Cardoso's two terms. Steady growth of 2.6 percent a year isn't so bad. The United States became a wealthy country by growing about that much every year for 100 years. But in 2006, the world was in the grips of a bubble mentality and Brazil was perceived as lagging behind countries such as China and India in closing the gap with the developed world.

Global markets were not an excuse, indeed international financial conditions were better than they had been during Cardoso's presidency. An econometric analysis estimated that "Brazil's growth of GDP during Lula's first term would have been about 70 percent lower than its realized growth rate if worldwide growth of GDP were similar to what was observed during the Cardoso administration."[243]

When they were in the opposition, Lula and the Workers' Party had attacked the "neoliberals" for slow growth and promised that they would do better. Now Lula's critics demanded that he deliver on his long-delayed promise of accelerated economic growth. Brazil's leading news magazine, *Veja*, featured his somber portrait on its November 8, 2006, post-election edition. The headline was: "The Last Chance: His first term was second-rate, now he has four more years to leave a legacy of greatness."[244]

Lula responded with a surprise announcement; he said he would make the economy grow at least 5 percent per year. His economic advisers were shocked; they thought that making such a promise was risky.[245] Economic growth depended on many factors no president can control, including the weather and trends in the global economy.

---

[243] Jocildo Bezerra and Tiago V. de V. Cavalcanti, "Brazil's Lack of Growth," in Joseph Love and Werner Baer, editors, *Brazil Under Lula*, New York: Palgrave, 2009, p. 75.

[244] Veja, November 8, 2006. http://veja.abril.com.br/arquivo.html.

[245] Kennedy Alencar and Valdo Cruz, "Lula já admite que país não cresce 5%," *Folha Online*, December 14, 2006. http://www1.folha.uol.com.br/folha/dinheiro/ult91u113114.shtml.

They thought that Lula could no more guarantee a 5 percent growth rate than Fidel Castro could guarantee a ten-million-ton sugar harvest. His economists were predicting a 4 percent growth rate at best for 2007. Lula promised his advisers he would not mention specific numbers in future speeches, but the cat was out of the bag. His second term would be judged, in large part, by how close he came to the 5 percent target.

What would he do to make this happen? Would he relax fiscal constraints and spend borrowed money to stimulate the economy? This "Keynesian" approach appealed to many despite the risk of reigniting inflation. Tarso Genro, Lula's minister of Institutional Relations, tried to get the ball rolling in this direction when he publicly stated that, "the era of Palocci is over in Brazil. The preoccupation with inflation without thinking of development has ended."[246] Genro, the former Workers' Party mayor of Porto Alegre, who had lost his campaign for governor of Rio Grande do Sul, was Lula's strongest link to the left of the Workers' Party.

Lula quickly popped Tarso Genro's trial balloon, saying that the government's fiscal policy had always been his, not Antonio Palocci's, and that it would continue. He said he would keep Henrique Meirelles as head of the Central Bank and that Meirelles would continue to report directly to him. After Heloísa Helena's crushing defeat in the 2006 elections, Lula no longer needed to worry much about forces on his left.

But what would mainstream economists suggest to accelerate Brazil's growth rate? In May, 2006, the Lula government's bank for economic development sponsored a conference in Rio de Janeiro on the topic "Why is Brazil Not a High Growth Country?" The organizers had just returned from the 2006 World Economic Forum in Davos, Switzerland, and they were chagrined to report that China and India had dominated the discussions. They said that Lula's enthusiastic speech was largely ignored because Brazil was not seen as a powerful emerging economic force. This was not China or India's fault, in their opinion, it was Brazil's. Why, they asked, had Brazil suffered at least two decades of wrong turns, frustrating experiences and lost opportunities?[247]

---

[246] Traumann, Os próximos cuatro anos," *Revista Época*, November 6, 2006. http://revistaepoca.globo.com/Revista/Epoca/0,,EDG75672-5990-442,00.html.
[247] XVIII Fórum Nacional, http://www.forumnacional.org.br/forum/pforum2.asp.

The conference participants were concerned that the modest economic growth in Lula's first term had depended on high world market prices for Brazil's agricultural and mineral exports. It is fortunate when a country gets good prices for its products, they warned, but it is dangerous to count on them. There is a temptation to rely on the high prices for primary products instead of developing industrial and high technology exports. This can lead to a crash when commodity prices go down. The economists wanted sustainable growth, not a short-term boom followed by a bust. They argued that important reforms were still needed if lasting growth and development were to continue.[248] These reforms included cutting spending, especially on personnel, a proposal that went against the grain for a president whose roots were in the labor movement.[249]

Lula had gotten through the re-election campaign the without pinning himself down to a detailed economic program, much to the frustration of some commentators.[250] But he did make elements of his thinking clear in a series of speeches to different audiences. His plans were in the mainstream, closer to the platform of the Social Democratic Party than that of his own party. They emphasized stability, fiscal responsibility, lessening bureaucracy and cutting taxes. One of the most innovative ideas was a set of simplified tax rules and regulations for small businesses. It came to be known as the "SuperSimples" law and everybody agreed it was a good idea. Congress passed it unanimously.

The Accelerated Growth Plan. Three weeks into his second term, as Brazilians returned from the summer holidays, Lula released the specifics of his Accelerated Growth Plan for Brazil. This was a precursor to economic stimulus plans in the United States and many other countries after the economic crash of 2008. But Lula's was not a response to a crisis. It was an attempt to get a sluggish economy

---

[248] Affonso Celso Pastore and Maria Cristina Pinotti, "Política Macroeconômica, Choque Externo e Crescimento," http://www.forumnacional.org.br/publi/ep/EP0141.pdf.

[249] Marcos Mendes, "Gasto Público Menor e Mais Eficiente como Condição Necessária ao Crescimento Acelerado da Economia Brasileira," http://www.forumnacional.org.br/publi/pestpq3.asp?codep=EP0146 and Raul Velloso, "Escancarando o Problema Fiscal: é preciso controlar o gasto não-financeiro obrigatório da União," http://www.forumnacional.org.br/publi/ep/EP0159.pdf.

[250] Padre Cesar, "O Segundo Mandato," *Radio Aparecida*. October 30, 2006. http://www.radioaparecida.com.br/cesar/30102006.htm.

growing more quickly. It was a balanced, mainstream plan including:[251]

- An investment of R$504 billion in infrastructure by 2010, including spending on energy, health, housing and transportation.
- Targeted tax cuts for small and medium businesses and individual taxpayers, and on companies building factories or working on infrastructure projects. Cuts on taxes for importing capital goods, including computers.
- Fiscal adjustments, including cutting the primary surplus used to pay the nation's debts from 4.25 percent to 3.75 percent, and management changes in the social security system
- Limits to future increases of the minimum wage and of spending on public employees' salaries

The plan had to be modest because Lula insisted on giving priority to maintaining fiscal stability which limited how much could be spent. Much of it was just repackaging things the government was already doing and using proposed spending that was already in the budget. Many of the infrastructure projects had also been in Fernando Henrique Cardoso's "Forward Brazil" plan. Brazilian presidents routinely announce such plans in the hope of building enthusiasm and self-confidence. In this vein, Lula boldly announced that "Now the game is going to take off. Now we will know who is with us and who is against us."[252]

When critics complained there were no dramatic changes in the plan, finance minister Guido Mantega said that "The ship hasn't changed course. It was on the right course and now it is going to

[251] Discurso do Presidente Lula e Apresentação do ministro de Fazenda Guido Mantega na solenadide de lançamento do PAC, January 22, 2007.
http://www.fazenda.gov.br/audio/2007/janeiro/a220107.asp. Ana Paula Ribeiro, "Lula anuncia hoje pacote para acelerar o crescimento," *Folha Online*, January 22, 2007. http://www1.folha.uol.com.br/folha/dinheiro/ult91u113872.shtml. Folha Online, "Veja as medidas que podem entrar no pacote econômico do governo," January 21, 2007.
http://www1.folha.uol.com.br/folha/dinheiro/ult91u113873.shtml. *Revista Época*, "Vai Funcionar?," Edition 454, January 29, 2007.
http://revistaepoca.globo.com/Revista/Epoca/0,,EDG76266-6009-454-2,00.html
[252] Blog de Josais de Souza, *Folha Online*, January 21, 2007.
http://josiasdesouza.folha.blog.uol.com.br/arch2007-01-21_2007-01-27.html#2007_01-21_23_37_40-10045644-0.

accelerate."[253] João Pedro Stédile, leader of the Landless Farmers Movement, responded that "Brazilian politics has entered a deadly calm such that nothing can change the direction of the ship from the hegemony of the political and economic commanders."[254] Most economists said the plan was a step in the right direction, but not a very big step. Notably absent were significant tax or social security reforms. Former Finance Minister Mailson da Nóbrega said "the mountain will give birth to a mouse. It is a mouse dressed in a lion's costume, but if people squeeze it they will find a mouse."[255] José Francisco Lima Gonçalves, the chief economist for a leading bank, said it would raise growth to no more than 3.5 percent a year. A former director of the Central Bank, Luiz Fernando Figueiredo, thought that the impact of the plan on growth rates would be negligible.[256]

Many economists thought the plan relied too heavily on government spending instead of on incentives to private enterprise. Mailson da Nóbrega thought that "the Accelerated Growth Plan is the product of a government hostage to the idea that development must be led by the state, using fiscal incentives. It is an old fashioned plan that ignores the true causes of low growth." The true cause in Mailson's view was high taxes: "This is what suffocates business."[257]

José Serra, from his new offices as governor of the state of São Paulo, opined that the plan was not really a new development plan, just a reorganizing of federal spending plans, most of which were already in the works. In his judgment, a significant increase in growth would depend primarily on increased private investment, and the recent announcement that interest rates would be reduced by only .25 percent suggested that there would not be enough of it.[258] Serra

[253] Lu Aiko Otta, "Pacote do crescimento divide a equipe e cria desconfiança," *Estado de São Paulo*, January 21, 2007.
http://www.estado.com.br/editorias/2007/01/21/eco-1.93.4.20070121.30.1.xml.
[254] João Pedro Stédile, "Segue a calmaria, preocupante … ," Movimento dos Trabalhadores Rurais sem Terra, February 23, 2007,
http://www.mst.org.br/mst/pagina.php?cd=2877.
[255] *Estadão.com.br*. "Para economistas, PAC é "remendo" para o crescimento," January 21, 2007.
http://www.estadao.com.br/arquivo/economia/2007/not20070121p19195.htm.
[256] Ibid.
[257] Ibid.
[258] Portal do Governo do Estado de São Paulo, "Para José Serra, PAC não é um plano de desenvolvimento," January 25, 2007.
http://www.saopaulo.sp.gov.br/sis/lenoticia.php?id=81677.

appeared to be positioning himself to the "left" or "developmentalist" side of the Lula government with a view to the 2010 elections. But he is a respected economist as well as a politician, and he made similar criticisms when Fernando Henrique Cardoso was in office. His criticism of the Cardoso government's policies of supporting the *real* turned out to have been correct.

Serra's reaction mirrored that of many other observers, including the Federation of Industries of the State of Rio de Janeiro, who saw the plan as "the right direction for the country" but as not doing enough. The Federation of Industries criticized the lack in the plan of "stronger structural measures, such as the reduction of public spending, and tax, labor and welfare reforms."[259]

Riding High on the Global Bubble. Given the almost total lack of enthusiasm from economists, the amazing thing was how quickly Lula's plan seemed to start working. A statistical fluke helped get things started. In March 2006, the Brazilian Institute of Geography and Statistics (IBGE) released new estimates of gross national product. In the new and more accurate data series, the average growth for Lula's first term was 3.4 percent instead of 2.6 percent.[260] It wasn't a real change, just a statistical correction, and the estimates for growth under Cardoso also increased. But the new numbers made the 5 percent target much more realistic. After all, by the new numbers, the economy had grown 5.3 percent in 1994, when then Finance Minister Fernando Henrique Cardoso implemented the anti-inflation plan that won him the presidency.

It wasn't just the revised numbers; the economy really was growing. The government statistical office recorded growth as 4.8 percent in the last quarter of 2006, 4.3 percent in the first quarter of 2007 and 5.5 percent in the second quarter of 2007.[261] Strong growth continued through 2007 and into 2008.[262]

---

[259] Alana Gandra, Agência Brasil, PAC leva país a direção correta, mas ainda evita "encontro marcado" com questões estruturais, diz Firjan," January 22, 2007. http://www.agenciabrasil.gov.br/noticias/2007/01/22/materia.2007-01-22.2836337144/view.

[260] Leonardo Carvalho and Marco Cavalcanti, "Outlook for the Brazilian Economy – 2007/2008", Project Link Meeting, Beijing, May 14-17, 2007. Instituto Brasileiro de Geografia e Estatística, "IBGE atualiza cálculo do Produto Interno Bruto e retrata com detalhe a economia do país," March 1, 2007, http://www.ibge.gov.br/home/presidencia/noticias/nota_nova_metodologia.shtm.

[261] Instituto de Pesquisa Econômica e Aplicada, *Boletim de Conjuntura*, July 2007 "Indicações e Projeções."

The growth was strongest in agriculture and commerce, but it was felt across the economy. In September, 2007, the Brazilian Institute of Geography and Statistics released the result of a household survey showing that unemployment had declined from 9.4 percent in 2005 to 8.5 percent in 2006. This was the largest annual decline in ten years, although it was still higher than the 1997 figure of 7.8 percent.[263]

Lula was quick to take credit for the good economic news, and the public was ready to give it to him. All talk of his "second-rate" first term was forgotten. Lula's opinion-poll ratings skyrocketed. Criticism from the left of his "neoliberal" model was muted because it was not only the wealthy that were doing better. Income was being redistributed and all the social indicators were improving. Average income was up 3.2 percent from 2006 to 2007 and the GINI index of inequality declined to .534 from .588 in 1997.[264] The income distribution improved slightly with the richest 10 percent of the population having 43.2 percent of the income, down from 44.6 percent in 2004. Illiteracy declined from 10.4 percent in 2006 to 10.0 percent in 2007. The average Brazilian woman had 1.95 children, down from 6.3 in the 1960 census, putting Brazil below the zero-population growth rate. Workers' Party leader José Genoino couldn't resist a jab at the naysayers of Lula's first term:

> Brazil has found its path. Our economic growth is accompanied by re-distribution of income; we have achieved fiscal sustainability and have greatly reduced our vulnerability to external forces. In addition to all the indices being positive, they are homogeneous. This is to say they improve in a uniform manner whether you break them down by social strata, age group or other classification. Without any doubt, we are liv-

---

http://www.ipea.gov.br/sites/ooo/2/boletim_conjuntura/boletim_77/bc_77a_Res umo.pdf.

[262] Statistics from www.ibge.gov.br and http://www.ibge.gov.br/home/estatistica/indicadores/pib/pib-vol-val_200804comentarios.pdf.

[263] Clarice Spitz, "Desemprego tem maior queda em 10 anos e renda sobe, diz IBGE," Folha Online. September 14, 2007. http://www1.folha.uol.com.br/folha/dinheiro/ult91u328290.shtml.

[264] Jornal do Brasil, "IBGE: Renda média melhorou no país," September 18, 2008. http://jbonline.terra.com.br/extra/2008/09/18/e180914659.html . IBGE, Pesquisa Nacional por Amostra de Domicílios, http://www.ibge.gov.br/home/estatistica/indicadores/sipd/segundo_aspectos.sht m. Thanks to Laura Randal for a useful summary to the Columbia Brazil Seminar.

ing in an extraordinary historical moment which is molding the future of Brazil.

Some of the disoriented opposition and the "speechless" commentators look to the supernatural and superstition to explain this. For them, Lula is just "lucky." … Few speak of the conflicts and tensions of the first years of the government. The search for an increase in the budget surplus and for equilibrium in the budget, the policies adopted in relation to the foreign debt and the International Monetary fund; the establishment of public-private partnerships; the expansion of microcredit, the approval of the bankruptcy law, the SIMPLES [simplified regulations for small businesses], and so many other actions taken in the first two years of government were the measures that prepared the conditions for the current level of growth. Measures that were fiercely combated by the opposition and by sectors of the media. [265]

The public shared Genoino's enthusiasm and gave Lula the highest presidential popularity ratings in Brazilian history in September, 2008: 64 percent "excellent or good" in the Datafolha poll and even higher in some others. [266] Lula was ecstatic, telling interviewers:

Brazil is living through its best historical moment. Brazil today is experiencing an almost magic time: combining economic growth with redistribution of income, with the improvement of the quality of life of the poor, raising the poor up into the middle class. It has a political process with a reasonable import and export policy, it has 200 billion in reserves, it no longer owes anything to the International Monetary Fund. I would say we are living in a glorious moment. [267]

Things were certainly going well, but why? It was much too soon for the spending increases or tax cuts in Lula's accelerated growth plan to have had an impact. The most obvious explanation is simply that market economies are cyclical. When an economy has been slow for a few years, it is due to cycle up. Presidents can do things to help manage these cycles, but they can't really control them. The economic fluctuations in the Cardoso and Lula years were actually more

[265] Jozé Genoino, "Nota 13: Não é sorte, é projeto!" Outubro 2008. http://genoino.org/opiniao.php.
[266] "Governo Lula é aprovado por 64% dos brasileiros, recorde histórico," *Datafolha Opinião Pública*, Sept 12, 2008. http://datafolha.folha.uol.com.br/po/ver_po.php?session=725.
[267] Lula da Silva, Entrevista exclusiva concedida pelo presidente da República, Luiz Inácio Lula da Silva, ao jornal *Clarín.* Palácio do Planalto, September 4, 2008. http://www.info.planalto.gov.br/static/inf_briefdiscusos.htm.

modest than those in the previous decades, as can be seen in the following table.

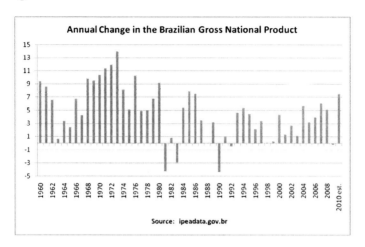

Annual Change in the Brazilian Gross National Product

Source: ipeadata.gov.br

Lula's inaugural speech had promised to bring about a new era of economic growth. Now that the economy was finally picking up, he naturally accepted the credit. But how much credit does Lula deserve for the upturn in 2006 and 2007? Would he also take responsibility if the economy went into a bust, as it did in 2009? Economists often disagree about such things, but among the most respected and impartial are those at the Institute of Applied Economic Research (IPEA) of the Ministry of Planning. The IPEA economists believed that Lula was finally reaping the reward for sticking to orthodox policies throughout his first term.[268] The continuity with Cardoso's policies, in their opinion, had given investors and businessmen confidence, leading to increases in production. In effect, they said that both Cardoso and Lula deserved credit for keeping the economy on track for growth.

Another important factor, which the IPEA economists and everyone else noted, was very favorable prices for Brazil's agricultural and mineral products in world markets. Relying on these prices was risky, but it seemed likely that global shortages of raw materials would continue as demand increased in China, India and elsewhere.

---

[268] Instituto de Pesquisa Econômica e Aplicada, *Boletim de Conjuntura*, July 2007, "Panorama Conjuntural." http://www.ipea.gov.br/sites/000/2/boletim_conjuntura/boletim_77/bc_77b_Pan orama.pdf.

At the time, no one fully appreciated how much these prices were distorted by a global bubble caused by irresponsible banking practices in the United States.

Instead of calling for more stimuli for growth, the IPEA economists warned of the risk of overheating the economy and re-igniting inflation. This might lead to rapid growth on paper in the short term, they said, but it would be followed by a strong cyclical downturn in the future because the country's real productive capacity could only grow so fast. They observed that Brazil had suffered greatly from the boom and bust cycle in the past, and it should not succumb to the temptation to overheat the economy."[269]

The IPEA economists warned that the country's technology, infrastructure, educational level and other resources had to keep up with the growth in financial activity to avoid crises in the future. This was music to Lula's ears. He could be remembered as the president who ushered in a new era of economic growth by rebuilding Brazil's infrastructure. He happily promised to transform Brazil into "a veritable incubator of public works."[270]

Compared to many of the world's economies, the Brazilian economy was in good shape. It was growing across the board rather than being driven by a "bubble" in any single sector. The largest sector, commercial agriculture, grew very rapidly during Lula's presidency; exports increased 16.3 percent a year on average from 2002 to 2007.[271] Agrarian reform continued, with 67,535 families settled in 2005, but this was a social inclusion program, not a major contributor to the national income. Brazil's agriculture benefited greatly from a global increase in food prices and in demand for ethanol from sugar cane. China has become a large consumer of Brazilian foodstuffs and raw material exports, and also a large supplier of imported consumer goods.

But Brazil was not just importing manufactured goods. Manufacturing exports grew 11.9 percent in 2007, compared to 2006, reaching a total of US$89.4 billion. Brazil's largest export market for manufactures continued to be the United States, but the proportion going to China and Europe was increasing. Exports to Argentina and Brazil's

[269] Ibid., p XI.
[270] Folha Online, "Vamos fazer deste país um verdadeiro canteiro de obras", diz Lula," August 6, 2007.
http://www1.folha.uol.com.br/folha/brasil/ult96u317886.shtml.
[271] Lula da Silva, Mensagem ao Congresso Nacional, Brasília: Presidência da Repuública, 2008. http://www.info.planalto.gov.br/static/inf_briefdiscusos.htm.

other South American partners were also increasing, as were Brazil's internal markets. Brazil seemed to have found its path. No longer the country of the future, it was doing very well in the here and now. It seemed too good to be true, and perhaps it was. **The Crisis of 2008.** During the Cardoso government Brazil had weathered economic storms from Mexico, Russia and Argentina. This time the blast came from the heart of the beast. The bubble broke in the United States and Wall Street banks and insurance companies started to topple. The George W. Bush administration went into shock, bailing out some firms, allowing others to fail. Panic set in and financial and equity markets nose-dived all over the world.

Lula's first reaction was to go into denial. Caught by reporters at a university inauguration ceremony in the northeastern state of Rio Grande do Norte, Lula quipped: "When people ask me about this crisis, I answer: 'Go ask Bush, it's his crisis not mine.' " He reminded the interviewer that Brazil had $200 billion US dollars in its reserves and was well prepared to weather the shock from the north. He said, "Imagine if this had happened ten years ago. If the United States had sneezed as it did in this real estate crisis, Brazil would have caught pneumonia."[272]

All concerns about accelerating economic growth were put aside; under these conditions any growth at all would be an accomplishment. The most urgent priority was to prevent a collapse of the banking system such as the United States had experienced. Fortunately, Brazil's banking system had already gone through its crisis, in the 1990s when hyperinflation was ended, and it had been reformed by the Cardoso government. Many of the large banks owned by state governments were insolvent and were privatized. But Brazil also has very large banks owned by the federal government, and these continued to play a very important role in the economy.

The largest bank in the country, the *Banco Nacional de Desenvolvimento Economico e Social* (BNDES), lends money to projects that are deemed important for the development of the country. It loaned out R$64 billion in 2007.[273] This included funding many cooperatives and micro-businesses. In the past it had helped to fund privatization ef-

[272] Mariana Jungman, "Lula volta a dizer que a crise é dos EUA e o Brasil está resguardado," Agência Brasil, September 19, 2008.
http://www.agenciabrasil.gov.br/noticias/2008/09/19/materia.2008-09-19.4529706998/view.
[273] Lula da Silva, Mensagem ao Congresso Nacional, op cit.

forts; its priorities depend on the government in power. The *Caixa Economica Federal*, entirely controlled by the federal government, finances construction and infrastructure projects. The *Banco do Brasil*, the largest bank by assets, is partly privatized and its shares trade on the stock market, but it is government controlled. The *Banco Central* is the national monetary authority and regulates the money supply in much the same way as the American Federal Reserve bank.

Due to strict regulations coming out of the reforms in the 1990s, Brazilian banks lend out only approximately 10 times their capital, while American commercial banks lent out approximately 20 times their capital and American investment banks 50 times their capital (prior to the crisis of 2008).[274] Brazilian banks do not generally make the risky, sub-prime loans that brought down so much of the American financial sector in 2008.

So, although Brazil could not wall itself off from a global downturn, Brazil's bankers and regulators had a lot of experience dealing with crises and they had built systems to weather them. No Brazilian banks or insurance companies were threatened with collapse. Brazil was even in a position to offer the United States some reassurance. Brazilian entrepreneur Roberto Medina published an "Open Letter to Wall Street" as a full page advertisement in the New York Times on October 6, 2008:

Open Letter to Wall Street

First of all, this crisis will be over for sure. Just like many others have in several different places in the world. A crisis is part of a strengthening and maturing process of all institutions. We learn to walk by falling ...

It is always through moments of crisis that the best opportunities come up. And we would like to talk about one of these opportunities: Brazil. Brazil is one of the biggest emerging markets in the world. We are the biggest food producer on the planet. We have the richest biodiversity on Earth and we have recently found out that we will soon become one of the biggest oil producers in the world. We are part of a 180 million potential consumers' market and one of the most desired tourist destinations. Our democracy is consolidated, our industry is strong, our inflation has been under control for many years, and our vast territory assures that we have many places for investments. Therefore, as we know, soon people will start considering where to invest, we tell you, invest in Brazil.

---

[274] Edmar Bacha, "Talk to Columbia University Seminar on Brazil," October 8, 2008.

This was advertising puffery from a man best known for promoting Rock-in-Rio concerts.[275] But it had a ring of plausibility at a time when investors were eager for good news. A global survey of business leaders by PricewaterhouseCoopers in January 2008, found that Brazilian businessmen were less pessimistic than those in any other country: 33 percent thought their firms' revenues would increase in 2009 as compared to the global average of 21 percent.[276] Not that anyone expected to escape the crisis unscathed. Brazil's central bank had to infuse capital into the banking sector just as the Europeans and North Americans did. The São Paulo stock exchange nose-dived like the others around the world, and the managers invoked the "circuit breaker" to pause trading several times. But Brazilians first reaction was to be pleased with how well their system weathered a storm that was not of their making. In October of 2008, Lula observed:

> This crisis may hit Brazil much more lightly than it hit the countries where it originated. We must not forget that this is the first crisis that hit first in the rich countries and is later coming to the periphery. The countries that are giving solidarity to the world economy are precisely the peripheral countries such as Brazil, China, India, South Africa, Mexico, Latin America and others. We are not involved in this financial crisis, but we may receive as a result of this financial crisis the second step which is a possible recession in the developed world which will cause problems with the exports of all the world's countries, including Brazil. But even in this way, I think Brazil will suffer less because we have greatly diversified our international partners. Ten years ago we had practically 27 percent of our commercial balance with the United States. Today we have a little more than 14 percent with the United States...
> We have a credit problem, because I don't know where all these trillions of dollars went, that are flying from bank to bank, from paper to paper... Do you know that game with chairs, where there are five chairs for six people, and quickly five sit down and one is left standing? I think the bankers are doing this, because suddenly the money has disappeared. There is no credit in Germany, no credit in France, no credit in England, no credit in Brazil. Where did all this money go?

[275] "Dono da Artplan publica anúncio no The New York Times propondo o Brasil como solução," CidadeBiz,
http://cidadebiz.oi.com.br/paginas/45001_46000/45667-1.html
[276] Folha Online, "Brasileiros estão entre os menos pessimistas com a crise, mostra pesquisa," January 28, 2009.
http://www1.folha.uol.com.br/folha/dinheiro/ult91u493318.shtml.

We, thank God, have very strong public institutions – The Bank of Brazil, Caixa Economica, BNDES – therefore we are buying shares from investment banks that had problems, and we will buy more. We are reducing the banks' compulsory deposits with the government so they can increase their lines of credit. Even Bush is talking about buying shares of banks. This means that the heart of the capitalist regime is beginning to have a taste for the role of the state, which has been demoralized for the last 30 years. We still have an important instrument to face the crisis which is the potential of the domestic market. This is why I don't want to cut credit, because people need credit. And I have said at meetings … "They are talking about a crisis, but no one has to stop buying their television or their refrigerator." Because if people aren't buying, the factories won't be producing, the stores won't be selling, and then we really will be in a recession.[277]

As the world crisis worsened, the magnitude of the effects on the Brazilian economy began to sink in. Prices for commodities fell and industrial exports declined. Brazil didn't go into a real recession, but economic growth was down sharply. Lula's ratings in the polls were less phenomenal, and pundits speculated that his chances of electing his chosen successor were weakened.

Lula was frustrated; he had followed all the rules and done everything the international establishment had wanted and now they were dragging him down. British Prime Minister Gordon Brown visited in March 2009, and during the visit Lula told the press, "This crisis was caused by the irrational behavior of white people with blue eyes, who seemed to know everything, but now it turns out they didn't know anything." Prime Minister Brown ignored Lula's comments about white people with blue eyes (he has brown eyes). Brown agreed with Lula's larger point about the need for government action to help the developing countries.

Questioned about his remark about blue-eyed bankers by the British press, Lula insisted, "I've never known a banker who was black." He insisted that "this is not an ideological bias. It is stating a fact. Along with the economic indices and unemployment, what we see is that, once again, the great part of the poor of the world, who

---

[277] Lula da Silva, "Speech to the Brazilian Society for Progress in Science," 21 October 2008, http://www.info.planalto.gov.br/static/inf_briefdiscusos.htm.

are hardly beginning to participate in the development caused by globalization, are the first victims."[278] **The Boom of 2010.** Economic growth was slightly negative for 2009 as a whole, but it picked up in the last quarter of the year. Then it picked up sharply in the first quarter of 2010, leading economists to predict a growth rate of 7.5 percent for the year, a rate they thought too high to be sustainable.[279] The Brazilian economy was booming again, despite the continuing crisis in the United States and Europe. Lula's approval ratings zoomed up into the 80's, and his chances of electing his choice of successor seemed very good indeed.

The strong banking regulations explain why the crisis was not as severe as elsewhere, but what accounts for the boom of 2010? The economists at the Institute of Applied Economic Research may have been as surprised as anyone, but looking at the data for their quarterly newsletter *Conjuntura Economica* they found a number of explanations.[280]

First of all, the Lula government applied very strong economic stimulus in response to the crisis, including major acceleration in spending on infrastructure programs. Brazil has no significant ideological groups similar to the Tea Party or the Libertarians in the United States that oppose government intervention in the economy on principle. Increased spending in these circumstances was not controversial, although there was concern that it not be allowed to reignite inflation.

A second factor was the diversification in Brazil's foreign trade, especially its export of primary products to China and many other countries. Brazil was not as vulnerable to a crisis in the United States as it had been. The Chinese economy remained strong, and prices for commodity exports remained high, so the shock of the crisis in the United States was soon absorbed.

[278] Chico de Gois, "Lula diz que crise é causada por 'gente branca de olhos azuis'.*O Globo*, March26, 2009. http://oglobo.globo.com/economia/mat/2009/03/26/lula-diz-que-crise-causada-por-gente-branca-de-olhos-azuis-755003398.asp. For video: http://www.youtube.com/watch?v=D_-31OLowhU.
[279] Ricardo Leopoldo and Raquel Landim, "FMI diz que PIB de 7,5% no Brasil não é sustentável," Estadão.com.br, November 22, 2010.
http://economia.estadao.com.br/noticias/not_42581.htm.
[280] IPEA, "Carta de Conjuntura," no 11, September 2010; no 10, June 2010; no 9, March 2010.
http://www.ipea.gov.br/portal/index.php?option=com_alphacontent&view=alpha content&Itemid=59

A third factor was the beginning of oil production from the deep "pre-salt" fields off the Brazilian coast. In addition to the stimulus this provides to the economy now, it has the potential to make Brazil a major oil exporting nation in the future. This greatly contributed to optimism about the Brazilian economy which attracts investment.

A fourth factor was the enthusiasm with which the Brazilian domestic economy responded to the first three, encouraged by Lula's optimistic cheerleading. Consumer optimism and buying power were up and consumer credit was easy. Commentator Maria Fernanda Delmas, writing in August 2010, described it as euphoria that was winning the 2010 election for the Workers' Party.

> Unless there is a surprise along the road, it is the economy that is deciding this election. The economy? More precisely, specialists say, consumers' buying power. Easy credit, facilitating buying real estate, high income and employment, increases in the minimum wage and in the Family Allowances, have paved the way for the Workers' Party candidate, Dilma Rousseff, to take off in the polls. Overloaded with household goods, the voter doesn't think of collective problems such as health or transportation. And he or she thinks even less of more abstract questions, such as the fiscal situation…
>
> As James Carville said, "It's the economy, stupid." Consumer buying is the motor of this euphoria. Just between December 2008 and last month, the most common kinds of consumer credit went up 35 percent… "People are voting with their pocket book. They are consuming at a level not seen in 30 years," says economics Claudio Frischtak. Sergio Vale, chief economist of MB associates, says the biggest factor in the election is not Lula's charisma but the pocket of the consumer. "The combination of more consumption with a President who communicates very well with two thirds of the population is very strong," says Frischtak.
>
> The Social Democratic opposition was not able to make political capital out of its having stabilized the economy. The pattern of consumption in the country changed beginning with the Real Plan; before that, with inflation at 80 percent a month it wasn't possible to choose products, research prices or obtain credit, recalls Renato Meirelles, co-director of the Popular Data Institute. Along with inheriting this benefit of a country with low inflation, the Lula government surfed the good waves of the world economy and took good measures.[281]

---

[281] Maria Fernanda Delmas, "Crédito farto e poder de consumo fazem eleitor querer continuidade do governo e não pensar em bens coletivos, *O Globo*, August 28, 2010. http://oglobo.globo.com/pais/eleicoes2010/mat/2010/08/28/credito-farto-poder-

Lula was happy to take credit for the boom in consumerism especially since it included lower income Brazilians. In his presidential address after the 2010 elections, he said that:

As we all know, Brazil today is living in a magical moment, of economic growth, social inclusion, a strong generation of employment, distribution of income and reduction of regional inequalities. I am convinced that in the years ahead Brazil will consolidate itself as a land of opportunities and prosperity, transforming itself into a developed nation.[282]

Lula had achieved his promise of a 5 percent annual growth rate, and more, and the electorate was happy. Other than warnings from professional economists, little thought was given to the possibility that this was a bubble that might eventually burst. Nicolas Eyzaguirre, Western hemisphere director for the International Monetary fund, expressed concern that "a 7.5 percent increase in growth in Gross Domestic Product is not sustainable" and that the economy was in danger of overheating.[283] Many specialists, including former Central Bank head Affonso Celso Pastore believe that, given the structural constraints built into the economy, a 4 percent annual growth rate is sustainable. Lula's economic advisers shared these concerns, and quietly cut back on the explosive growth that had reached an annualized rate of 8.9 percent in the first half of 2010.[284]

---

de-consumo-fazem-eleitor-querer-continuidade-do-governo-nao-pensar-em-benscoletivos-917502437.asp.
[282] Lula de Silva, "Pronunciamento em cadeia de rádio e televisão, sobre as eleições 2010," Brasília, November 5, 2010.
http://www.info.planalto.gov.br/static/inf_briefdiscusos.htm.
[283] Ricardo Leopoldo and Raquel Landim, "FMI diz que PIB de 7,5% no Brasil não é sustentável," Estadão.com.br, November 9, 2010.
http://economia.estadao.com.br/noticias/not_42581.htm.
[284] IPEA, "Carta de Conjuntura," no 11, September 2010,
http://www.ipea.gov.br/portal/index.php?option=com_alphacontent&view=alpha content&Itemid=59

CHAPTER THIRTEEN
SOCIALISM, ECONOMIC SOLIDARITY, AND MICRO-CAPITALISM

Lula's election in 2002 and re-election in 2006 were widely interpreted as part of a "turn toward the left" in Latin America. No one, however, knew exactly what "left" meant in this context. In her book *Rebuilding the Left*, Marxist theorist Marta Harnecker denounced "social democratic reakpolitik" and bemoaned the fact that:

> People assign more and more importance to the search for comfort and question the legitimisation of consumerism less and less, tendencies which the credit system encourages. People are not content to live within their means, but prefer to live in debt and therefore need to have a steady job.[285]

If being on the left means being against steady jobs, living in comfort and buying on credit, Lula would hardly qualify. Indeed, the phrase "social democratic realpolitik" fits his politics pretty well. But Harnecker included his government as part of a "red tide" in Latin America. This "red tide" included leaders as diverse as Hugo Chávez in Venezuela, Michelle Bachelet in Chile, Néstor Kirchner in Argentina and Evo Morales in Bolivia. Lula and Bachelet were often said to be of the moderate or responsible left, while Chávez and Morales represented the radical or populist left. Chávez called himself a "twenty-first century socialist," but never clearly defined what that meant.[286]

So is Lula a leftist? A twenty-first century socialist? Or a social democratic realpolitician? If the latter, how is he different from his opponents in the Social Democratic Party? Many journalists have asked Lula to pigeon-hole himself, but he always resists doing so as in this interview with a Brazilian magazine:

> Interviewer: Do you believe South America is moving toward the left?
>
> Lula da Silva: I believe it is moving toward the left.

[285] Marta harnecker, *Rebuilding the Left*, London: Zed Books, 2007, p. 17.
[286] Margarita López Maya, *Ideas para Debatir el Socialismo del Siglo XXI*. Caracas: Editorial Alfa, 2007.

Interviewer: Are you on the left?

Lula da Silva: You know I never like to label myself as on the left. I am a lathe mechanic and I arrived at the Presidency of Brazil through hard work and a lot of patience.

Interviewer: Why not accept the definition of Norberto Bobbio? To be on the left is to fight for equality?

Lula da Silva: I don't have to be on the left to fight for equality... If fighting for equality is the great definition of being on the left, there is no one more leftist than me in the world. In truth, I fight for everyone to be able to enjoy the results produced by the nation. And I think this can be achieved.[287]

Mário Soares, a former president of Portugal representing that country's Socialist Party, raised a similar question in an interview:

Mário Soares: Tell me one thing, Mr. President. With your experience as a labor leader and as a politician, from the beginning until now, do you believe there is still a division between right and left in the world or is it ending?

Lula da Silva: I believe it exists. We have a lot of people on the right and a lot of people on the left. What has happened is that the experiences that we have had, for example, of socialism implanted in the world, if we take the revolution of 1917 and others, people have come to perceive that the dream, that of socialism...

Mário Soares: Totalitarian ...

Lula da Silva: Has not survived, because at some point the mistake ...

Mário Soares: But the utopia, equality, is maintained.

Lula da Silva: The utopia continues. Why did my party never want to define itself as a socialist party? It is because every time we had this discussion, we raised the question: what kind of socialism? This is a discussion sociology will have to have to deal with in more depth. But I think the left continues to exist, the utopia continues to exist. We still want to construct the just world we dreamed of. But when you reach the presidency, of a state or a city, you no longer have the right to dream, you have the right to do things, because the mandate is for four years and if you dream too much you end up not doing anything. So I resolved to adopt, first of all, an administrative pragmatism.[288]

---

[287] Entrevista do presidente da República, Luiz Inácio Lula da Silva, à *Revista Carta-Capital,* Palácio do Planalto, 07 de dezembro de 2005.
http://www.info.planalto.gov.br/static/inf_briefdiscusos.htm.
[288] Mário Soares and Lula da Silva, "Entrevista exclusiva concedida pelo presidente da República, Luiz Inácio Lula da Silva, ao ex-presidente de Portugal, Mário Soares,

In 1997, Lula told an interviewer, "I am not and have never been a socialist. How can one support a system in which a person who produces eight bottles of beer earns the same as one who produces ten?"[289] In 2006, he told a group of businessmen that "things evolve in proportion to the number of white hairs and the responsibilities that one has," and that "if you meet someone very old who is still a leftist, he must have problems." Two days later, when a group of activists urged him to follow a "leftist" policy in his second term, Lula told them he was a social democrat, not a socialist.

This drew a flurry of angry comments from Brazil's gray-haired left intelligentsia. Marxist philosopher Leandro Konder accused Lula of never having been a sincere leftist. Poet Ferreira Gullar accused him of being an opportunist, and predicted that "tomorrow he will say something else. Lula will say anything at any time, depending on the audience and what is convenient. He has no commitment to anything except holding power." Sociologist Francisco de Oliveira said "I am 73 years old and I continue to be a leftist, with much pride. What Lula said is regrettable."[290] In response, Lula said that the best path was to "take the middle road" and seek an "equilibrium" rather than going to extremes of right or left.

The intellectuals were surprised that Lula called himself a social democrat because that term has been staked out in Brazil by the Social Democratic Party. Calling himself a social democrat was tantamount to admitting that he and Fernando Henrique Cardoso are competitors in the same political space, not ideological opponents. But, as the term is used internationally, Lula and his majority faction of the Workers' Party actually are social democrats. They are "socialists" in the same way as leaders of the French, Spanish, Chilean and Portuguese Socialist Parties are today.

This has nothing to do with the gray hairs that make Lula look mature and distinguished in his tailored suits. As a youth, he followed Frei Chico into the labor movement but not into the Communist Party or any other socialist organization. He condemned the excesses of both Soviet socialism and corporate capitalism in his in-

para a Rádio e Televisão de Portugal," Pálacio do Planalto, February 20, 2008. http://www.info.planalto.gov.br/static/inf_briefdiscusos.htm.
[289] *Veja*, August 13, 1997.
[290] *La Jornada*, "Lula genera malestar tras afirmar que a cierta edad ya no se es de izquierda," December 14, 2006. http://www.jornada.unam.mx/2006/12/14/index.php?section=mundo&article=03 7n1mun.

augural speech as a union president in 1975. As Frei Chico told Denise Paraná: "Lula was never a communist. He was a socialist: at the most he had a vision of a just society that might be socialist or might be something else."[291] **Redefining Socialism**. Yet, Lula is the leading figure of a party which, as recently as August 2007, reaffirmed its commitment to "socialism" as its guiding principle.[292] This is less of a contradiction than it might appear because the Workers' Party defines "socialism" as a system with competitive multiparty elections, full respect for human rights, and a mixture of private, cooperative and state ownership of property.[293] This view evolved through long years of debate between factions within the Workers' Party. Political scientist and Workers' Party activist André Singer explains:

> Up until 1990, the Workers' Party could be seen at times as a democratic party committed to ample liberty to dispute government offices through elections, and at other times as a party for which the electoral struggle is only a step towards the conquest of hegemony, after which only the parties which do not oppose the working class will persist...
>
> State ownership of the means of production has never been a typical theme of Workers' Party socialism. With regard to property, the Workers' Party position has been to privilege social ownership without eliminating, by decree, private ownership...
>
> The defeats of Lula in 1994 and 1998 were felt as hard blows by the party and the party's attention was turned towards the immediate tasks of government, or to the Democratic Revolution. Socialism was not discussed after 1991, and beginning in 1995 the Democratic Revolution became the name of the reforms the Workers' Party wanted for Brazil. Socialism continued to be "a possibility open to humanity in the era of capitalism" according to the 1999 program.
>
> The theme of socialism only returned to the Workers' Party through a series of debates organized in the first semester of 2000 ... and directed by Lula.[294]

These debates took place at a conference on the "Socialist Economy" sponsored by a Workers' Party think tank. Kicking off

[291] Interview with Denise Paraná in *Lula: O Filho do Brasil*, São Paulo: Perseu Abramo, 2002.

[292] Partido dos Trabalhadores. Socialismo. 3º Congresso do PT. August 2007. http://www.pt.org.br/sitept/index_files/fotos/file/Socialismo%20Petista.zip.

[293] Partido dos Trabalhadores. Socialismo. 3º Congresso do PT. August 2007. http://www.pt.org.br/sitept/index_files/fotos/file/Socialismo%20Petista.zip.

[294] André Singer, *O PT*. São Paulo: Publifolha, 2001, p. 42-43.

the conference, Lula said, "I think that, in this forum, we are constructing, together, an understanding of socialism which will be really at the level required by the demands of the new century and that this will prepare us to struggle for victories that are imperative and unavoidable in the grave scenario of social crisis, injustice and inequality that have been imposed on Brazilians for a long time."[295]

The principal speaker at the conference was Paul Singer, a University of São Paulo economist who has long been one of the Workers' Party's principal theorists, and the father of André Singer, quoted above. Paul Singer advocates a vision of socialism as worker self-management with worker-owned firms competing in a democratic marketplace. He opposes the Soviet model of socialism as a state monopoly of the means of production because it led to a monstrous concentration of power, the exact opposite of the withering away of the state that Marx and Engels had anticipated.

The kind of "socialism" Singer advocates is often referred to as employee ownership, but the term used most in Brazil is "economic solidarity." Singer insists that every citizen has the right to organize his or her economic activities as he or she chooses, with only slavery and indentured servitude prohibited. This means that socialism must emerge gradually from within capitalist societies by winning voluntary converts. In his view, true socialism cannot be imposed by a revolutionary party with a monopoly of state power. This means that:

> The socialist economy will probably suffer (for how long no one knows) competition with other modes of production. It will be permanently challenged to demonstrate its superiority in terms of self-realization of products and satisfaction of consumers. This leads to the conclusion that the struggle for socialism will never cease. If this is the price which socialists must pay to be democrats, I venture to say that it is not too much.[296]

After Paul Singer's address at the conference, Lula criticized the activists for spending too much time on theoretical argumentation in the false expectation that everything would be taken care of once the Workers' Party took power. He observed that even after many dec-

[295] Luiz Inácio Lula da Silva, "Apresentação," Paul Singer and João Machado, editors, *Economia Socialista*, São Paulo: Editora Fundação Perseu Abramo, 2000, p. 6.
[296] Paul Singer and João Machado, *Economia Socialista*. São Paulo: Editora Fundação Abramo, 2000.

ades of dictatorial power, the Cuban and Soviet governments had not solved the problems. He thought the Workers' Party should put more effort into setting good examples in the towns where they held the mayor's office or in non-governmental settings. He stated that:

> I think that actually existing socialism – speaking here of the real and not the utopia – has never resolved a crucial problem in its relationship with society, with production, which is how to deal with inequalities. The human being is eminently competitive. To the extent to which one blocks the competitive capacity of the human being and makes it that everyone receives the same thing within a factory, you cut off the possibilities of that factory being successful. People are leveled off at the bottom instead of at the top. Socialism was not able to resolve this problem.
>
> I am a great fan of the Cuban Revolution. I think that everyone in the PT [Workers' Party] is. But they have not resolved the crucial problem of democracy and of some liberties without which there is no socialism. I am the greatest deliverer of medals to Cuban workers. Every time I go there I am invited to a ceremony at the Central Organization of Cuban Workers. They have a worker there with thirty medals on his chest. That is his prize for production. If there were some improvement in his quality of life, he would be more pleased.
>
> I believe Paul Singer exaggerated on the question of the value of markets, because the market only works when there is a very strong state that regulates the market and makes it comply with social commitments. Just the market by itself doesn't resolve anything. Harmonizing the market with a regulating state, capable of guaranteeing that the market attends to all of people's needs, which would be the ideal.
>
> The Soviet Union lasted 70 years and whenever you questioned someone, they would say "Socialism is a process." A process that lasted 70 years. Cuba, if you go there and ask, but when will it get better? They say, "It is a process." A process that has been there for 40 years! We are not going to wait 40 years to reach power. In my opinion we will reach it sooner than that. But what will we then do in practice? What government action and what party action? I think the Workers' Party could do infinitely more than it does.[297]

Just two years after this conference, Lula was in power. He appointed Paul Singer to run a new Secretariat of Economic Solidarity within the Ministry of Labor.[298] Singer didn't have to start from

[297] Ibid, pages 72-74.
[298] Paul Singer, "A Economia Solidária no Governo Federal," Instituto de Pesquisa Economica Aplicada, Mercado de Trabalho, Vol 24, pages 3-5.

scratch. The Economic Solidarity movement had been mobilized in the 1980s and 1990s under the auspices of the Caritas movement and the Landless Farmer's Movement. It had first been institutionalized in the state government of Rio Grande do Sul in 1999. Paul Singer's Secretariat brought renewed energy and national scope to the movement. As of 2007, there were 21,859 employee owned enterprises in Brazil. The largest number, 9,498, were in the impoverished northeastern region of the country. These enterprises had 1,687,496 employees, including 645,504 in the northeast. Of these, 63 percent were men and 37 percent women.[299]

The Economic Solidarity movement has focused on the underprivileged sector of the population including the approximately 45 percent of Brazilian workers who are in the "informal" sector without the protection of the country's extensive labor legislation. Economic Solidarity enterprises help these workers integrate into the formal structure of society. Economic Solidarity also works with individuals released from mental hospitals and prisons. Funding is raised through federal and community banks, credit cooperatives and rotating funds. More than 30 Brazilian universities maintain incubators for popular cooperatives, providing technical assistance and support.

Many of these employee-owned firms are small and economically vulnerable. Only 14 percent are formally organized as cooperatives, 55 percent are more loosely organized associations, and 27 percent are just informal groups. In some cases, small businesses reorganize as cooperatives to get a break from Brazil's restrictive tax and labor legislation. In other cases, the workers take over an enterprise that the original owners have abandoned. The emphasis of Paul Singer's secretariat has been on working with poor and impoverished populations that have few alternatives, not on competing with viable private enterprises in more lucrative segments of the economy.

The Economic Solidarity movement comes out of a socialist tradition but the word is not used because it has too many other meanings. If it is a form of socialism, it is market socialism; the enterprises compete in the marketplace and the workers decide on pay scales and incentives. They may or may not all be paid the same. Economic Solidarity is not a frontal assault on capitalism, it is an alternative for

http://www.mte.gov.br/ecosolidaria/conf_textopaulsinger.pdf.
[299] Lula da Silva, Mensagem ao Congresso Nacional, Brasília: Presidência da Repuública, 2008. http://www.info.planalto.gov.br/static/inf_briefdiscusos.htm.

those who have not found inclusion in the capitalist economy or who prefer working in a cooperative environment. If it ever replaces capitalism, it will be by building a better world one enterprise at a time.

Microcredit for Capitalist Inclusion. Another way to build a better world one enterprise at a time is the microcredit program. This was inspired by the work of Muhammad Yunus in Bangladesh whose Grameen Bank pioneered by offering very small loans to poor people to start small businesses. Sometimes these businesses employ only one person; sometimes they hire a few employees. They are capitalist in the sense that they are privately owned, but much of the labor is provided by the owner.

In Brazil, there are 150 different banks and other entities offering microcredit loans, small loans to people who do not qualify for ordinary bank credit. Between 2003 and 2007, R$926 million in consumer loans and R$253 million in micro-entrepreneurial loans were given out. The average micro-entrepreneurial loan was R$964.63. The Banco Popular do Brasil alone has given out 3.2 million loans.[300] The microcredit initiatives are part of a program of making banking services more accessible to people of low income so they can use bank accounts and debit cards to handle their money and to obtain small loans.

The economic solidarity and microcredit programs are a modest segment of the Brazilian economy. The economic solidarity firms employ approximately 1,600,000 people in a labor force of approximately 100,000,000. There are no precise figures on the number of people employed in microcredit operations, but it may be of the same approximate magnitude. These programs are most valuable for building the culture of transformation among people who have been mired in the culture of poverty. For Lula, the important thing is that people are getting the help they need to take control of their own lives, not whether they do it in a "capitalist" or a "socialist" manner.

Brazilian Fabianism. Frei Chico tells us that Lula's father was a supporter of Getulio Vargas, the president who modernized Brazil in the 1940s by building a strong state that gave organized labor a role in an emerging industrial economy. Although Vargas did not call himself a socialist, he did participate in something close to the socialism advocated by Sidney and Beatrice Webb of England's Fabian

[300] Lula da Silva, Mensagem ao Congresso Nacional, Brasília: Presidência da Repuública, 2008. http://www.info.planalto.gov.br/static/inf_briefdiscusos.htm.

Society. In Fabian socialism small- and medium-sized businesses are left to the private sector, but the "commanding heights" of the economy are owned by the government.

Brazil's ventures into Fabian socialism were mostly a matter of necessity, not theoretical preference. The country needed to industrialize and there simply were not enough private investors, domestic or foreign, to build large industrial enterprises or the infrastructure to support them. So the government built them and used them to develop the country. The national oil company, *Petrobras*, was formed in 1953 and given a monopoly on oil exploration. Many utilities and telecommunications and railroads were operated as state-owned companies, as was the country's largest iron ore producer, the *Companhia Vale do Rio Doce*. And most Brazilian state governments established state-owned banks to finance economic development.

These state-owned companies were an important element of national pride. They were supported by the anti-Communist military governments as well as by the left. They provided secure, well-paying employment to the workers lucky enough to get jobs in them. Many of these workers joined labor unions that supported the Workers' Party.

Over the years, however, these companies sometimes became bureaucratic and inefficient and more of a burden than a stimulus to the country's development. The telephone companies, for example, simply did not provide the service a growing country needed, in large part because government regulations kept the rates from rising with inflation. People waited years to get a telephone line for their home or office, bought one from someone who had one, or inherited one when their parents died.

People began to look for new ways to stimulate development, and in the 1980s and 1990s, plenty of global corporations were eager to invest in Brazil. So the Brazilian governments of the time decided to auction off or privatize most of the major state-owned companies. Petrobras remained state controlled, but it sold a majority of its non-voting stock to private investors and gave up its monopoly status. It competes like a private corporation. Most banks owned by Brazilian state governments were privatized when they went into crisis with the end of inflation.

This privatization process was vehemently denounced by the left, including the Workers' Party, which has a great many members from public employee unions. Sociologist Francisco de Oliveira argues that the privatization of firms such as *Telebras* and *Companhia*

Vale do Rio Doce was an egregious case of "corruption" even though it was done perfectly legally and government officials made no personal gain from it.[301] In his view, they had no moral right to sell off the "crown jewels" of the Brazilian people without submitting the issue to a referendum. He calls this "legalized stealing" and considers it just as bad as taking bribes.

On the other side, supporters argue that privatization gave the government money to help stabilize the financial system without resorting to inflationary spending. And many of the privatized firms did quite well. Both wired and cellular telephones became widely available from private firms that invested large amounts of capital in expanding the networks. Petrobras became a competitive player in the international energy industry, developing huge natural gas fields in Bolivia and discovering vast underwater oil fields off the Brazilian coast. The *Companhia Vale do Rio Doce* expanded and paid more to the government in taxes than it had earned as a state-owned corporation.

This success did not placate many of the critics; sometimes it seemed to anger them more. Economist Fabio Giambiagi observed that the success of the *Companhia Vale do Rio Doce* after privatization was often taken as evidence that "there must have been some funny business in the sale price when it was privatized." He says that it never occurs to critics that the company might be "harvesting the fruits of a strategy that any competitor could have followed if it had had the courage to offer a higher bid for the company when it was sold in open auction open to all."[302]

In 2007, the Workers' Party joined with the Landless Farmer's Movement, the Catholic Church and other organizations in a campaign to renationalize the *Companhia do Vale Rio Doce*.[303] Their argument was that the privatization was fraudulent because it was sold for R\$3 billion and was worth R\$50 billion a few years later. Instead of buying it for its current value, they organized a national plebiscite to demand that the original sale be canceled. Lula brushed the proposal aside, stating that renationalizing the company was not a na-

[301] Personal interview, December 2006.
[302] Fabio Giambiagi with Marcelo Nonnemberg. *Brasil: Raízes do Atraso*. São Paulo: Elsevier, 2007, p. 198.
[303] Fábio Amato, "Protesto do MST quer reestatização da Vale," *Folha Online*, September 7, 2007.
http://www1.folha.uol.com.br/folha/brasil/ult96u326423.shtml.

tional priority and that no such proposal had crossed his desk.[304] He was not one to quarrel with success and a failure to honor contracts with investors would have had a powerful chilling effect on any further investment.

In the Brazilian system government and private enterprise are contributors to a common goal. This goal is expressed in the theme of Lula's annual report to Congress: "sustainable development with social inclusion." The state plays its most critical role in the financial sector where it maintains stability and channels significant credit to agricultural settlements, micro-enterprises and worker-owned companies. The state also operates redistributionist programs, the most important of which is the Family Stipend. Worker owned and managed enterprises are part of the picture, as are small and micro-businesses. Both play important roles in including marginal and excluded populations. But the largest engine that drives the economy, with all its "socialist" and social democratic elements, is the corporate "capitalist" economy that generates much of the economic growth and pays taxes to help support the rest.

There is still some nostalgia among intellectuals and activists for the era when purely socialist ideals seemed more plausible. Articles on socialism are still posted on the Workers' Party Web site, but they are mostly historical discussions, not visions of the future. In 2007, the Party posted a sophisticated YouTube video promoting its socialist project.[305] The video is full of inspiring clips from the party's militant past. But the ending is anti-climactic. It just says that socialism must be democratic and claims that the discussion about how to accomplish it is about to begin. Party activists would like to go beyond "neoliberalism," but they are acutely aware that they don't have a clear idea of what to put in its place. Party documents acknowledge that the struggle to "overcome neoliberalism on the plane of ideas and, more important, on the level of concrete alternatives ... is today obscured by impasses in the thinking and practice of socialism."[306]

[304] Renata Giraldi, "Lula diz que reestatização da Vale não é prioridade do governo," *Folha Online*, September 6, 2007.
http://www1.folha.uol.com.br/folha/brasil/ult96u326265.shtml.
[305] "Socialismo Petists," YouTube video,
http://www.youtube.com/watch?v=VNPjmoqfByc.
[306] 3º Congresso do PT, "Socialismo,"
http://www.pt.org.br/sitept/index_files/fotos/file/Socialismo%20Petista.zip.
O Globo, "PT aprova tese socialista de crescimento com distribuição de renda," August 31, 2007. http://oglobo.globo.com/pais/mat/2007/08/31/297536964.asp.

Lula does not worry about these theoretical issues. He would be happier if the party just stopped talking about socialism. He never talks about it unless an interviewer pushes the point. The words "socialism" and "capitalism" do not appear in his reports to Congress. Without saying so, Brazil is gradually becoming more and more capitalistic if one defines capitalism as a system where people work for private enterprise instead of for the government. Brazilian popular culture is still adjusting to these trends. Brazilians have never bought into the "the less government the better" ideology common in the United States. A March, 2006, survey commissioned by a Workers' Party think tank found that 49 percent of Brazilians thought that "socialism continues to be an alternative to resolve social problems," while 24 percent thought that "socialism was a good solution but it no longer has a future;" 16 percent thought that "socialism never was a good solution for social problems" and 13 percent did not know. [307] Support for "socialism" was not consistently related to income or educational level; it was common in all social classes.

The term "socialism" was not defined in the survey, but the respondents seem to have had some kind of democratic socialism in mind since 59 percent agreed that "democracy is always better than any other form of government; only 17 percent said that "under certain circumstances a dictatorship is better than a democracy;" 16 percent said that it makes no difference and 7 percent said they don't know.

But this comparatively favorable attitude towards socialism did not imply a negative attitude towards capitalism. In a 2002 Pew survey, 70.5 percent of the respondents thought that the impact of "large companies from other countries" was good for the country. [308] Fifty-six percent agreed that "most people are better off in a free market economy, even though some people are rich and some are poor." Only 30.7 percent were willing to support the closing of large, inefficient factories when it was necessary for economic improve-

[307] Núcleo de Opinião Pública da Fundação Perseu Abramo. 2006. Imagen Partidária e Cultura Política.
http://www2.fpa.org.br/portal/modules/wfdownloads/viewcat.php?cid=51.
[308] Pew Research Center. "Views of a Changing World," June 2003,
http://pewglobal.org. The Brazilian survey was a face-to-face probability sample of 1,000 adults 18 years of age and older. The interviews were conducted between July 2 and August 8, 2002, the last year of the Fernando Henrique Cardoso administration.

ment. The rest agreed that this was too much of a hardship for people. Lula is very much in the mainstream of Brazilian culture on these issues. His stated goal of "sustainable development with social inclusion" is accepted, at least in principle, by virtually everyone. Brazil made good progress on these goals during his presidency with a combination of market incentives, financial regulations, infrastructure development and social programs to redistribute income, increase skills, improve health and encourage enterprise on the part of those on the lower margins of society.

These goals and approaches are shared by the leading opposition parties. Brazil's development under Lula compares quite favorably to Venezuela's under Hugo Chávez, especially after the collapse of oil prices in 2008. It has much in common with successful policies in Chile, Mexico and several other Latin American countries, and provides some lessons for post-2008 economic policies in the United States.

Ironically, the 2008 financial crises forced the "neoliberal" government in the United States into a thinly disguised form of "lemon socialism" when it was forced to buy interests in failing enterprises, including major automobile companies, to keep them from collapsing. The more "socialist" elements of the Brazilian system, especially the strong government regulation and control of the financial system, protected it from having to do the same and helped protect the capitalist elements of its system.

CHAPTER FOURTEEN
ELECTING A SUCCESSOR

Although many of his supporters wanted him to seek a constitutional amendment permitting a third term, Lula ruled it out saying, in August 2007, "it is not a matter of the people asking. My term will end on December 31, 2010. I will give the presidential sash to another President of the Republic on January 1, 2011, and I will make my roasted rabbit which I have not done for five years." In an obvious reference to Hugo Chávez he said "when a political leader begins to think that he is irreplaceable or unsubstitutable, this is the beginning of a little dictatorship."[309]

But who would succeed Lula? The governors of the largest states have traditionally been leading contenders for the Brazilian presidency. The two most important of these at the time, José Serra of São Paulo and Aécio Neves of Minas Gerais, were both members of the opposition Social Democratic Party. The traditional response would have been for the Workers' Party or one of its allies to nominate one of its governors or former governors or perhaps a senator. Several were qualified, but none stood out above the crowd, so choosing one would have meant a struggle for the nomination. Instead of going that route and perhaps weakening his coalition, Lula made the surprising decision to give his support to his chief of staff, Dilma Rousseff.

Lula made the decision to anoint Dilma in 2006, soon after his second term began, but confided it only to close advisors.[310] Dilma had been active in the underground resistance to the military dictatorship when she was a youth. She was captured and jailed and reportedly tortured between 1970 and 1972. Later, she was able to go back to university to earn an undergraduate degree in economics and to begin graduate studies. When democracy was restored, she became very active in politics and rose to the positions of treasury sec-

[309] Lula da Silva, Interview with the *Estado de São Paulo*, August 26, 2007. http://www.estadao.com.br/estadaodehoje/20070826/not_imp41136,0.php.
[310] Leila Suwwan, "Em comício com Dilma, Lula acusa a elite de tentar 'dar um golpe a cada 24 horas', *O Globo*, July 30, 2010. http://oglobo.globo.com/pais/mat/2010/07/30/em-comicio-com-dilma-lula-acusa-elite-de-tentar-dar-um-golpe-cada-24-horas-917277901.asp.

retary in the city of Porto Alegre and energy secretary in the state of Rio Grande do Sul. She left the Brazilian Labor Party for the Workers' Party in 1986.[311] She had never, however, run for elective office.

When Lula began his first term, he surprised many in his entourage by appointing Dilma as minister of Energy, because he thought her to be very efficient and practically oriented. He was impressed by the way she always brought a computer to meetings. His finance minister, Antonio Palocci, agreed that she would be effective and easy to work with.[312] Her success as minister of Energy led to Lula's appointing her to the very powerful position of chief of staff when José Dirceu was forced to resign.

Lula revealed his support for Dilma to the public in December, 2008, joking that she might be surprised when she heard about it because he hadn't told her about the announcement.[313] Lula's choice avoided a primary contest within the Workers' Party and negotiations with coalition parties. Everyone knew that Lula's popularity was the key to winning the election, so none of the leaders of the major coalition parties contested his choice.

Although they couldn't oppose him, many Workers' Party leaders were skeptical of Lula's choice. Tarso Genro was one of the best known Workers' Party leaders and could have been a good candidate for the presidency. He was first elected mayor of Porto Alegre in 1992. He served as Minister of Institutional Relations and Minister of Justice in the Lula government. In 2005, he took over leadership of the Workers' Party and led its recovery from the monthly payoff scandal. When he heard about Lula's choice of Dilma, in 2009, he publicly questioned her lack of charisma and electoral viability. He said that her choice by Lula was the fruit of a vacuum in the party after the monthly payoff scandal.[314]

But Dilma's lack of name recognition wasn't a problem in Lula's view, it was an advantage. He said there was plenty of time for the people to get to know her. The fact that Dilma had never held elec-

---

[311] http://en.wikipedia.org/wiki/Dilma_Rousseff.

[312] Carvalho, Luís Maklouf (July 2009). "Mares nunca dantes navegados: Como e por que Dilma Rousseff se tornou a candidata de Lula à sucessão presidencial". *Revista Piauí*, nº 34, p. 26-33.

[313] Agência Brasil, "Lula diz que nunca falou com Dilma sobre candidatura à Presidência," December 19, 2008.
http://www.direito2.com.br/abr/2008/dez/19/lula-diz-que-nunca-falou-com-dilma-sobre-candidatura-a-presidencia.

[314] Ibid.

tive office and had no political following meant she could be a stand-in for him with little baggage of her own. Later, when the Workers' Party convention rubber-stamped his choice, he told them that "there is going to be a blank space on the ballot, and to fill this space, I changed my name and put Dilma on the ballot."[315] He and Dilma wore identical bright red shirts to symbolize the continuity. The sound system in the hall played a jingle with the words "Lula is with her, and so am I; look how Brazil has changed."

Brazilian electoral campaigns are tightly regulated by law and campaigning is not supposed to begin until the candidates are officially nominated and the free television time allocated to each party is available. But Lula chose to begin Dilma's campaign early in violation of the election law. When the Social Democrats complained to the Supreme Electoral Tribunal, Lula made fun of them for whining about technicalities, saying:

> The President of the Republic can't violate the laws. But it is important for people to be attentive, because I am surrounded by adversaries who are afraid they can't match me in the campaign, so they try to win on technicalities. This country is going to follow democracy to its last consequences. I think we all have to follow the law, we all have campaign rituals that are permitted or prohibited by legislation, and I think no one should disobey the law. If there are excesses, obviously each of us has to be punished. But I've heard some people talking too much; I've heard some people jeering too much. You have people saying things they shouldn't say, because you have a kind of people you shouldn't have. The citizen opens his refrigerator in the morning to get a glass of water, and he gives an interview thinking he is on television. He goes into the bathroom to shave and he turns on his razor and thinks it is a microphone and starts talking. I think you have people talking too much about this question, making too many insinuations, and I think this isn't good for democracy.[316]

Lula and Dilma were fined by the Supreme Electoral Tribunal for early campaigning, but this is a common occurrence and the Social Democrats were also fined for similar offenses. The fines are

[315] Carol Pires and Rodrigo Alvarez, "Lula diz que mudou de nome e será Dilma na cédula de votação," *Estadão.com.br.* June 13, 2010.
http://www.estadao.com.br/noticias/nacional,lula-diz-que-mudou-de-nome-e-sera-dilma-na-cedula-de-votacao,565950,0.htm.
[316] Lula da Silva, "Entrevista à Rádio Jangadeiro FM," Fortaleza, June 8, 2010.
http://www.info.planalto.gov.br/static/inf_briefdiscusos.htm.

very small in comparison to the cost of television time and they are treated like penalties imposed by an umpire in a sporting event. The early campaign publicity was well used. It featured a television advertisement where Lula introduced Dilma to the public. The transcript of this video, which featured both Dilma and Lula, captures the theme and tone of the campaign:

> Lula: One day they asked me why I admire Dilma so much.
>
> Dilma: Does my being a woman make a difference? I think it does, it makes a big difference.
>
> Lula: The person certainly thought it was because Dilma helped me so much in my government.
>
> Dilma: Each of the three times the president asked me to help in his campaign was a surprise and a challenge. First, to help with the transition to the new government. Then to be minister of Energy, and principally, as chief of staff.
>
> Lula: Certainly I admire very much what she did in my government. But what I admire most is her own history. It is a history of a woman who lived everything with great intensity, with great courage and competence, and who got where she is today on her own merits. It is a great life history. Dilma was born and grew up in Belo Horizonte. She was 16 when the military *coup d'état* ended democracy. Like thousands of youth, Dilma saw no other solution but to join the struggle against the dictatorship.
>
> Dilma: It was a very difficult time. We lived in the darkness, everything was prohibited. Press freedom, freedom of speech and opinion were not respected. Unions were not even allowed to struggle for higher salaries and students didn't even have the right to organize. Yes, I fought. I fought for liberty and democracy. I fought against the dictatorship from its first day to its last day with the means I had at my disposal. At that time many people were killed, others went into exile, others were killed. When Brazil changed, I changed, but I never changed sides.
>
> Lula: Part of Dilma's history reminds me very much of [Nelson] Mandela. I remember one time Mandela told me that he was only for confrontation because they didn't give him any other choice. Time passed and what happened? He became one of the greatest symbols of peace and unity in the world. No one has done more for unity than Mandela in South Africa after spending twenty-seven years in prison and later becoming president of the Republic. [317]

---

[317] http://www.dilma2010.blog.br/veja-o-otimo-depoimento-de-lula-para-dilma/.

Lula went on to praise Dilma's accomplishments as minister of Energy, including bringing the Light for All campaign to poor rural communities. He praised her exuberance in coordinating his government as chief of staff and concluded that "a large part of the success of the government is due to the capacity for coordination of comrade Dilma Rousseff."

Lula's introduction of Dilma was successful; she pulled three points ahead of the chief opposing candidate, José Serra of the Social Democratic Party, in the Vox Populi poll.[318] José Serra had lost to Lula in 2002 and he was reluctant to run again in 2010, thinking that Lula's popularity and the economic boom might make his candidate unbeatable.[319] Running meant giving up the governorship of the state of São Paulo, perhaps the second most important position in the country. In January, he almost decided not to run, but he went ahead, hoping that the public would want a tested, experienced leader to succeed Lula.

In his 2002 campaign against Lula, Serra had distanced himself from then-outgoing President Fernando Henrique Cardoso, of his own party, and tried to portray himself as a candidate of change. It didn't work because most of the voters who wanted change voted for Lula. In 2010, he couldn't portray himself as a candidate of change because Brazilians were happy with the results of Lula's two terms and wanted continuity. To win, he would have to persuade voters who wanted continuity that he would be able to provide it better than Lula's own chief of staff.

Serra didn't deny that Brazil had done well during Lula's eight years. But he pointed out that much of Lula's success, especially in the economy, came from continuing policies from previous administrations going back to the end of the military dictatorship in 1988. What needed to be continued, he argued, were not new policies Lula had invented, but policies Lula had continued. He also argued that some things Lula had done that were new ought not be continued, especially Lula's support for authoritarian governments in Cuba and Iran, and his use of rhetoric that encouraged hostility between rich and poor. He said, "I do not accept the rationale of us versus them. This has no place in the life of a nation. We are all brothers in the

[318] O Globo, "Vox Populi aponta Dilma à frente de Serra Diferença de três pontos, May 17, 2010.
[319] Demétrio Magnoli, "A escolha de Serra," Estadão.com.br, July 8, 2010. http://www.estadao.com.br/estadaodehoje/20100708/not_imp578225,0.php.

same fatherland. We will fight for the unity of Brazilians, not to divide them."[320]

Serra's key talking point was that he had more experience in governing than Dilma. He was a tried and true leader; everybody knew him and what he could do. While this was true enough, it wasn't very exciting and it hadn't worked in 2002. In his losing 2002 race against Lula, he often spoke dryly about complex policy issues, rather than about his feelings and motivations. In 2010, he strove to present a warmer, more human image, telling the television audience that "I come here today to speak of my love of Brazil, to speak of my life, to speak of my experience, to speak of my faith, to speak of my hopes for Brazil." He adopted the slogan, "Brazil can do more," and presented himself as the best prepared candidate to continue the progress Brazil has made.

By voting for either José Serra or Dilma Rousseff, Brazilians would be opting for continuing the country's fundamental economic and social policies. There were other choices for those who really wanted change. They could vote for the Green Party candidate, Marina Silva or for the candidate of the Party of Socialism and Liberty, Plínio Arruda Sampaio. Both Marina and Plínio were former Workers' Party leaders who had left the party for ideological reasons. Neither candidate had a chance of winning the election; Marina generally ran about 8 percent or 9 percent in the pre-election polls, Plínio was lucky to get 1 percent. Their goal was to advance ideas for the future.

Marina Silva argued that both the major candidates were mired in the developmentalist perspectives of the twentieth century instead of the environmentalist perspectives needed for the twenty-first century. She raised the issue of global warming and advocated increased funding for health care, sanitation and education. She also advocated hiring 300,000 to 500,000 "development agents" to work with the Family Allowances program to help recipients learn ways to increase their incomes.[321] She was supported by singer Gilberto Gil, who had been minister of Culture in the Lula government up until 2008.

[320] Fábio Portelo, " Com a casa em ordem, Serra vai à luta," *Veja,* April 21, 2010.
[321] Ricardo Noblat, "Verde lança programa de governo amanhã," *O Globo,* July 26, 2010.
http://oglobo.globo.com/pais/noblat/posts/2010/07/26/verde-lanca-programa-de-governo-amanha-311025.asp.
Marcelle Ribeiro, "Marina promete ampliar programas sociais ," *O Globo,* June 4, 2010.

Plínio was a 79-year-old intellectual who had been active in the Catholic left and a founding member of the Workers' Party. He ran to keep a socialist vision alive. He advocated confiscating all farms larger than one thousand *alqueires* in size (about 6,000 acres as the term is used in the state of São Paulo). He said, "This will not be done to increase the productivity of Brazilian agriculture. No. It will be done to redistribute the land. The redistribution of wealth and of income is the central theme of our program of government."[322] Plínio was counting mostly on the Internet to promote his ideas because his party was entitled to only 44 seconds of free television time based on its weak showing in previous elections.

And there were candidates from even smaller parties[323] including José Maria de Almeida of the United Socialist Workers' Party, who advocated not paying the domestic or foreign debt, breaking with the International Monetary Fund and nationalizing the banks, the financial system, the large corporations, the large farms and all companies that exported natural resources. Ivan Pinheiro of the relaunched Brazilian Communist Party advocated nationalizing all financial institutions, oligopolies and strategic companies. Rui Costa Pimenta of the Workers' Cause Party advocated going beyond the capitalist model, but also criticized "ecological demagoguery" which he said inhibited development. José Maria Eymael of the Christian Social Democratic Party advocated the right to happiness and opposed pornography and violence in the media. His principal claim to fame is his theme song, "Ey Ey Eymael, A Christian Democrat," first popularized during his campaign for mayor of São Paulo in 1985. He is said to keep contesting elections so as to keep his song on the air. Clips of the campaign songs are available online.[324]

Plínio qualified for the televised debates, and was thought to help Dilma by making her look more moderate by comparison. He was especially critical of the Workers' Party's land reform efforts,

https://conteudoclippingmp.planejamento.gov.br/cadastros/noticias/2010/6/4/m
arina-promete-ampliar-programas-sociais.
[322] Agencia O *Globo*, "Plínio, do PSOL, promete distribuir riqueza," July 1, 2010.
https://conteudoclippingmp.planejamento.gov.br/cadastros/noticias/2010/7/1/pli
nio-do-psol-promete-distribuir-riqueza/.
[323] O *Globo*, "Nanicos anunciam suas propostas e apostam na internet," July 5, 2010.
http://www.linearclipping.com.br/fecomerciodf/detalhe_noticia.asp?cd_sistema=7
&codnot=1211279.
[324] For campaign theme songs of Dilma Rousseff, José Maria Eymael, José Serra and
Marina Silva go to:
http://www.youtube.com/watch?v=UPMMT7_n9Cw&feature=related.

saying they had done even less than the Fernando Henrique Cardoso government. His criticisms seemed plausible because he had had a central role in forming the Workers' Party's land reform plans in the era before Lula was elected. The other minor party candidates did not qualify for the official television debates and had no discernable impact on the election.

Election Controversies. In many ways, the 2010 presidential campaign was like a rerun of the 2002 and 2006 campaigns. Dilma set this tone by focusing her rhetoric on Fernando Henrique Cardoso instead of on her actual opponents. Repeating the theme of the 2006 election, she said that under Cardoso "Brazil was on its knees and had to ask for help from the international fund. Before Brazil was broken, now it is no longer broken."[325] This argument was for domestic consumption only. When speaking with investors in New York at an event sponsored by the São Paulo stock exchange, Dilma correctly credited the country's economic success to the governments "of the last twenty years" and gave much praise to Antonio Palocci who had resolved the crisis in 2002 by continuing Cardoso's economic model.[326]

José Serra focused his rhetoric on his opponent, Dilma Rousseff, not on Lula. His fundamental argument was that Dilma was inexperienced and not ready to be president. In response, Dilma pointed out that she had lots of experience, just not as an elected official. Her political career had begun 25 years ago when she was finance secretary for the Mayor's Office in Porto Alegre.

Serra's political advisors told him to avoid criticizing Lula at all costs because of Lula's extremely high popularity figures. Taking this advice to an extreme, the campaign went so far as to broadcast advertisements showing Serra and Lula together in the past, implying that they were working together now. They tried the slogan, "When Lula is gone, I want Zé to be there." (Zé is a nickname for José.) Serra also modeled himself on Lula by publishing a "Social Letter to the Brazilian People" similar to Lula's "Letter to the Brazilian People" in 2001. The slogan was, "Brazil can do More with Social Assis-

[325] Flávia Salme, "No Rio, Dilma diz que FHC deixou o Brasil de joelhos," *Jornal do Brasil Online*, May 19, 2010.
http://jbonline.terra.com.br/pextra/2010/05/10/e100512441.asp.
[326] Dona Flor, "Dilma credita conquistas do Brasil a "governos dos últimos 20 anos," *Folha Online*, May 21, 2010.
http://www1.folha.uol.com.br/folha/brasil/ult96u738728.shtml.

tance with Serra as president."[327] None of these efforts caught on with the public. There were also corruption issues similar to those in the 2006 election. Newspaper stories told of a false *dossier* being prepared to undermine Serra, similar to those that had been discovered in the 2006 campaign. The revelations came as a result of internal conflicts within the Workers' Party and were published in the newsmagazine *Veja* and in leading newspapers, as in 2006. One principal target was Serra's daughter Verônica whose income tax records were violated.

The Social Democratic Party went so far as to petition the Supreme Electoral Tribunal to investigate the incident and to cancel Dilma's candidacy if it found that she was involved in these illicit schemes.[328] There was no doubting that confidential records had been illegally released. The head of the income tax department admitted that Verônica Silva's signature had been forged and falsely notarized, and the clerk who released the information said it was because "somebody wanted to harm Serra,"[329] But there was no proof of a direct link to the Dilma campaign, so the Social Democrats' lawyers relied on journalistic accounts and the claim that this was a pattern of violations dating to the 2006 election.

Lula, Antonio Palocci and José Eduardo Dutra, the Workers' Party president, met with Dilma in the Presidential Palace to advise her on weathering the scandal.[330] They told her to say that criminal matters had to be investigated by the proper authorities, and that any officials guilty of leaking or selling information should be prosecuted. Lula made the following comment:

> I have no reason to doubt the word of the tax department who say that
> a request was filed, and I have no reason to doubt the word of ex-

[327] Silvia Amorim, "Serra assinará 'Carta' para o social," *O Globo*, July 2, 2010. http://oglobo.globo.com/pais/noblat/posts/2010/07/02/serra-assinara-carta-para-social-304950.asp.

[328] Carlos Pires, "Oposição vai ao TSE e mira tornar Dilma inelegível," *estadão.com*, September 2, 2010. http://www.estadao.com.br/estadaodehoje/20100902/not_imp604021,0.php.

[329] Aduari Barbos, et al, "Receita confirma falsificação de documento de filha de Serra, e contador diz que era para prejudicar tucano," *O Globo*, September 1, 2010. http://oglobo.globo.com/pais/eleicoes2010/mat/2010/09/01/receita-confirma-falsificacao-de-documento-de-filha-de-serra-contador-diz-que-era-para-prejudicar-tucano-917532366.asp.

[330] Vera Rosa, "Lula discute estratégia para blindar Dilma," *estadão.com*, September 2, 2010. http://www.estadao.com.br/estadaodehoje/20100902/not_imp604003,0.php.

governor Serra's daughter's word that it was falsified. Now it is necessary to prove that it was falsified, if it was falsified, and to find the falsi-
fier, because he committed a grave crime in Brazil – ideological false-
ness. We are going to find out what is happening, because there is no
lack of people trying to cause problems at election time. I have great
confidence in the seriousness of the Tax Department, I have great confidence in the seriousness of the Federal Police, and, if it is the case
that someone has caused damage, a falsification, you can be certain that
it will be made public.[331]

Lula and Dilma repeatedly claimed that this was an electoral ma-
neuver and that the Serra campaign was trying to win the election on
a technicality because they couldn't win at the ballot box. The public
seemed largely content with this argument.

Serra's biggest hope was that he could outperform Dilma sufficiently in the televised debates to shift opinion. In the first debate,
Serra was more composed and fluent, especially at the beginning,
while Dilma seemed a little awkward. Dilma made some mistakes
including getting some statistics wrong, admitting that she had not
read the party's campaign program before it was submitted to the
election officials, and stating that Iran already had an atomic bomb.
But viewers made allowances for this being her first debate, against
an experienced opponent. Both candidates did their best to be per-
sonable and folksy, although neither one is naturally that kind of person. Commentators agreed that they both did reasonably well but
that this helped Dilma because it proved she could hold her own
against an experienced politician.

José Serra started with strong name recognition, and dominated
the very early polls more than a year before the election. But at that
time, 25 percent of the voters thought they would vote for Lula, not
realizing that he would not be running. It took time for many voters
to learn that Dilma Rousseff was Lula's candidate, and to become
comfortable with the idea of passing his mantle on to her. In the
public opinion polls, the big shift in favor of Dilma came in August,
2010, after the debates, when voters had a chance to watch Dilma in
action.[332] This was very discouraging to Social Democratic Party ac-

---

[331] Luiza Damé, "Lula sai em defesa da Receita Federal no caso sobre a quebra de
sigilos," *O Globo*, September 1, 2010.
http://oglobo.globo.com/pais/eleicoes2010/mat/2010/09/01/lula-sai-em-defesa-
da-receita-federal-no-caso-sobre-quebra-de-sigilos-917530036.asp.
[332] In the earliest Datafolha presidential preference survey, respondents were first
asked who they would vote for without being given any names from which to

tivists who thought Serra did well and expected his poll numbers to go up.

Voters knew who José Serra was and they preferred Lula. Since they couldn't vote for Lula, they wanted to be reassured that Dilma was competent to carry on in his place. Datafolha, one of Brazil's leading survey research companies, reported that the debates and campaign broadcasts served mainly to reassure voters that Dilma was competent to be president.[333] She did well enough to reassure them.

Some blamed Serra's rapid decline in the polls on the strategies recommended by his political consultant, journalist Luiz Gonzales. But this was Monday-morning quarterbacking; there were no obvious errors on his part, and his plans were vetted by experienced Social Democratic politicians. In the opinion of Brazil's best known political consultant, Duda Mendonça, Serra was simply unable to overcome the climate of the times. Mendonça said:

---

choose. In response, 25 percent said they would vote for Lula, 6 percent for Serra and 3% for Dilma; 49 percent said they did not know and the rest were scattered among other possible candidates. Although much of the campaign focused on issues understood by well-informed voters, the election may have depended more on getting less-informed voters to know that Dilma Rousseff was Lula's candidate. In the March 2009 Datafolha poll, 95 percent of the respondents said they knew who José Serra was and 52 percent said they knew who Dilma Rousseff was. But most who said they knew Dilma said they did not know her well, and few apparently thought of her as a presidential hopeful. When asked to choose among a list of likely candidates, 38 percent chose Serra, 20 percent chose Ciro Gomes of the Brazilian Socialist Party, 15 percent chose Heloisa Helena of the Party of Socialism and Liberty, and only 3 percent chose Dilma. (As it turned out Helena's party nominated Plínio Arruda Sampaio and the Brazilian Socialist Party supported Dilma once Lula made his choice clear).

By December 2009, the parties' choices were narrowing and Datafolha asked for a choice between three candidates: Serra had 37 percent, Dilma had 23 percent and Marina Silva of the Green Party had 11 percent (the remainder not knowing or planning to vote blank). By April 2010, Serra had 42 percent, Dilma 30 percent and Marina 12 percent. In July 2010, 70 percent of the respondents reported that they knew that Dilma was President Lula's preference. Dilma and Serra were in a virtual tie, with Serra at 38 percent and Dilma at 37 percent with Marina holding on to her 10 percent. By August 2010, 85 percent knew that Dilma was Lula's candidate and she pulled decisively ahead with 47 percent compared to Serra's 29 percent and Marina's 9 percent. All these poll data are from reports posted at http://datafolha.folha.uol.com.br/eleicoes/2010/2010_index.php. Reports from other polling companies were very similar

[333] *Datafolha*, "Exposição eleva imagem de Dilma," August 30, 2010. http://datafolha.folha.uol.com.br/po/ver_po.php?session=1025.

In this campaign, it was foreordained that Dilma would win. It wasn't Serra's time. Dilma will win in the first round of the election, and it is not [Serra's] political consultant's fault. A political consultant can maximize a candidate's potential, but he can't decide the election.[334]

As it turned out, Mendonça was wrong in predicting that Dilma would win in the first round. But he was right that the climate of the times were favorable to Dilma. Two reasons were given: Lula's popularity and the country's economic boom. One letter to the editor said "President Lula's popularity is so great that he can elect any successor, even a post."[335] This remark was repeated so widely that Dilma felt she had to respond to it:

> I know that some people say I am a post. Now I don't believe that this makes me a post. I am going to want the president's help to pass important reforms. I want him to give me his counsel. But I am clear that the president will participate as ex-president.[336]

Lula's personal history and personal charm explain much of his popularity, but that kind of personal charisma is hard to transmit from one person to another. And Lula's popularity slumped when the economy seemed to be going into a recession in 2009. Much of his popularity could be attributed to the fact that the average consumer was living very well at the end of his eight years in office.

The government did everything it could to make sure the economy would be booming at election time: loosening credit, increasing spending on pork-barrel projects in districts and hiring large numbers of new state employees from among its party members and allies.[337] But the economy around the world was in crisis, so these actions were also justifiable as a stimulus plan to prevent a recession.

[334] Adriana Vasconcelos, "Duda Mendonça Defende Gonzales," *O Globo*, August 28, 2010. http://oglobo.globo.com/pais/moreno/diarioreporter/posts/2010/08/28/caiu-na-rede-duda-mendonca-defende-gonzalez-319907.asp.
[335] Letter to the Editor, *O Globo*, August 30, 2010.
[336] Reuters Brasil Online, "Dilma nega ser 'poste', mas quer ajuda de Lula se eleita," *O Globo*, June 28, 2010. http://oglobo.globo.com/pais/mat/2010/06/28/dilma-nega-ser-poste-mas-quer-ajuda-de-lula-se-eleita-917006798.asp.
[337] Cristiane Jungblut, "Indicações Políticas Crescem 40% no Governo Lula," *O Globo*, August 16, 2010. https://conteudoclippingmp.planejamento.gov.br/cadastros/noticias/2010/8/16/indicacoes-politicas-crescem-40-no-governo-lula. Gilberto Scofield, Jr. "Dinheiro Público, Herança em Votos? Cem milhões dependem de pagamentos do governo,"

By September things looked dismal for the Serra campaign. Dilma was 20 points ahead in the polls and seemed almost certain to win more than 50 percent of the vote in the first round of the elections on October 3. But it had looked the same in 2006, yet Lula failed to reach the 50 percent mark on the first round because dossier scandal hit the newspapers just before the election. The Serra campaign decided to focus on the income tax records scandal in the hope that something similar would happen. The press helped by giving the tax confidentiality issue extensive coverage with new revelations each day. If the Social Democrats could use the tax confidentiality issue to cut Dilma's lead to 10 percent, it would probably be enough to deny her a first round victory. Then they could try to get the public to perceive the second round as contest between Serra and Dilma rather than as a referendum on Lula.[338]

Workers' Party focus groups in the beginning of September suggested that the scandal could have a negative impact on the campaign.[339] Lula went into action immediately, meeting with Dilma and her campaign staff to strategize how to deal with this issue. Lula argued that Dilma should not reply directly to Serra's criticism, but should present a "friendly and happy face."[340] Lula decided to take on the "bad cop" role with a direct presidential attack on Serra. September 7 was Brazil's Independence Day and traditionally the president goes on television with an Independence Day Proclamation. Instead of the official proclamation, Lula decided to dress up in his formal presidential suit and tie and use two minutes of Dilma's campaign air time to attack Serra:

> Unfortunately, our adversary, the candidate of the just say no group, who turn up their nose at everything the people have accomplished in recent years, have decided to lower themselves by using personal at-

---

O Globo, July 18, 2010. http://www.aarffsa.com.br/noticias/18071001.html. Veja, "O aparelhamento do estado contra a oposição," September 8, 2010. http://www.veja.com.br/acervodigital/.

[338] Gerson Camarotti, "PT decidiu usar presidente para atacar Serra e blindar Dilma temendo efeitos negativos do escândalo da Receita," O Globo, September 8, 2010. http://oglobo.globo.com/pais/eleicoes2010/mat/2010/09/08/pt-decidiu-usar-presidente-para-atacar-serra-blindar-dilma-temendo-efeitos-negativos-do-escandalo-da-receita-917586639.asp.

[339] Ibid.

[340] Christiane Jungblat, "Lula blinda Dilma e parte para o ataque," O Globo, September 8, 2010. http://oglobo.globo.com/pais/noblat/posts/2010/09/08/lula-blinda-dilma-parte-para-ataque-322544.asp.

tacks. I regret this, I regret it very much. But I am sure that Brazilians will know how to repel this kind of attack. They think that the people can be fooled by any story. But it is they who are mistaken. The Brazilian people are mature and know very well how to separate the wheat from the chaff. To use lies and calumny against a woman of Dilma's quality is to commit a crime against Brazil, and especially against the Brazilian woman ...

For this reason, I ask for a calm and prudent response to those who insult Dilma, motivated by desperation, and by bias against women and against me. I ask also that they have more love for Brazil ... It is possible to dispute an election in an honest, democratic and civilized way.[341]

Speaking as if he were giving a formal presidential proclamation, Lula framed the attack on Dilma as an insult to Brazilian womanhood. He didn't mention the income tax confidentiality issue, as if mentioning such a thing would be like airing dirty laundry in public. He argued that a "strong, just and independent nation" cannot be made by those who "think only to destroy" and who "place their personal interests ahead of those of the country."

The risk of relying on Lula to lead the attack was that it could make Dilma appear weak, as if she needed Lula to defend her. Portraying it as an attack on womanhood implied that a female candidate couldn't stand up for herself in a debate with a man. What would she do, Serra wondered, if she were attacked by someone after the election, call on Lula to defend her? Serra quickly made these arguments:

Dilma has sub-contracted her attacks and arguments, including, now, to the president of the Republic, who despite being president of the Republic and of all Brazilians, has now become the spokesman for one candidate who, apparently, is unable to speak for herself or to go on the attack. Because what happened yesterday was not a defense, it was an attack ...

It is absolutely original to accuse victims, who complain of being victims, of dirty tricks. The dirty tricks, the invasion [of privacy], just shows the nature of those who committed the crime.[342]

[341] Ibid.
[342] Breno Costa, "Serra diz que violações são 'trabalho de quadrilha' e Dilma está 'terceirizando' artilhari," Folha.com, Sept 8, 2010.
http://www1.folha.uol.com.br/poder/795650-serra-diz-que-violacoes-sao-trabalho-de-quadrilha-e-dilma-esta-terceirizando-artilharia.shtml.

The bank account issue didn't catch on with the masses of people, only with people wealthy enough to have significant bank accounts. The Serra campaign reluctantly concluded that the average Brazilian either didn't understand the issue or didn't think it was very important.[343] Raising the issue didn't cut into Dilma's lead in the opinion polls, although there was some change in the class base of her support. Datafolha reported that she lost some support among classes "A" and "B", the two wealthiest of Brazil's five classes as pollsters categorize them. Instead of going to Serra, however, their support shifted to Marina Silva of the Green Party, who went up slightly. Dilma made it up with increased support especially from class "C".[344]

With only a few weeks to the election Dilma seemed to be coasting to a first-round victory. Then a more serious corruption issue arose. Erenice Guerra, Dilma Rousseff's successor as Lula's chief of staff, was accused of influence peddling by giving government contracts to family members and business associates.[345] Guerra was Dilma Rousseff's close assistant for many years, and it appeared that the corruption had been going on for years. The Social Democrats seized on the case, posting YouTube videos portraying Workers' Party activists as rottweilers and linking the 2010 scandal in the chief of staff's office to the 2005 scandal with José Dirceu in the same office. Dilma brushed off the accusations, saying she had seen no proof of wrongdoing by Erenice. Lula dismissed Erenice from office only five days after the allegations emerged, in the hope of ending the story in the press.

Lula also lashed out at the Social Democrats for focusing on this issue at the key point in the campaign. Speaking at a rally in Campinas, São Paulo state, he referred to the Social Democrats by their party icon, the toucan, a colorful Brazilian bird with a prominent beak:

[343] *O Globo*, "Serra diz considerar impossível explicar o caso na televisão," September 9, 2010.
http://www.linearclipping.com.br/fecomerciodf/detalhe_noticia.asp?cd_sistema=7&codnot=1308714.
[344] *O Globo*, "Datafolha: Dilma cai entre mais ricos," September 12, 2010.
[345] Alexei Barrionuevo, "Scandal Puts Bumps in Path of Brazil Leader's Protégée," *New York Times*, September 20, 2010.
http://www.nytimes.com/2010/09/21/world/americas/21brazil.html?scp=3&sq=Brazil&st=cse.

Nothing irritates a toucan more than having such a big beak to talk with and so little to say. Some things must be said. You know toucans will even eat their own babies in the nest. When [Aloizio] Mercadante is elected governor [of the state of São Paulo] we are going to create a family allowance so the toucans don't go hungry.[346]

This was good-humored partisan squabbling. Lula's attack on the press was more troubling to many Brazilians. Workers' Party activists have a history of calling for "social" controls on the press, alleging that it is biased in favor of the Social Democrats and the affluent social classes. Lula picked up on this theme, saying:

There are days when the some sectors of the press are shameful. The owners of the papers should be ashamed. We are going to defeat some of the papers and magazines that behave like political parties. We don't need formers of public opinion. We are public opinion.[347]

The Brazilian press association and the Brazilian legal association expressed their concern that he had lost sight of the importance of the free press. A group of noted Brazilian jurists and intellectuals organized a protest rally in front of the law school in downtown São Paulo, some of them attacking Lula as a fascist, caudillo, authoritarian, oppressor and violator of the constitution.[348] They circulated an online petition with the slogan "we don't need a sovereign with paternal pretensions, we need convinced democrats."[349] A few days later, a second group of equally distinguished jurists came to Lula's defense with a statement that the Lula government had always observed democratic values, and noting that despite his 80 percent popularity ratings Lula had not tried to modify the constitution to his advantage.[350]

---

[346] Rogerio Alvares, "'Nós somos a opinião pública', afirma Lula," *estadão.com*, September 18, 2010. http://www.estadao.com.br/noticias/nacional,nos-somos-a-opiniao-publica--afirma-lula,611876,0.htm.
[347] Martha Beck, "ANJ e OAB condenam ataque de Lula à imprensa," *O Globo*, September 20, 2010. http://oglobo.globo.com/pais/noblat/posts/2010/09/20/anj-oab-condenam-ataque-de-lula-imprensa-325881.asp.
[348] Fausto Macedo, "Após ataques de Lula, juristas lançam 'Manifesto em Defesa da Democracia'," *estadão.com*, September 23, 2010.
http://www.estadao.com.br/estadaodehoje/20100923/not_imp613986,0.php.
[349] "Manifesto em Defesa de Democracia," September 23, 2010.
http://manifestoemdefesadademocracia.wordpress.com/.
[350] Sérgio Roxo, "Carta de juristas defende Lula de críticas," *O Globo*, September 29, 2010.

All in all, the 2010 election had been a pretty dull affair up until the first round of voting on October 3. The final debate before the election was especially dull, with both major candidates doing their best to be pleasant and avoid alienating anyone. The only excitement was in Marina Silva's Green Party camp. Her poll numbers kept creeping up, and the crowds at her rallies kept growing. Her supporters called it The Green Wave, and even hoped that she might come in second and get a chance to go up against Dilma in the final round. The Social Democrats hoped she would get enough votes to deny Dilma a first run victory.

And, surprise of surprises, she did, with 19 percent of the vote. Dilma got 47 percent and Serra 33 percent. Despite a lively Internet campaign, Plínio Arruda Sampaio of the Party of Socialism and Liberty got only the 1 percent he had in the polls all along. Exit poll analysts said the main changes were Marina's surge, renewed strength for the Social Democrats in São Paulo and a weakening of support for Dilma among the middle-income group that had grown so much during Lula's presidency.[351] Social Democrat Geraldo Alckmin took the São Paulo governorship on October 3, despite Lula's strong support for Aloizio Mercadante.

The Democrats [formerly the Liberal Front Party], a more conservative party allied with the Social Democrats, had an especially sweet victory in the state of Santa Catarina. They elected Raimundo Colombo governor after Lula had visited the state and called the Democrats "wolves" who should be "uprooted from Brazilian politics."[352] The Democrats also elected a governor, Rosalba Ciarlini, in the state of Rio Grande do Norte.

Marina Silva is best known as an environmentalist, but there was no indication of a sudden increase in green consciousness to account for her success. Nor were other Green Party candidates equally successful. The party's other well-known candidate, Fernando Gabeira, lost his campaign for Rio de Janeiro governor, while Marina ran very strong in the state. In addition to being an environmentalist, Marina

http://oglobo.globo.com/pais/eleicoes2010/mat/2010/09/29/carta-de-juristas-defende-lula-de-criticas-922663571.asp.

[351] Fernando Canzian, "Arrancada de Marina, voto de SP e queda de Dilma na classe C explicam o 2º turno," *Folha.com*, October 4, 2010.
http://www1.folha.uol.com.br/poder/809281-arrancada-de-marina-voto-de-sp-e-queda-de-dilma-na-classe-c-explicam-o-2-turno.shtml.

[352] Claudio Leal, "Lula diz que o DEM precisa ser extirpado da política brasileira," *O Globo* September 13, 2010.

is an evangelical Christian who strongly opposes abortion. Much of her vote surge came from evangelical voters bothered by Dilma's secularism and weak opposition to abortion. An extensive Internet campaign by religious and anti-abortion voters cut into Dilma's vote. Workers' Party activists suspected the Social Democrats of manipulating the issue behind the scenes.

Marina is a charming woman who seems to genuinely say what she thinks. She is similar to Lula both in personality and in her social-class background. Neither Serra nor Dilma are known for their charisma. Serra's nickname is "the grave-digger" because some find his looks and mannerisms ghoulish. Dilma's nickname is the "Iron Lady" because she is known as a sober taskmaster who imposes discipline on bureaucrats. Their debates were described as a conversation between nuns.[353]

The only politician who made extensive use of Fernando Henrique Cardoso in his television advertisements was Aloysio Nunes Ferreira, a candidate for the Senate from São Paulo. He started at the bottom of the list of candidates and ended on top.[354] Fernando Henrique, interviewed as he left the voting booth on October 3, said that in his view Lula had failed to transfer enough of his popularity to Dilma. He opined that Dilma was too dependent on Lula and had not asserted herself as a leader in her own right, and concluded that "what we need is real leaders, not puppets."[355] He also criticized Lula for abusing his role as president of Brazil by becoming too closely involved in Dilma's campaign, blurring the distinction between government and electoral politics.

But Lula had no intention of stepping back from the campaign. He immediately canceled the foreign trips he had planned and took personal control of Dilma's campaign for the second round of the election.[356] The leadership's thinking was that Dilma had done well in

[353] John Paul Rathbone and Jonathan Wheatley, "Green candidate may play kingmaker in Brazil," *Financial Times*, October 4, 2010. http://www.ft.com/cms/s/0/b1c86336-cf59-11df-9be2-00144feab49a.html.

[354] *O Globo*, "E FH, no final, foi um bom cabo eleitoral," October 4, 2010. http://clipping.radiobras.gov.br/clipping/novo/Classes/SinopsesDetail.php.

[355] Fausto Macedo, "FHC chama Dilma de fantoche," *Estadão.com.br*, October 3, 2010. http://blogs.estadao.com.br/radar-politico/2010/10/03/fhc-chama-dilma-de-fantoche/

[356] Gerson Camarotti, "Lula comandará campanha de Dilma," *O Globo* October 4, 2010. http://oglobo.globo.com/pais/eleicoes2010/mat/2010/10/04/lula-comandara-campanha-de-dilma-922693853.asp.

the polls throughout the month of August, when Lula had been campaigning intensively for her, and that she had dropped a bit when he turned his attention to other matters. Campaign leaders also thought that Lula had been more effective in the early part of the campaign, when he was in his "Lula: Peace and Love" mode. Later on, his nasty attacks on the press and on the Democrats shocked some voters. Dilma never went into the nasty mode, leaving that to Lula. But neither was she terribly good at sweetness and warmth. Marina was.

For their part, the Social Democrats were critical of their own presidential campaign for a slow start, for delays in choosing a vice president, and for its reluctance to confront Lula. They thought that Serra had acted too much on his own without relying on party leaders. But they thought that they had a chance to win the second round, and they moved quickly to re-energize their campaign.

Social Democratic leaders believed that they had been too deferential to Lula and not assertive enough about their own heritage. After the first round voting, they corrected this mistake and gave full credit to their own accomplishments. Social Democrat Aécio Neves, who won a landslide victory in his own campaign for senator from Minas Gerais, expressed this view:

> We are going to show that we have the best project for the country, a project that recognizes the advances that we have made in the last eight years, as in the eight years that preceded the Lula government. Because we would not have had a Lula government if we had not had President Itamar [Franco] with the *real* plan, and President Fernando Henrique, with the modernization of the economy.[357]

Dilma and her team realized that they had underestimated the effectiveness of the Internet campaign of rumors about her antiabortion view. She insisted that "it was a perverse campaign of untruths about what I said and what I believe."[358] She declared herself

[357] Adriana Vasconcelos and Thiago Herdy, "Serra: Aécio é pessoa-chave no 2º turno," *O Globo*, October 5, 2010. http://www.senado.gov.br/noticias/opiniaopublica/inc/senamidia/notSenamidia.asp?ud=20101005&datNoticia=20101005&codNoticia=472863&nomeParlamentar=Marina+Silva&nomeJornal=O+Globo&codParlamentar=59&tipPagina=1.

[358] Cristiane Jungblut, Gerson Camarotti e Maria Lima, "Campanha de Dilma planeja reconquistar evangélicos e católicos para o segundo turno," *O Globo*, October 4, 2010.

to be a Catholic, forgetting doubts she had expressed in the past about the existence of God. Speaking in the parking lot of a chapel next to the traditional market in Belo Horizonte, she defined abortion as an act of violence against women and made reference to the recent birth of her first grandchild:

It would be very strange when there has been a manifestation of life in my family because my grandson was just born, for me to defend a position in support of abortion. I am against abortion because abortion is violence against women.[339]

This was a bizarre argument; feminists view a woman's right to choose an abortion as a response to violence, especially after a rape. But the Workers' Party campaign quickly changed the topic and focused its rhetoric on accusing the Social Democrats of favoring privatization, especially of Petrobras. This had worked in 2006, after Alckmin forced the election into a second round, and they thought it would work again in 2010. In 2006, Alckmin had apparently lost ground by being too aggressive and defensive, so Serra avoided that approach. He even came to the defense of the Fernando Henrique Cardoso government, especially for privatizing telephone service. He said that before Cardoso, Brazilians had to line up at telephone booths to make calls because there was a great shortage of telephone lines. Now everyone has their own cell phone, and wired phone lines are available. Dilma responded that cell phones were a new technology that had solved the problem, not the privatization.

The newsmagazine *Veja* published some new allegations tying Dilma to contracts given out by her subordinates, but they seemed like more of the same and didn't attract much attention. Both campaigns also paid a little more attention to the issues in the second round of the campaign, in response to widespread criticism that the electioneering had been too focused on sound bites. The sponsor of the last television debate, the *Globo* television network, invited a sample of undecided voters to ask questions of the candidates. This

http://oglobo.globo.com/pais/eleicoes2010/mat/2010/10/04/campanha-de-dilma-planeja-reconquistar-evangelicos-catolicos-para-segundo-turno-922703673.asp.
[339] Eduardo Kattah, "Dilma nega aprovar aborto e ataca PSDB por privatização," *Estadão.com.br*, October 7, 2010.
http://www.estadao.com.br/noticias/nacional,dilma-nega-aprovar-aborto-e-ataca-psdb-por-privatizacao,622031,0.htm.

was successful in generating more serious discussion of issues, although probably not in changing many voters' minds.

A top priority for both campaigns was to capture the support of Marina's voters, since it was thought that few voters who had voted for Dilma or Serra in the first round would change in the second round. The Green Party was allied with the Social Democrats in many states, and Fernando Gabeira immediately came out in support of Serra. Marina called for a meeting of the Green Party activists to discuss what to do. She was thought to be more sympathetic to Serra, but the Green Party was split on which candidate to support and Marina decided to remain neutral in the second round. Polls found that Serra was attracting more of Marina's voters, but not enough more to shift the election. As the election settled down to the final days, most voters seemed to settle into the positions they had formed early on.

When the second round of voting finally came, on October 31, 2010, Dilma won, as expected, with 56 percent of the vote against Serra's 44 percent. Her vote was strongest among the lower social classes and in the northeast. Serra's vote was strong enough to maintain the credibility of the Social Democrats, and the opposition remained in control of São Paulo, Minas Gerais and other key states. The opposition's representation in Congress was weakened, but not to the extent that had been expected earlier in the campaign.

A Frustrating Election. The 2010 elections were frustrating even to those in the winning camp. Lula was frustrated when Dilma failed to win in the first round because of corruption scandals and the unexpected surfacing of the abortion issue. Dilma turned out to be a weak campaigner, as anticipated, and Lula had cancel his foreign trips and devote full time to campaigning as if he were running for re-election himself. His frustration led him to lash out against the press and the Democrats in a way that violated his own rule about not making enemies.

There was really no good answer to the corruption revelations. All they could do was attack the press for bringing them up and pretend they had no idea what was going on in their own administration. The fact that the press may have dug the cases up for political reasons didn't mean they weren't true. But, just as in 2006, the majority of voters just didn't care enough about corruption when compared to economic issues. This attitude was expressed by liberation theologist and Franciscan Friar Leonardo Boff in an interview about why he supported Dilma in the second round:

Boff: The Workers' Party is the political space that best attends to the
marginalized and the excluded, as it did in including 30 million people
into Brazilian society.

Interviewer: And the scandals such as the monthly payoff and the Erenice case?

Boff: I don't have a moralistic view of politics. The world of politics is
the world of differences, in which there was always corruption I
condemn the errors, society should denounce them. But we can't destroy the project for this reason, it is still valid.[360]

Dilma had to compromise her personal beliefs about abortion
and claim to be much more religious than she actually seems to be.
And she repeated the old story about how the Workers' Party saved
Brazil from the disastrous policies of the Fernando Henrique Cardoso government when she clearly knew better. There is no way of
knowing how many voters actually believed these statements and
how many didn't care. To some observers, the whole campaign
seemed dishonest. Filmmaker José Padilha observed:

This campaign has been marked by the lack of ethics and by lying on
all sides. Dilma lies when she says she is against abortion. Serra lies
when he says he believes in God. I, at least, don't believe either of
them.[361]

The Social Democrats were frustrated because they betrayed
their own history and beliefs by marginalizing Fernando Henrique
Cardoso, and got nothing for it. They corrected this mistake after the
first round of voting, but wasn't enough. Serra promised to raise the
minimum wage to R$600 a month and to give the Family Allowance
recipients an extra month's payment as a Christmas bonus. But these
populist appeals didn't seem true to the Social Democrat's history of
sober, market-friendly policies. Their supporters had a hard time
maintaining enthusiasm for a campaign that seemed willing to com-

[360] Sérgio Roxo, "Eleitores de Marina, Bicudo e Boff se dividem entre Serra e Dilma,
O Globo, October 19, 2010.
http://oglobo.globo.com/pais/eleicoes2010/mat/2010/10/19/eleitores-de-marina-
bicudo-boff-se-dividem-entre-serra-dilma-922826476.asp.
[361] Luiz Antônio Novaes, "Entrevista com o cineasta José Padilha, que teve o nome
indevidamente incluído numa lista pró-Dilma," *O Globo*, October 19, 2010.
http://oglobo.globo.com/pais/eleicoes2010/mat/2010/10/19/entrevista-com-
cineasta-jose-padilha-que-teve-nome-indevidamente-incluido-numa-lista-pro-dilma-
922826574.asp.

promise its principles and still couldn't win. Asked to defend his se-cond-round vote for Serra, jurist Hélio Bicudo said:

You have two candidates. One is Lula, the other is the diverse of Lula. I think the alternation of power is fundamental to democracy. If one group is in power too long, you have the Mexicanization of Brazilian politics, because giving everything to one group, things will deteriorate. They have already been deteriorated by corruption. In addition to that, Serra has a respectable curriculum vita.[362]

Marina Silva was the only one who came out of the campaign stronger than she went in. In her analysis, both the Workers' Party and the Social Democrats had become so consumed with the prag-matics of winning elections that they lost sight of their founding mis-sions. Both parties had begun as innovators, she said, seriously dedi-cated to solving Brazil's problems. And both parties still had strong leaders who had been involved since their founding. But she thought they had lost the ability to come up with new ideas and new solu-tions to problems. In her view, both parties "sacrifice any utopia in the name of unlimited pragmatism."[363]

Sociologist Bernardo Sorj thought that José Serra, as the opposi-tion candidate, was primarily responsible for the uninspiring nature of the campaign:

The 2010 election should go into the annals of Brazilian history as the "anti-election," thanks to an opposition candidate who chose not to present himself as such but preferred to present himself as a continuer of the Lula government. Even when it is defeated, the opposition should play its role of informing/alerting/politicizing the citizenship and defining its future line of conduct in Congress, positioning itself for the next elections. The Lula government, in favorable global eco-nomic conditions and with a macroeconomic policy that gave continui-ty to that of Fernando Henrique, managed to satisfy the elites and am-ple popular sectors and to co-opt the militants of the Workers' Party, the base allied with the social movements. In the middle of the sand-

[362] Sérgio Roxo, "Eleitores de Marina, Bicudo e Boff se dividem entre Serra e Dilma, *O Globo*, October 19, 2010. http://oglobo.globo.com/pais/eleicoes2010/mat/2010/10/19/eleitores-de-marina-bicudo-boff-se-dividem-entre-serra-dilma-922826476.asp.
[363] Bernardo Mello Franco, "Em carta, Marina acusa PT e PSDB de 'pragmatismo sem limites', Folha de São Paulo, October 17, 2010. http://www1.folha.uol.com.br/poder/815926-em-carta-marina-acusa-pt-e-psdb-de-pragmatismo-sem-limites.shtml.

wich was the taxpaying middle class, which is concerned about issues such as freedom of expression, transparency of the state and corruption. This vector will determine the future of Brazilian democracy. Either a party will emerge that is capable of mobilizing these concerns, or it will continue to be an apathetic mass vulnerable to whatever demagogues may arise.[364]

Sorj isn't quite fair to the Social Democrats. They did raise the issues of transparency and freedom of expression, as did the Green Party. But there are other important differences between the two parties that could have been made more explicit in the campaign. The Social Democrats are more concerned about lessening the tax burden on business and the middle class so as to stimulate economic development. The Workers' Party is more willing to increase taxes to fund health care, education and social programs, e.g., by reinstating the financial transactions tax, even if it may inhibit growth. Stressing that difference would not have changed the election results because the economic boom made it look as if additional concessions to business weren't necessary. But it might have set the Social Democrats up for the 2014 elections if the economic cycle changes.

By coincidence, the Workers' Party's victory came only two days before the midterm elections in the United States. In the United States, the economy was still in crisis and the voters turned away from the incumbents. The contrast was not lost on the Brazilian media as a leading newspaper observed:

> The two elections ... reaffirm a thesis from the political marketer James Carville that was made famous with the election of Bill Clinton, "It's the economy, stupid." It was the economy that determined the results in both countries. Dilma Rousseff's election was leveraged by Lula's popularity, but most of all by the feeling of well-being brought by economic growth, which is also largely responsible for the president's popularity. In the United States, President Barack Obama lived through an opposite moment.[365]

If the election was predetermined by the economic boom, there was no need for Lula to sully his legacy by threatening the press and the Democrat Party. His supporters could have treated José Serra

---

[364] Bernardo Sorj, "A Massa Apática," *O Globo*, September 12, 2010.
[365] *O Globo*, A economic e a politica, November 4, 2011.
http://oglobo.globo.com/pais/noblat/posts/2010/11/04/a-economia-a-politica-337954.asp.

with respect instead of disrupting his rallies with thrown objects and cries of "assassin." Neither of these tactics helped their electoral cause. As soon as the election was over, Lula went on television with an implicit apology, hoping that the bitterness of the campaign would soon be forgotten:

> With the elections passed, when it is understandable that the heat of the dispute generates stronger conflicts, it is important that government and opposition, without giving up their opinions, respect each other and differ in a mature and civilized way.[366]

---

[366] Lula de Silva, "Pronunciamento em cadeia de rádio e televisão, sobre as eleições 2010," Brasília, November 5, 2010.
http://www.info.planalto.gov.br/static/inf_briefdiscusos.htm.

CHAPTER FIFTEEN
THE SON OF BRAZIL IN POWER

Lula was elected in 2002 with a fuzzy promise of "change." He promised an intensified effort to end hunger. Other than that, his only certain promise was to be better than the previous government. Many Brazilians were tired of Fernando Henrique Cardoso and the crises the country suffered during his presidency. Cardoso's presidency was an historical fluke brought about by a remarkably successful solution to a hyperinflation crisis, as he explains in his book, *The Accidental President of Brazil.*[367] He was a sober intellectual who sounded like a college professor lecturing a class about inconvenient truths. He was widely respected, but many Brazilians were relieved to see him retire. They looked forward to a more cheerful, less demanding leader.

Lula was anything but an accidental president. He had campaigned for the job for decades. After three losing campaigns, he had perfected his message. When he spoke on television he was like a cheerleader, emphasizing the bright side and building team spirit. The public had always liked Lula as a personality and were proud of his personal achievements, but in previous elections many thought he was a bit too radical to trust with the presidency. In 2002, most were convinced that he had matured and settled down and was finally ready to run the country.

Lula had the luck to be elected at a good time in the economic cycle. There was a short-term crisis in the year before he was elected, caused largely by concerns in the investment community that he might implement radical policies. Publicly, he blamed the crisis on Fernando Henrique Cardoso and the elite, but his advisors actually thought the policies Cardoso had put in place were fundamentally sound. They said he didn't need to impose radical changes, just tighten things up a bit. As soon as the investment community saw what he was doing, the crisis abated. Lula's strategy was to change the style of leadership without disrupting policies that were about to bear fruit.

---

[367] Fernando Henrique Cardoso with Brian Winter, *The Accidental President of Brazil,* New York: Public Affairs, 2006.

He succeeded brilliantly, ending his eight years in office with 80 percent of Brazilians rating him as "good" or "excellent" in the polls.[368] At the end of his term, Lula heralded his success, focusing on the results. The change he brought was simply to make things work better:

> We came, eight years ago, with the commitment to change Brazil. We came with the commitment to unlock this immense country which lived with the promises of a great future that never arrived.
>
> We came with the commitment to combat hunger and poverty, but also to confront the causes of inequality and make it steadily diminish.
>
> We came to promote the development of the whole country, while making the regions that had historically fallen behind grow more.
>
> We came to change the place of Brazil in the world, to win the respect our country deserves and to be able to influence the solution of international problems, looking to peaceful coexistence between nations.
>
> We came to do all this democratically, valuing the national Congress and at the same time amplifying the participation of society in decisions.
>
> We are happy to say clearly that all, all, sectors of Brazilian society improved their lives in these eight years, but that the poorest, who were treated with indifference or even with disrespect, improved more.
>
> We are extremely happy because we rescued the self-esteem of our people and because Brazilians today have more pride in Brazil.[369]

Lula's success was not so much in changing Brazil, as in presiding over a period when Brazil continued to improve. Much of the credit has to be shared with the governments that came before him, which laid the groundwork for success. His chosen successor, Dilma Rousseff acknowledged this when asked if she would continue the same mainstream economic policies:

[368] Associated Press, "Brazil's Silva sees record approval rating," *Washington Post*, December 16, 2010.
http://www.washingtonpost.com/wpdyn/content/article/2010/12/16/AR2010121
605223.html.
[369] Lula da Silva, "Discurso durante cerimônia de Registro do Balanço de Governo 2003-2010." December 15, 2010.
http://www.info.planalto.gov.br/static/inf_briefdiscusos.htm.

Interviewer: There are concerns in the US business community as to whether Brazil will continue on the economic path set out by President Lula.

Dilma Rousseff: There's no question about that. Why? Because for us this was the major achievement of our country. It is not an achievement of one sole administration - it is an achievement of the Brazilian state, of the people of our country. The fact that we managed to control inflation, have a flexible exchange-rate regime and fiscal consolidation so that today we are amongst the countries in the world that has the lowest debt-to-GDP ratio. Also, we have a not very significant deficit. I don't want to brag, but we have a 2.2 percent deficit. We intend in the next four years to reduce the debt-to-GDP ratio and to guarantee this inflationary stability.[370]

Unlike Dilma, Lula refused to share credit with his predecessors. He saw himself as different from the other presidents, although this was more a matter of style and background than of ideology or public policy. He portrayed the previous presidents as elitists, and portrayed himself as personifying the great mass of the Brazilian people. **The Son of Brazil.** Denise Paraná's characterization of Lula as the "Son of Brazil" has been widely accepted, but the 32 men who were president before Lula were, in different ways, also sons of Brazil. Lula was the son of a different Brazil, the Brazil that had been left out, the Brazil without college credentials or middle-class careers. From 1889, when the Republic was founded, until 1956, all of Brazil's presidents either had a law degree (19) or were military officers (9).[371] Since 1956, Brazilians have elected a physician (Juscelino Kubitschek), a media executive (Fernando Collor), an engineer (Itamar Franco), a sociologist (Fernando Henrique Cardoso) and an economist (Dilma Rousseff). All of them were children of the formally educated middle or upper classes. Brazil has no history of self-made men rising to the presidency.

[370] Lally Weymouth, "An interview with Dilma Rousseff, Brazil's president-elect," *Washington Post*, December 3, 2010. http://www.washingtonpost.com/wp-dyn/content/article/2010/12/03/AR2010120303241.html
[371] There were 34 presidents who lived to hold office, not including members of short-lived military juntas.
http://en.wikipedia.org/wiki/List_of_Presidents_of_Brazil
and http://pt.wikipedia.org/wiki/Presidente_do_Brasil for links to reference material. The longer list at
http://www.presidencia.gov.br/info_historicas/galeria_pres/ includes some who were in office for only a few days but who were not included in this analysis.

Despite his background, Lula was elected by Brazilians of all so-cial classes. He lost the first three elections when he ran as the candi-date of the working class, and won when he cultivated a moderate, middle-class image. He won when he personified the Brazil that sought to join the middle class, not to overthrow it. He won when he learned to personify what he called the Brazilian soul:

> The elite that governed this country knew the country theoretically but it didn't know, in practice, the soul of this country. And it is by soul, by song, and by culture, and by the way of smiling, of speaking, of crying, that a people build a nation as we built Brazil.[372]

Lula's is not the story of the working class rising up and seizing power from the bourgeoisie. It is not the story of landless farmers rising up against the latifundia or Amazonian rubber tappers rising up against lumber conglomerates. It is the story of a worker who struggled to be included in the middle class, to realize his mother's ambition that he should be something in society. The American ver-sion of this archetypal story, immortalized in the novels of Horatio Alger, glorifies the self-made entrepreneur. Lula's Brazilian version is broader. It includes the unionized worker, the educated professional, the member of a cooperative, the civil servant, even the recipient of government assistance whose children go to school. And it includes business people, a point Lula made by choosing a self-made entre-preneur as his vice president:

> I believe that José Alencar and I are, in the history of the world, the first president and vice-president without a college degree. José Alencar left home at 14 years of age, a poor boy, and became one of the great-est businessmen of this country. I left Garanhuns, became a unionist, and one fine day, the unionist met with the businessman and joined forces, and we won the elections. And José Alencar, like me, didn't have the chance to study.[373]

Like many of Lula's "first time in history" claims, this one is not quite true. Lech Walesa, an electrician and shipyard worker with no higher education, was elected president of Poland in 1990. Lazáro

---

[372] Lula da Silva, "Discurso durante cerimônia de entrega de títulos de cessão de uso de casas em vilas produtivas rurais do Programa de Reassentamento de Populações do Projeto São Francisco," Salgueiro, Pernambuco, December 14, 2010. http://www.info.planalto.gov.br/exec/inf_discursos.cfm.
[373] Ibid.

Cárdenas, president of Mexico from 1934 to 1940, left school at age eleven. Harry Truman, vice-president and president of the United States from 1945 to 1953, had no college degree. But Lula was the first in Brazil.

Lula often claimed the elites were attacking him because they didn't want a worker president to succeed. He reassured working people that he shared their hopes, and took pride in proving that a worker's child could be an effective president. He told an audience of longshoremen in 2010 that university training wasn't necessary to be president because:

> Intelligence is not measured by years of schooling. Years of schooling demonstrates knowledge and mastery of a specific body of material. Intelligence you are born with and you develop, because political skill is not learned in school, or the best president would be a political scientist, not a lathe mechanic.[374]

Not that he was against higher education; he took great pride in building 15 universities and 126 campuses in the interior of the country, along with 126 technical schools, and providing scholarships for 750,000 students in private universities.[375] He knew that working-class parents wanted nothing more than for their children to become professionals:

> Brazil went for centuries without making investments in education because the Brazilian elite, the elite that governed this country, since it already had access to education, thought the people didn't need it, they thought the people should be content to be a stonemason, to be a metallurgist, to be a stonemason's assistant, when, in truth, everyone wants to have a child who is an engineer, who wants to have a child who is a doctor, a child who is a dentist … We don't want to be treated as second-class citizens. "I'm a worker so my toilet paper has to be second class, my food is second class, my meat has to be the neck or the foot of the chicken." No! We want to eat chicken breast too; we want to eat tenderloin, not just ribs.[376]

---

[374] Lula da Silva, "Discurso na cerimônia de entrega da última fase das obras de reconstrução do cais do Porto de Itajaí, October 27, 2010,
http://www.info.planalto.gov.br/static/inf_briefdiscusos.htm.
[375] Lula da Silva, "Discurso durante cerimônia de Registro do Balanço de Governo 2003-2010," Brasília, December 15, 2010.
http://www.info.planalto.gov.br/static/inf_briefdiscusos.htm.
[376] Ibid.

Lula's Legacy. As the first president from the working class, Lula was reported to be "obsessed" with how he would be compared to other presidents. He hoped to be as influential as Getúlio Vargas (president from 1930 to 1945 and 1951-1954) and Juscelino Kubitschek (1956-1961), two presidents usually credited with having had a major impact on Brazilian society. Getúlio Vargas is remembered for starting state-led industrialization and institutionalizing labor unions. Juscelino Kubitschek (1956-1961) built Brasília and stimulated rapid economic growth. More surprisingly, Lula also hoped to rival Ernesto Geisel (1974-1979), a military president. Geisel is usually remembered for beginning the gradual transition back to democracy, but Lula said he admired him because "he was the last Brazilian president to make investments in infrastructure."[377]

Lula seldom, if ever, compared himself to his two immediate predecessors, Itamar Franco (1992-1994) and Fernando Henrique Cardoso (1995-2003). But his speeches often included thinly veiled criticisms of Cardoso, to the point that columnist Reinaldo Azevedo thought that Lula had an "obsession with deprecating Fernando Henrique Cardoso."[378] For example, in a speech in the northeast in 2009 Lula observed that:

> There are very-well-lettered people who became president of the republic, so well lettered that they forgot that this country has a majority of poor people, who never got to go to a university. When the elite had already finished their studies, sometimes even doing a post-graduate course abroad, the poor people were left out."[379]

Itamar Franco and Fernando Henrique Cardoso shared one major accomplishment that guaranteed their legacy; they slayed the dragon of hyperinflation that was stealing the workers' bread and butter. Cardoso developed the successful anti-inflation plan while he was finance minister in Itamar's government. Once he became presi-

---

[377] Thomas Traumann, "Os próximos cuatro anos," *Revista Época*, November 6, 2006.
http://revistaepoca.globo.com/Revista/Epoca/0,,EDG75672-5990-442,00.html.
[378] Reinaldo Azevedo, blog, *Veja.com*. May 14, 2007.
http://veja.abril.com.br/blogs/reinaldo/2007/05/lula-quer-agora-fundar-uma-religio.html.
[379] Lula da Silva, "Discurso durante cerimônia de inauguração dos campi do IFRN nos municípios de Apodi, Caicó, Ipanguaçu, João Câmara, Macau, Pau dos Ferros e Santa Cruz, Ipanguaçu, August 20, 2009.
http://www.info.planalto.gov.br/static/inf_briefdiscusos.htm.

dent, Cardoso maintained fiscal and monetary stability during several global crises, continued the privatization of state industries begun under the Fernando Collor administration, and worked to modernize government programs. It was a legacy that tangibly improved life for poor people and Lula and his advisors believed Brazil needed to build on it, not reverse it. But Lula had promised change, not continuity. So he simply denied that he was building on his predecessors' accomplishments. He frequently went further and claimed that he had received a "cursed legacy" (*herança maldita*) from Fernando Henrique Cardoso. But he never explained why, if the legacy he inherited was so "cursed," he did not change more of it. Surprisingly few journalists or political opponents confronted him on this. When one reporter surprised him with the question during a radio interview, he was flustered and evasive, retreating into abstractions and digressions:

> Journalist: What is the cursed inheritance from Fernando Henrique, if you would agree to look at the statistics in comparison with the *tucanos* (Social Democrats), the numbers for your government and for the *tucanos* in relation to the Brazilian economy, especially the question of employment and social inclusion?
>
> Lula: I think my government changed the paradigm of Brazil. Whoever governs after me won't be able to think small. This is what we want to confront, not just compare numbers. And the people will judge, the people will judge … Because the people who were born on the bottom floor of this society were not expected to rise to the top floor, and I climbed up. I climbed up, do you know why? Because the Brazilian people had consciousness, they matured and won't go backwards. I compare myself often with Mandela …[380]

Lula refused to discuss the statistical record, not because it was bad, but because it wasn't dramatic enough to support his story of a change to a "new paradigm." According to figures released in 2010, economic growth over his eight years as president averaged 4 percent a year. This compared to 4.64 percent for Latin America as a whole, 10.95 percent for China, 8.2 percent for India and 4.8 percent for Russia during the same period.[381] Brazil did reasonably well in many

[380] Lula da Silva, "Entrevista exclusiva concedida às rádios Emissora Rural AM e Juazeiro AM," Petrolina, Pernambuco, March 4, 2010.
http://www.info.planalto.gov.br/static/inf_briefdiscusos.htm.
[381] Bruno Rosa and Danielle Nogueira "Brasil cresceu na era Lula menos que emergentes e AL," *O Globo*, December 10, 2010. http://www.itamaraty.gov.br/sala-

other ways as well, but the statistics generally show continuity with improvements under the previous government, not a radical shift that could be characterized as a paradigm change. Lula's discomfort with Cardoso may also reflect personality differences. Cardoso is dispassionate and analytical, while Lula is warm and effusive. Cardoso is a critical thinker, Lula is a cheerleader. In explaining his differences with the Cardoso administration, Lula does not focus on specific policy changes but on changes in the national spirit. Here indeed there was a change attributable to Lula's personal leadership. The country's self-esteem did improve thanks to Lula's efforts.

Lula could have said that his predecessors made a good start by stabilizing the economy, giving him the opportunity to help it grow and to redistribute income and expand social programs. That's what other Workers' Party leaders and intellectuals say when asked, and it is the answer historians are likely to give. Lula's judgment about his own legacy is actually much the same; except that he insists on comparing himself to Vargas instead of to Franco or Cardoso. In 2008, at the height of the boom, he said:

> I am convinced that the social and economic policies and the national project can only be compared with the government of President Getúlio Vargas. The legacy of our government is the consolidation of social policies with economic growth in a solid macroeconomic situation.[382]

Expansion of social programs with solid macroeconomics and economic growth were just what the country needed in 2002, just as ending inflation and stabilizing government finances were what it needed in 1994. Lula's stubborn refusal to acknowledge that he was building on Franco and Cardoso's contributions is partly simple partisan expediency, but it may reflect some doubt about how momentous his contribution really was.

Itamar Franco is doubly miffed because people often give Cardoso most of the credit for the anti-inflation plan when it was done on his watch. Franco actually supported Lula in 2002. But he didn't get much recognition from Lula and complained, "I was the first to

de-imprensa/selecao-diaria-de-noticias/midias-nacionais/brasil/o-globo/2010/12/10/brasil-cresceu-na-era-lula-menos-que-emergentes-e 2010.
[382] Tiago Pariz and Alexandro Martello, "Só vou ser comparado a Vargas, diz Lula," *globo.com*, August 30, 2007. http://g1.globo.com/Noticias/Politica/0,,MUL96520-5601,00.html.

support him. Later, he disappointed me because he became arrogant. That humble man, who assumed the presidency of the Republic, no longer exists."[383] He complained that Lula was always saying "never before in the history of this country" as if nobody else in the history of the country had ever done anything.

When Cardoso was asked about Lula's legacy, he said, "I think he will be remembered for growth and continuity, and for putting more emphasis on social spending. He's a Lech Walesa who worked out." Comparing his own presidency to Lula's he said, "I did the reforms. Lula surfs the wave."[384]

Why, then, did Lula retire with approval ratings over 80 percent while Cardoso's ratings were so low that even candidates of his own party were afraid to mention him? Ending inflation and stabilizing the economy required cutting spending and imposing fiscal discipline, tasks that can make any president unpopular. Lula had the good fortune to take office when these difficult reforms had already been done and it was time to reap the benefits. The global markets were also much more favorable during most of Lula's presidency. This meant that he could concentrate on stimulating economic growth, hiring his supporters as government employees, building infrastructure and distributing benefits to the poor. These are tasks that are popular in any country, and he took full advantage of them. Surfing waves is more popular than weathering economic storms. Rather than thanking his predecessors for giving him an opportunity, he blamed them for giving him a "cursed inheritance" and took the credit for himself.

The Lula Paradox. But there is more to Lula's legacy than surfing the waves of a favorable economy. Lula's remarkable popularity puzzled some observers because it seemed out of proportion to his accomplishments. On Sunday, December 19, the influential newspaper *O Globo* published a special section called "The Construction of the Lula Myth."[385] Its argument was summarized by one of the writers:

---

[383] Luciano Lima, "De volta à política, Itamar Franco ataca Lula, FHC e Sarney," Agência Brasil, August 12, 2009.
http://www.agenciabrasil.gov.br/noticias/2009/08/12/materia.2009-08-12.0386843759/view.
[384] Jonathan Wheatley, "Lunch with the FT: Fernando Henrique Cardoso," *Financial Times*, September 24, 2010.
[385] "A Construção do Mito Lula," *O Globo*, Sunday, December 19. http://oglobo.globo.com/pais/mat/2010/12/20/especial-construcao-do-mito-lula-923329740.asp

President Lula ends his eight year mandate with popularity never before obtained by a president of this country despite a contradictory legacy. We did not have advances or improvements in education, health,
public security, basic sanitation, infrastructure and reforms. What
leaves me incredulous is that the people of a giant nation such as Brazil, the majority of whom are poor, would give up all these improvements in exchange for a basic food basket called the Family Allowance.
A government with 37 ministries and various secretariats did not succeed in advancing in anything. If it was a right-wing party that was leaving office, and a left-wing party was taking power, surely they would
say that they had received a cursed inheritance.[386]

Of course, this is an exaggeration. There were advances and improvements in all these areas. But they were modest advances, continuous with the past, not radical reforms of the sort Lula seemed to
have promised. *O Globo's* analysts relentlessly probed the flaws in all
of Lula's claimed accomplishments. If the economy grew phenome-
nally in 2010, that was only because it had crashed in 2009. If Brazil
grew an average of 4 percent a year during Lula's term, that was less
than the average for Latin America during the same economic cycle.
Despite his promises, the agrarian reform limped along slowly as it
had before. Conflict in the countryside increased. Lula formed political alliances with oligarchs such as José Sarney, the kind of leader the
Workers' Party had always denounced. Despite his talk of building
infrastructure, he left the highways, ports and aiprorts close to chaos.
His Zero Hunger program degenerated into a permanent dole leaving the poor no escape from dependence on welfare. Worst of all, *O
Globo* insisted, Lula maintained high interest rates and high taxes that
would continue to burden the country for years to come since there
was no social security or tax reform.

The *Blog do Planalto*, a public relations tool of the president's office, fired back:

Anyone who reads the special section of the journal *O Globo* on the Lula Era will have no doubt; the management of the journal, its editors
and anaysts, are among the 3% to 4% of Brazilians who rate the Lula
government as poor or awful.
    For them the approval of more than 80% achieved by President
Lula and his government at the end of eight years in office is a mystery.
Perhaps an illusion or a collective hypnosis which is keeping the public
from perceiving reality. For *O Globo* and its analysts, Brazil advanced

very little in the Lula Era, and the few advances have been in spite of the government and not because of its actions.

As the president said on the day when he released the documents on his legacy, the press has no interest in the government's constructive actions, preferring to focus on the destructive. It falls to the government to document the positive.[387]

And document it they did. Lula's secretariat of communication released a massive six-volume collection called the *Balanço do Governo 2003-2010* and Lula bragged about his government's accomplishments in a retirement speech on national radio and television.[388] The list was long. The minimum wage increased 67 percent. Hydroelectic dams, petroleum refineries and new railway lines were built. Two million people got electricity, one million got new homes. New health programs were established, as were 14 new universities and 126 technical schools. Brazil paid off its debt to the International Monetary Fund and is now lending the Fund money. It was a fine list, but no more impressive than the list in book the same bureaucracy prepared at the end of Fernando Henrique Cardoso's eight years in office.[389] Most of the accomplishments were continuous with programs the government had been working on before Lula took office. There was much steady progress, little dramatic change or reform.

The lack of dramatic change troubles observers on the left as well as on the right. In one of the most comprehensive scholarly appraisals, Fernando J. Cardin de Carvalho extends this criticism to Fernando Henrique Cardoso as well:

There is a significant leadership deficit with respect to both the ability to formulate clear strategies and, consequently, to commit to them. In the case of Cardoso, this anomie seemed to be rooted in his theory of dependence... In the case of Lula and the Workers' Party, the reasons for the absence of strategic thought are unclear... In the absence of

[387] "Balanço da Era Lula *O Globo*: Olho torto entorta a vista, Blog do Planalto, December 21, 2010. http://blog.planalto.gov.br/balanco-da-era-lula-no-globo-olho-torto-entorta-a-vista/.

[388] Balanço do Governo 2003 | 2010. Secretaria de Comunicação Social da Presidênca da República, 2010. http://www.secom.gov.br/sobre-a-secom/publicacoes/balanco-de-governo-2003-2010. Lula da Silva, Pronunciamento à nação em cadeia nacional de rádio e TV, por ocasião do final de ano," December 23, 2010. http://www.info.planalto.gov.br/static/inf_briefdiscusos.htm.

[389] Presidency of the Federal Republic of Brazil, Brazil: 1994-2002: *The Era of the Real*. Secretaria de Estado de Comunicação do Governo, Brasília, 2002.

clearly defined strategies, Lula's policies seem to have consisted mostly of surfing on the favorable winds of the international economy.[390]

Carvalho is right that neither Lula nor Cardoso were the kind of "strong" leader who imposes radical changes on society. But his explanations for their supposed weakness are wrong. Cardoso's academic writings were about how countries could overcome dependency, not apologies for it. Once in office, Cardoso formulated a clear strategy to end hyperinflation and stuck to it. Lula is a brilliant political strategist and organizer. His *Letter to the Brazilian People* made his political strategy in 2002 clear and he carried it out brilliantly. It is hard to think of two leaders better able to formulate strategies and carry them out.

Why then the failure to implement the social security and tax reforms that both Cardoso and Lula believed the country needed? The weakness is not in the leaders but in the democratic system itself. Cardoso and Lula are very different personalities, but they both entered politics as part of a democracy movement and are committed democrats. A democratic leader cannot simply impose dramatic changes. Cardoso was often stymied by opposition from the Workers' Party and others. Lula tried to implement many of the same reforms in his first two years, but he ran into opposition from unionized public employees and from the left wing of his own party, among others. His party tried to get around the legislative roadblocks by buying votes from his so-called allies. After the vote-buying scandal, he largely retreated from controversial reform efforts.

Critics are disappointed that Lula and Cardoso didn't impose their visions on Brazil. Carvalho is explicit about his expectations from a left-of-center government:

> Even a nominally left-wing government in a developing country should pursue at least four goals: full employment of labour; economic growth; income and wealth redistribution; and the empowerment of dispossessed groups, spreading out citizenship rights. A left-wing administration should not be 'generous'. On the contrary, it should advance a redefinition of duties and rights, redistributing power away from those used to rule towards those in position of subordination.[391]

---

[390] Fernando J. Cardim de Carvalho, "Lula's Government in Brazil: A New Left or the Old Populism?" in Philip Arestis and Alfredo Saad-Filho, eds, *Political Economy of Brazil*, New York: Palgrave, 2007, p. 33.

[391] Fernando J. Cardim de Carvalho, "Lula's Government in Brazil: A New Left or the Old Populism?" in Arestis and Saad-Filho, op cit, p. 30.

Lula shares these four goals and made progress on all of them. The progress was not as rapid as he would have liked, but it compares favorably to that made by more dictatorial left-wing governments, such as Hugo Chávez's Venezuela or Evo Morales' Bolivia. The problem seems to be with what Cardin de Carvalho's calls Lula's "generosity." Lula's impulse is to get along with everybody. The radical left wanted him to berate the wealthy and powerful, as Hugo Chávez does. Both Cardoso and Lula preferred to cajole and persuade them.

A Christian World View. For Lula, getting along with people from all walks of life is a matter of personality and philosophy of life, not political ideology. Lula's worldview is fundamentally Christian, not Marxist. This is obscured by the fact that he keeps his religious life private and respects the separation of church and state. A Roman Catholic, he repeatedly emphasizes his appreciation of all Brazil's religious groups, including the evangelicals and the Jews. He chose an evangelical Protestant as his running mate. His is not a narrow, sectarian Christianity; it is a theology of compassion for other human beings.

Frei Betto tells us:

A devotee of Jesus and of Saint Francis of Assisi, Lula likes to pray, he has the habit of making the sign of the cross before his meals, and he never misses the Mass of the Worker celebrated every first of May at the central church in São Bernardo do Campo. At the same time he protects his faith with the same discretion that he protects his family from the scrutiny of the media.[392]

Lula says he has a strong aversion to making enemies:

I am a man who learned not to have enemies. Obviously, someone can be my enemy, but I am not his. When someone reaches 60, he is already thinking of the other life; anyone who is Catholic has this preoccupation. I do not want to create any animosity that might cause the "Man" to be in doubt about receiving me there above; I want to guarantee my space. Therefore I do not have time to make enemies. I do not care if a governor is from the PMDB, if he is of the PT, the PSDB, the PFL [*political parties*], I don't want to know if he is Jewish, if he is evangelical, if he is … . I want to know the following: does he govern?

[392] Frei Betto, "O Amigo Lula," *America Latina en Movimiento*, October 28, 2002. http://alainet.org/active/2675&lang=es.

Are there people in that state, in that city? Then they have equal rights with everyone else in this country. That's how it is. [393]

This is a personal value, rooted in his admiration for his deeply religious mother, *dona* Lindu, from whom he also inherited his admiration of the dignity that comes from not needing the trappings of wealth or power. He remained loyal to her values by continuing to live simply in an apartment in a working-class suburb of São Paulo, without domestic servants, long after he could have afforded more.

Lula's Christianity strikes a deep chord in Brazilian culture; this is another sense in which he is a son of Brazil. Listening to his inauguration speech, Frei Betto was reminded of the legend of the "good king" *dom* Sebastião who disappeared in battle in 1578 and whose return was promised during the War of Canudos in 1897. Betto thought, "From this day forward the future will no longer await *dom* Sebastião's return." [394]

Social scientist Deborah Pereira says that Lula was a Messiah figure for many Brazilians, especially during the long years of his struggle for election:

> In a certain way, president Luis Inácio Lula da Silva inhabits the Brazilian imagination as the man who emerged from the most excluded part of the population precisely to bring redemption to these same people. They believed, perhaps in part because his chances of election were always reduced, that he really was the Redeemer who was time and again impeded from working his miracles by the forces of evil.
>
> Lula's association with the Catholic Church only accentuated this characteristic by giving him a religious nuance. At this time [before his election] it was common for priests involved with the Theology of Liberation to include a prayer for him in their dominical masses. This contributed to the Workers' Party having been for years the political reference for ethics in Brazilian politics. From this perspective, the politicians of the Workers' Party were just, incorruptible and above good and evil. They would be the retinue of good and pure men who frequently follow a Messiah ...
>
> The socialist/Marxist discourse that had been the foundation of the Workers' Party, and consequently of all of Lula's electoral campaigns, almost disappeared in favor of a discourse that was almost meek. Lula was incongruous when he said he was "against everything

---

[393] Lula da Silva, "Discurso na cerimônia alusiva à coleta do primeiro óleo da camada do pré-sal na Plataforma P-34," September 2, 2008.
http://www.info.planalto.gov.br/static/inf_briefdiscusos.htm.
[394] Frei Betto, *A Mosca Azul*. Rio de Janeiro: Rocco, 2006, p. 26.

that is here," and at the same time calmed, principally, the market by following a neoliberal economic policy, we could say a reformed version – everything would stay the same except the most excluded social strata would receive more significant help in the form of money or food.[395]

A Mother's Boy. Perhaps just as important as Lula's class or religious background is the fact that he was a mother's boy. He refused to model himself on his father who he viewed as a failure. Having a father who is a failure can have advantages in life; research shows that father failure is common in the childhoods of eminent people.[396] Two American presidents, Barack Obama and Bill Clinton, were also angry and resentful of their fathers (or stepfathers) and had very close relationships with their mothers. Juscelino Kubitschek's father died when he was two, and he was raised by his mother.

Successful mother's boys learn to share their feelings and empathize with others, and develop practical skills in human relations and problem solving. Not having to compete with their fathers for their mothers' attention in childhood may help them build self-confidence. Not having to submit to their fathers' authority, or rebelling against it, may help them to move quickly through adolescence into career paths that suit their own talents and inclinations. Of course, in Lula's case, his father returned to his life when he was nine and he had to deliberately rebel against him, with his mother's support. Lula is quite explicit about adopting a maternal model of leadership. In a 2010 campaign speech he said:

> The best example I can give of the art of governing is the art of being a mother. Governing is nothing more than acting like a mother taking care of her family, assuring everyone the right to have opportunities. Incidentally, the word "govern" is really wrong. I don't know which philosopher invented the word "govern," it should be "to care for" [*cuidar*].[397]

[395] Deborah Pereira, "Publicidade e religião: o governo Lula." UNIrevista, vol 1, no 3, July 2006. http://www.unirevista.unisinos.br/_pdf/UNIrev_DPereira.PDF.
[396] Victor, Mildred and Ted Goertzel and Ariel Hansen, *Cradles of Eminence*, 2nd ed. Scottsdale, Arizona: Great Potential Press, 2003.
[397] Malá Menzes, "Lula fala em Deus e vingança no Piauí," *O Globo*, October 15, 2010.
http://www.senado.gov.br/noticias/OpiniaoPublica/inc/senamidia/notSenamidia.asp?ud=20101015&datNoticia=20101015&codNoticia=481646&nomeOrgao=&nomeJornal=O+Globo&codOrgao=47&tipPagina=1.

According to the dictionaries, the word "govern" implies exercising authority and enforcing rules. This is a stereotypically masculine approach to life, implicit in the legal and military training of most of Brazil's past presidents. Lula is a feminist, not just in ideology but in his personal style. He freely shares tender feelings and is uninhibited about breaking into tears on public occasions. This is very much the opposite of the stereotype of the Latin American ruler. Lula did not get this style from his regional or social class background or from being raised in Brazil; he got it from his mother. He is not so much the son of Brazil as the son of a Brazilian single mother.

The Republic of Hustlers. Lula's easygoing attitude towards corruption is yet another way in which he is a son of Brazil. The belief that the Workers' Party was different was shattered when the second cash-box scandal revealed practices that had been going on for years in the Workers' Party's proudest strongholds.[398] But maintaining second accounts to avoid legal constraints was not uncommon in Brazil. The vote-buying scandal went beyond the usual political norms because of its scale and the fact that it was run directly by the Party itself. When the political pressure got too hot, Lula blamed it on advisors who had "betrayed" him.[399] But as soon as the pressure abated he brought these advisors back into his inner circles. By the end of his administration, he described the vote-buying scandal as "attempted coup d'état" against his government.[400]

As president, Lula maintained political alliances with two former presidents, José Sarney and Fernando Collor, who were caught up in corruption scandals. Collor was impeached, which is a kind of indictment, but never convicted. On his Web site, he claims that he was "accused of corruption by his political opponents and by those who felt threatened by the modernization of the Brazilian economy," and that he was found innocent of all charges, making him "the only politician in Brazil to have an officially clear record validated by an

[398] Wendy Hunter, *The Transformation of the Workers' Party in Brazil, 1989-2009*. New York: Cambridge University Press, p. 103.
[399] Wikinoticias, "Lula se diz traído e pede desculpas ao povo brasileiro," August 12, 2005. http://pt.wikinews.org/wiki/Lula_se_diz_tra%C3%ADdo_e_pede_desculpas_ao_povo_brasileiro.
[400] Lula da Silva, "Discurso durante a 36ª Reunião Ordinária do Pleno do Conselho de Desenvolvimento Econômico e Social da Presidência da República: Celebração dos oito anos de funcionamento do CDES," December 2, 2010. http://www.info.planalto.gov.br/static/inf_briefdiscusos.htm.

investigation of all interests and sectors of the opposition government."[401]
José Sarney, of the Democratic Movement Party, was Senate leader in 2009 and his party was a key part of Lula's coalition. Sarney was caught up in a corruption scandal when he allegedly gave jobs and favors to friends and relatives.[402] Lula was counting on Sarney and his Party of the Brazilian Democratic Movement as key allies in the 2010 election. He defended Sarney vigorously; remarking that "I believe Sarney has enough history in Brazil that he cannot be treated as an ordinary person."[403] He criticized the "process of making denunciations," and said he did not know who "was trying to weaken the Legislative Power."[404]

In an essay called "The Republic of Hustlers [*malandragem*]," Fernando Henrique Cardoso asked "how is it possible, confronted with such a moral disaster, for the people to vote to consolidate a governmental situation whose sins are expressed without any remorse and even with jubilation?"[405] He found an answer in writer Antônio Candido's description of Brazil as a country where "people do things which could be considered worthy of reproach, but they also do things worthy of praise, which compensate for them. Since all have their faults, no one should be censured ... Remorse does not exist, because acts are evaluated according to their efficacy."[406]

Lula expressed exactly this attitude at a speech summing up the accomplishments of his administration. With a nod to José Dirceu in the audience, he said:

[401] http://www.collor.com/didyouknow.asp.
[402] Alexei Barrionuevo, "Scandal Puts Pressure on a Brazilian Leader to Step Down," *New York Times*, August 7, 2009. http://www.nytimes.com/2009/08/07/world/americas/07brazil.html?scp=1&sq=Sarney%20scandal&st=cse.
[403] *O Globo*, "Lula critica 'onda de denuncismo' e defende Sarney," June 17, 2009. http://oglobo.globo.com/pais/mat/2009/06/17/lula-critica-onda-de-denuncismo-defende-sarney-756378108.asp.
[404] Andrei Netto, "Sarney não é uma 'pessoa comum', diz Lula," *estadao.com.br*, June 17, 2009. http://www.estadao.com.br/noticias/nacional,sarney-nao-e-uma-pessoa-comum-diz-lula,388706,0.htm.
[405] Fernando Henrique Cardoso, "República de Malandragem," *O Estado de São Paulo*, September 3, 2006. http://www.ifhc.org.br/files/pdf/artigos_fhc/2006-09.pdf. The word "malandro" is often translated as "scoundrel" but "hustler" seems better.
[406] Quoted by Cardoso, ibid, from "A Dialéctica da Malandragem," in *O Discurso e a Cidade*, São Paulo, Duas Cidades, 3rd ed.

We all, together, go through difficult moments. We all, together, go through glorious moments. The concrete data is that the sum of the errors we may have committed and the sum of the things we may have done right is such that in synthesis we can finish our mandate with more than 80 percent approval.[407]

This attitude toward corruption is rooted in the mismatch between the ideals of Brazil's legal system and the limitations of its social realities.[408] Brazilian legislation expresses noble aspirations that go beyond the country's capabilities. Detailed regulations govern every aspect of business and labor relations, and of land use and housing construction, but many employers, builders and landlords do not have the resources to follow them. So people find a way to make things work despite the rules and regulations, a practice captured in the expression *dar um jeito*, or "find a way." Historian José Murilo de Varvalho writes:

> I think it is almost a consensus opinion that transgression is the national sport; it is as Brazilian as *feijoada* [the national black bean stew]. In fact, there is a folklore about the Brazilian as a systematic violator of the law. The *malandro* [scoundrel or hustler] and the *jeitinho* [finding a way around the law] are part of this folklore.[409]

This culture of transgression is found in the Brazilian labor movement as much as in other sectors of society. Especially under the military governments, union activists resisted laws that were imposed by an undemocratic ruling class. As Lula said at the time, "If I do only what the law says I won't do anything, I will be gagged. I prefer not to know and not to find out. If a problem comes up, we'll hire a lawyer to deal with it."[410] Strikes were often illegal, but the workers were powerless without them and they often came to be recognized by the authorities.

When the Workers' Party won control of municipal and state governments, they began to receive illegal contributions or kickbacks

[407] Lula da Silva, "Discurso durante cerimônia de Registro do Balanço de Governo 2003-2010," Brasília, December 15, 2010.
http://www.info.planalto.gov.br/static/inf_briefdiscusos.htm.
[408] Fernando Henrique Cardoso and Marcílio Marques Moreira, editors, Cultura das Transgressões no Brasil. São Paulo: Saraiva, 2008.
[409] José Murilo de Carvalho, "Quem Transgride o Quê?" in Cardoso and Moreira, op cit., p. 73.
[410] Interview with Denise Paraná in *Lula: O Filho do Brasil*. São Paulo: Perseu Abramo, 2002.

from contractors and from operators of illegal gambling operations. These off-the-books contributions are very widely used in Brazilian election campaigns and the party would have been at a disadvantage if it didn't use them. But they are usually handled by the candidate personally. The Workers' Party and its allies were apparently the first to use the party organization itself as a vehicle for this kind of activity.[411]

The Son of Brazil in Power. Lula promised "change" but he knew that the change Brazilians really wanted most was relief from change. Brazilians were tired of being told their institutions needed to be reformed, tired of losing the security of government jobs and early retirements, tired of being hectored from environmentalists and other activists. They wanted a president who was a cheerleader, not a critic. They liked being paid in money that held its value and they wanted to enjoy spending it. It was Lula's good fortune to be elected at a point in time when the Brazilian economy could provide economic growth with some redistribution of income and without reigniting inflation. He seized the opportunity and took full credit for giving Brazilians what they wanted.

Far from being an agent of radical change, Lula built on the legacies of past presidents. As commentator Cesar Sanson observed:

> Lula is a mixture of policies that go from Getúlio Vargas, passing through Juscelino Kubitschek and the military presidents, until arriving at Fernando Henrique Cardoso. His government has developmentalist policies which remind us of Vargas, policies of favoring transnational capital that remind us of Kubitschek, policies that please the military such as rearmament, and the maintenance of Fernando Henrique Cardoso's macroeconomic orthodoxy. What we see are happy businessmen, even happier transnational capital, and the military the same. All of this is viewed by a perplexed political right and a national left without direction.[412]

Sanson was too kind to mention the corruption scandals, but these also remind us of past presidents, especially Collor and Kubitschek.

---

[411] Personal correspondence from Fernando Henrique Cardoso.
[412] Cesar Sanson, "Governo Lula, de Vargas a FHC," Radioagência Noticias do Planalto, November 19, 2007.
http://www.radioagencianp.com.br/index.php?Itemid=43&id=3352&option=com_content&task=view.

The public is comfortable with this continuity and delighted that it has brought results. Dilma Rousseff was elected because the overwhelming majority wanted it to continue. But it is not clear how long it can continue without actually carrying out some of the tax and social security reforms that Cardoso, Lula and Rousseff have all agreed are needed. Politics tends to be cyclical, and Brazil may be approaching a cyclical turning point. Cristovam Buarque, one of Brazil's most imaginative left-of-center politicians, believes that Brazil is finishing a cycle and poised to begin another.[413] He calls the current cycle, which began with the transition to democracy and the stabilization of the currency, one of "timid social democracy" that made only modest reforms. He argues that the next cycle should be one of more aggressive social democracy to make politics less corrupt, to build a high technology economy, to promote equality of opportunity and to make the cities safer. If social democracy cannot do this, he believes, the next cycle could be either a swing to the right or a swing to populism.

Brazil has two strong social democratic parties still largely led by a generation of leaders who understand the need for reforms. Rather than joining forces, however, these two parties, the Social Democrats and the Workers' Party, have allied with more traditional parties and retreated into what Marina Silva, the Green Party environmentalist, calls "unlimited pragmatism." She argues that:

> It is an irony of history. Two parties born to affirm the diversity of Brazilian society, to break the social duality existing at the time of their formation, have allowed themselves to be captured by the logic of the struggle between themselves ...
>
> By leaving the umbrella of the Brazilian Democratic Movement, these parties enriched the Brazilian political universe by creating democratic alternatives based on strong personal histories [of the leaders] and collective political struggles and public ethics.
>
> Today, the subversion of these parties in the pragmatism of the old political logic makes it less likely that the country will be able to make the essential policy changes the country demands.[414]

---

[413] Cristóvam Buarque, "O Ciclo Dilma," Blog do Noblat, *O Globo*, December 23, 2010.   http://oglobo.globo.com/pais/noblat/posts/2010/12/18/o-ciclo-dilma-350289.asp.

[414] Bernardo Mello Franco, "Em carta, Marina acusa PT e PSDB de 'pragmatismo sem limites'," *Folha.com*, October 17, 2010.

http://www1.folha.uol.com.br/poder/815926-em-carta-marina-acusa-pt-e-psdb-de-pragmatismo-sem-limites.shtml.

Lula's successor has expressed her commitment to leading a more active reform process to make the lasting changes that Brazil needs. Her party's dependence on the alliance with the Party of the Brazilian Democratic Movement, however, may make this difficult. The Social Democratic Party reconsidered its strategies after losing the presidential election in 2010, and is also well aware of the needs for reforms. It is too much to hope that these two progressive, social democratic parties could join forces, but the Social Democrats in Congress cooperated with the Lula government on many issues, putting the needs of the country ahead of short-term partisan advantage. Dilma Rousseff was part of this process when she was chief-of-staff, and she should be ready to continue to work with the Social Democrats and other progressive forces. In a democratic system, however, really significant reforms may be difficult until or unless the country goes into a crisis that makes the need for them more apparent.

Oddly enough, it may be the editorial writers from *O Globo*, after reconsidering their own analysis, who came up with the best statement of Lula's legacy:

> President Lula should leave office satisfied with his legacy. In fact, he may not have done everything he should have done, but what he did qualifies him to enter into history as the president who raised the self-esteem of the Brazilian people. This says it all!
>
> It is clear that Brazilians of all income and educational levels and age groups massively approved of this government and its president. Considering that the mainstream press was consistently and strongly against him, a question cannot be ignored: can it be that these people have all been fooled and only the three percent or four percent who disagree have a monopoly on the truth? That is very pretentious.[415]

Lula chose to go into retirement with popularity ratings in the 80s rather than use his popularity to pressure for controversial reforms. He also chose not to try to get the constitution amended so he could become one of Latin America's "presidents for life." He was especially pleased that the country would be hosting both the Olympic Games and the soccer World Cup, and observed that Brazil

---

[415] *O Globo*, "Era Lula," December 22, 2010 (Kindle edition).

had discovered that "there is no greater conquest than to recuperate the self-esteem of its people."[416]

Lula will go into history as the first president to make raising the country's self-esteem a national priority. The motto on the Brazilian flag is "Order and Progress," taken from the writings of French sociologist Auguste Comte. The son of Brazil in power acted very much in that positivist tradition, maintaining order through continuity of economic policies and progress through increased redistribution of income.

Two decades of effective, pragmatic government have made Brazil a much better place, and perhaps given it the confidence it needs to pursue the further reforms its leaders recognize as necessary. Lula ended his term as the constitution required, and he stepped back from the limelight for a few years to give Dilma Rousseff a chance to establish herself as the country's leader. But there is no constitutional impediment to his running for the presidency again.

---

[416] Lula da Silva, Pronunciamento à nação em cadeia nacional de rádio e TV, por ocasião do final de ano," December 23, 2010.
http://www.info.planalto.gov.br/static/inf_briefdiscusos.htm.

INDEX

Note: This index follows the Brazilian convention of alphabetizing individuals by their first name or nickname.

Abílio Diniz, 111
Abortion issue, 182, 183
Advisory councils, 95–98
Aécio Neves, 119, 165
Ahmadinejad, Mahmoud, 112
AIDS, 103
Akbar Ganji, 112
Alberto Amadei, 69
Aloizio Mercadante, 35, 122, 181
Anthony Garotinho, 117, 119
Antônio Palocci, 43, 50, 166, 173
Aristides da Silva (Lula's father), 5–8
Arlindo Chingalia, 114
Barack Obama, 114, 205
Benedita da Silva, 54
Bernardo Sorj, 187
Bill Clinton, 205
Blairo Maggi, 92, 93
Bolivia, 104
Carlos Cachoeira, 54
Carlos Minc, 92, 94
Celso Amorim, 105, 107, 110
César Benjamin, 50
Cesar Sanson, 209
Charles Burke Elbrick, 31
Chico Buarque, 129
Chile, 106
China, 142
Colombia, 106
Corruption, 53–68, 121–23, 127, 129, 173, 206–9

Council on Foreign Relations, 101
Cristovam Buarque, 28, 119, 124, 210
Cuba, 109
Denise Paraná, 2
Dilma Rousseff, 3, 88, 193, 210, 211
corruption allegations, 173, 184
political campaign, 165–89
Dorothy Stang, 90
Drew Westen, 129
Duda Mendonça, 33, 36, 128, 175
Economic policy, 40–41, 133–49
Eiiti Sato, 115
Environmental issues, 88–94
Erdogan, Recep Tayyip, 113
Erenice Guerra, 179
Ernesto Geisel, 196
Ethanol, 106
Evo Morales, 2, 104, 106, 151, 203
Family allowances, 78–80
Fernando Collor, 53, 125, 193, 209
Fernando de la Rúa, 41
Fernando Gabeira, 89, 93, 181
Fernando Henrique Cardoso, 2, 23, 25, 28, 34, 50, 121, 129, 136, 153, 186, 191, 193, 196, 197, 199, 202, 209

Fernando J. Cardin de
  Carvalho, 201
Fernando Mitre, 48
Ferreira Gullar, 153
Fidel Castro, 106
Foreign policy, 99–116
Francisco de Oliveira, 40, 153
Free Trade Area of the
  Americas, 100, 103
Frei Betto, 1, **8**, 72, 73, 74, 77
Frei Chico (Lula's brother),
  15, 18, 19, 153
Freud Godoy, 123
George W. Bush, 104, 106
Geraldo Alckmin, 117–32,
  181
Getúlio Vargas, 196, 198, 209
Gilberto Gil, 170
Giselle Bündchen, 73
Gordon Brown, 146
Guido Mantega, 35, 136
Haiti, 102
Helena, 120, 124, 125
Hélio Bicudo, 187
Heloísa Helena, 49, 119, 123
Henrique Meirelles, 42
Honduras, 107
Hugo Chávez, 2, 106, 151,
  163, 165, 203
Inflation, 25–28, 138
Iran, 113
Iraq, 104
Israel, 108–9
Itamar Franco, 25, 193, 196,
  198
Ivo Poletto, 74
James Carville, 148
Jânio Quadros, 23
João Goulart, 23
João Pedro Stédile, 87, 137
João Roberto Rodrigues, 88

João Siscu, 49
José Dirceu, 31, 44, 53, 166
José Eduardo Dutra, 173
José Genoino, 30, 35, 41, 139
José Graziano, 72, 73, 76, 78,
  82
José Padilha, 186
José Serra, 117, 118, 122, 137,
  165
  political campaign, 165–89
Josias de Souza, 129
Juscelino Kubitschek, 193,
  196, 205, 209
Labor movement, 12–13, 19
Land reform, 81–88
Landless farmer's movement,
  81–88, 137
Leandro Konder, 153
Leonardo Boff, 185
Letter to the Brazilian People, 41
Lindu da Silva (Lula's
  mother), 6, 5–8, 9, 11
Luciana Genro, 49
Luís Fara Monteiro, 91
Luiz Fernando Figueiredo,
  137
Luiz Gushiken, 36
Lula da Silva
  adolescence, 11–13
  childhood, 5–8, 9
  children, 14
  corruption allegations, 53–
    68
  economic policies, 51, 133–
    49, 151–58, 158–61
  election campaigns, 83
  inauguration, 1, 23, 40
  labor activism, 13, 19
  leadership style, 3, 5, 191,
    198
  legacy, 212

loss of finger, 12
political campaigns, 25, 28,
    32–38, 86, 117–32, 165–
    89
political philosophy, 80,
    158, 162
relationship with his
    mother, 206
religious beliefs, 8, 205
sexual initiation, 12
social policies, 194–95
Lurdes da Silva (Lula's first
    wife), 13
Luriam Cordeiro (Lula's
    daughter), 14
Magalhães Teixeira, 79
Mailson da Nóbrega, 137
Manuel Zelaya, 107
Marcos Azambuja, 107
Maria Fernanda Delmas, 148
Marilena Chaui, 49
Marina Silva, 88–94, 170, 181,
    185, 187, 210
Mário Covas, 118
Marisa da Silva (Lula's second
    wife), 14, 15
Marta Harnecker, 151
Marta Suplicy, 122, 130
Mexico, 103, 106
Michelle Bachelet, 151
Microcredit, 158
Military government, 17, 19–
    20, 23
Miriam Cordeiro (Lula's
    girlfriend), 14
Moisés Naím, 109
Movimento sem terra. *See*
    Landless farmer's
    movement
Mozambique, 103
Namibia, 103

National self-esteem, 99–116,
    212
Neoliberalism, 50, 49–51, 132,
    139
Néstor Kirchner, 151
Oded Grajew, 72
Orestes Quércia, 17
Orlando Zapata Tamayo, 109
Palestinians, 108–9
Participatory budgeting, 95–
    98
Patrus Ananias de Sousa, 76
Paul Singer, 32
Plínio Arruda Sampaio, 170
Political parties, 3, 17, 21, 20–
    21, 26, 46, 94, 95, 119, 120,
    171, 181, 210, 211
Political prisoners, 111
Race differences, 131
Rafael Correa, 106
Raimundo Colombo, 181
Roberto Medina, 144
Roberto Micheletti, 107
Rosalba Ciarlini, 181
São Tomé and Príncipe, 103
Sean Burgess, 101
Social security reform, 47
Socialism, 17, 28–32, 151–58,
    158–61, 162
South Africa, 103
Souza Martins, 83
Tarso Genro, 166
Tax reform, 49
Trevisan Vedoin, 122
Uruguay, 106
Vote buying scandal, **62**
Waldomiro Diniz, 54
Workers' Party, 3, 17, 21, 32,
    35, 41, 43, 45, 49, 69, 95–
    98, 99
World Bank, 79, 80

World Economic Forum, 99,
106
World Social Forum, 99, 106
World Trade Organization,
102, 104

Zander Navarro, 84
Zeca do PT (José Orcírio
Miranda dos Santos), 35
Zero hunger campaign, 39,
69–78

CPSIA information can be obtained
at www.ICGtesting.com
Printed in the USA
FFOW03n0652221114
8887FF

9 781612 335056